W9-CDS-096

THE ECONOMIC IMPACT
OF THE
AMERICAN CIVIL WAR

THE Economic Impact o

SP co SCHENKMAN Publishing Co. CAMBRIDGE 1 9 6 2

EDITED BY **Ralph Andreano**

Chairman,
Department of Economics
Earlham College

HE American Civil War

TABLE OF CONTENTS

EDITOR'S INTRODUCTION

I.

The glamour of the military and political events of the Civil War years have long obscured the events of social and economic history. The sordid legacy of the political and economic reconstruction (and the character of historical writing about this period) have contributed to the lack of a dispassionate evaluation of the impact of the Civil War on the development of the American economy. Characterized by easy clichés and deceptively simple historical explanations, the subject has eluded several generations of able students and scholars. It is hoped that the eleven selections reprinted in this volume will redress this long overdue imbalance.

The readings are divided into four parts and focus on the major influences of the War on the American economy, Union and Confederate: 1) the internal economic readjustments necessitated by wartime conditions, 2) the monetary and physical cost of the War, 3) the impact of the War on post-war economic policy, and 4) the role of the War in increasing the industrialization of the American economy. A fifth part of the book brings together some of the major quantitative information on American economic history. This is useful for the critical reader who tries to evaluate the range of viewpoints presented in the various selections.

The book as a whole is directed to teachers, students, and scholars, particularly historians, as a source book for classroom and seminar discussion and for student topics in research. The readings should be helpful to instructors teaching courses that deal with the history of the South and of the Civil War and Reconstruction, but should be valuable also to instructors and students in general courses in American history. Consideration is already given to the causes of the War but too little concern has been shown by scholars for the War's long-term economic impact and its social impact. It is hoped that the quality of the research and writing collected here in one book will make this volume rewarding reading.

II.

The great glamour, and tragic impact, of the political and military events of the period have tended to obscure the fact, in our study of the American Civil War, that the study of war can point up the importance of the underlying market forces in an economy. But the fundamental economic and social changes that the Civil Wartime economy wrought on the entire United States must be more widely understood. In order to appreciate these changes, it is useful momentarily to forget political forces. (To be sure, the relationship between economic forces and political results has been explored in a number of instances; consider, for example, the literature on the so-called "wheat thesis.")

What do we find when we try to understand the changes wrought by the Civil War? These are some of the facts: There was a sudden increase in the demand for war goods, and producers strove to meet these demands. Government spending rose. The substitution of wartime for peacetime goods forced consumers, who now had higher money incomes, to bid up the prices for consumption goods. In general, a whole causative chain of economic pressures was set in motion, and it was difficult to predict where it would all end. Some industries, income groups, and production methods were appreciably enhanced by the new wartime demands for goods and services; others felt the pinch either because labor was in tight supply or because material was short.

The strength of market forces tends to offset to some extent imbalances of the economy during a war by bringing forth substitute goods and services, workers, and production techniques for those siphoned or rerouted into the war economy. People never before in the work force enter the wage-earner class. Consumer tastes are changed by the overpowering dictates of the war and the market. And the search for new, and hopefully cheaper, production techniques is accelerated, especially where bottlenecks occur in industry.

Effective government control of the economy and the use of monetary and fiscal policy can minimize most of the serious distortions created by war. Nevertheless, the operation of market forces usually produces a drastic reordering of economic life. Even within a controlled situation, wartime conditions and responses can restructure an entire economy in a relatively short time period. The inner tensions and readjustments generated by such wartime activity assume great importance in the study of the impact of war on a nation's economic development.

III.

So much which was dramatic and exciting had already affected the path and direction of the American economy before the Civil War that one must investigate carefully allegations that specific changes had been stimulated (or retarded) by the conditions of war. The urgent demands of war economics dictate that some industries will grow faster than others. But to shift irrevocably the direction and path of an entire economy is something more fundamental than this.

Professor Moses Abramovitz and others at the National Bureau of Economic Research have shown, in their pioneering studies of the American economy, that its growth may have taken place in a series of waves of acceleration and retardation of from 10 to 20 years' duration. Abramovitz has called these waves "long swings" in order that they not be confused with an ordinary business cycle. Some of his findings are reproduced in Part V. These investigations raise questions of central importance. Was the Civil War experience a watershed of the long swings dating from the two prewar decades? Was the American economy approaching the peak phase of a long swing at the time of the War? Did the War alter significantly the underlying growth trend of the economy?

There are other questions that must be asked. Are structural changes in a wartime economy likely to be permanent? Are the creative capacities of entrepreneurs and tastes of consumers altered fundamentally? Do the creation of new productive capacity, of new blocks of potential investable capital, of new business organizations and structures, outweigh the monetary costs of the War? Is the physical destruction of the War permanently damaging to the economy's resource base? These are but a few of the questions that must be raised for they all, in greater or lesser degree, influence the short and long-run course of a nation's postwar economic development.

The character, pace, and accomplishment of American economic life after the Civil War was from all appearances fundamentally different from that before this period in our history. But if the War restructured and reshaped the economy, how can the postwar levels of economic activity ever be precisely compared with prewar levels? Certainly the movement of a single production index, such as one focusing on a redistribution of income or on a shift in national economic policy, cannot alone give us our precise answers. Indeed, the fundamental complexity of the economy just before, during, and after the War can only be analysed by a judicious weighting of the quantitative and institutional elements central to the processes as well as results of economic change. Such analysis is necessary, even though it may not give us our full explanation.

IV.

The selections in this volume contain some of the most provocative discussions that scholars have given us on the impact of the Civil War on the economic development of the USA. The authors are, of course, by no means unanimous in their judgments. Indeed, few of them have taken into consideration all the relevant factors that bear on the issue. One conclusion which may be drawn from the articles reprinted here is that the standards of balance and perspective by which the impact of the War must be judged are still to be developed.

In actual fact, the economic consequences of the War in the long run may far out-weigh in significance the causes (moral or economic) of the conflict. But perspective and balance require that both causes and consequences be explored in depth. There is therefore a desperate need for new study and thought on this critical period of American history. It is hoped that this volume will stimulate new and objective research.

RALPH ANDREANO

The Economic Impact
of the
American Civil War

PART ONE

Internal Economic Adjustments During the War

The following four selections examine the inner strains of an economy created by a large-scale war effort. In the excerpt of Wesley Mitchell, the effects of monetary and price inflation on consumption patterns and business behavior in the North are appraised. Written nearly 60 years ago, Mitchell's study is still provocative and suggestive of new lines of research. Eugene Lerner's more recent study examines the economy of the South during the War in essentially the same terms as did Mitchell. Lerner's study shows that the South experienced even more drastic internal economic tensions and readjustments than did the North. What is most striking about the two selections, however, is the apparent uniformity of economic behavior in both sections of the country: businessmen reaped high profits, consumer living standards were depressed, and market forces continued to offer substitute goods and opportunities.

Victor Clark's article, written nearly a half-century ago, is a neglected classic. He was one of the first scholars to take a purely economic view of the impact of the War on the secular progress of industrialization and economic growth. Notice that Clark pays particular attention to changes in technology.

Emerson Fite's article exposes the adjustments the War caused in the agricultural sector of the economy and the pres-

1

sures exerted on the allocation and distribution of resources: the loss of markets for some goods set in motion forces that led to the development of other markets and commodities; the shift of resources into agricultural production, and increased agricultural productivity, released resources in other sectors and geographic regions for other uses, i.e., manufacturing. The political implications of increased agricultural production which resulted from the pull of the War on Western producers are also vividly re-created by Fite. Finally, living standards and consumption and production patterns of the West are described in detail.

FOR FURTHER READING

The economic aspects of the War in the United States are the aspects of the War least of all studied and this curious neglect is demonstrated by the paucity of research materials available. The selections in this unit, nevertheless, ought to be balanced by additional reading in the following selected studies:

Emerson D. Fite, *Social and Industrial Conditions in the North During the Civil War* (New York: Macmillan Company, 1910). Fite's study examines all the major income groups and industrial sectors of the economy. It is very institutional material and shows its age: yet, it is one of the best studies available.

Charles W. Ramsdell, *Behind the Lines in the Southern Confederacy* (Baton Rouge: Louisiana State University Press, 1944). Ramsdell's study is more penetrating. Ramsdell, both a superb historian and analyst, presents the most authoritative picture of social and economic conditions in the Confederacy.

Chester Wright, *Economic History of the United States*, Second Edition (New York: McGraw-Hill Book Company, 1949) is one of the few to treat the Civil War in purely economic terms. See especially, Chapter 28.

Harold F. Williamson (ed.), *The Growth of the American Economy*, Second Edition (New York: Prentice-Hall, Inc., 1951) is a standard economic history textbook. See especially, Chapter 17 and the Introduction to Part Four.

For the "wheat vs. cotton" thesis two classic articles should be consulted: (also see Tables VIII — 3, 4, 5 in statistical supplement)

Louis Schmidt, "The Influence of Wheat and Cotton on Anglo-American Relations During the Civil War," *Iowa Journal of History and Politics*, vol. XVI (July, 1918), pps. 400-439.

Eli Ginsberg, "The Economics of British Neutrality During the American Civil War," *Agricultural History*, vol. X (Oct., 1936), pps. 147-156.

Wesley Mitchell was one of the most distinguished American economists and was a pioneer in the application of quantitative methods to historical problems. In this selection he examines the effect of Greenback issues on the economic behavior of entrepreneurs and consumers. Was the illusion of "war prosperity" real? Did workers share in the "prosperity" to the same extent as other income groups? These are some of the critical questions explored by Mitchell.

THE PRODUCTION AND CONSUMPTION OF WEALTH

By Wesley C. Mitchell

DURING THE CIVIL WAR the question whether or not the loyal states were really "prosperous" was debated with much zeal. Supporters of the Greenback policy, like Spaulding and Hooper, were in the habit of claiming that the paper currency "operated very beneficially upon the business of the country" and promoted the general well-being of the people.[1] "It is an indisputable fact," said Hooper in January, 1863, "that the material interests of the North were never more prosperous than at present."[2]

From Congress such assertions passed on to newspapers and pamphleteers. Publicists of the prominence of Dr. William Elder, D. A. Wells, and Lorin Blodget employed their pens in drawing most cheerful pictures of the condition and prospects of the country. A brief citation from the first writer will suffice to indicate the general character of the conclusions at which these optimistic patriots arrived: "The knowledge of an immensely enhanced activity in all branches of industry," said Dr. Elder, "is brought home to everybody in the free states by the almost perfect distribution of its benefits. One class, and one class only, of the people, and that a class which the general prosperity always injures, suffers something — the class of annuitants, salaried officers, and people living upon accumulated capital."[3]

The general tone of all these pamphlets suggests that the primary object of the writers who prepared them was to encourage the public to accept heavy taxation without grumbling, and to invest their savings in government bonds without hesitation. Laudable as such a design may have been, it was not conducive to impartial selection of data or to successful analysis, and sober-minded critics had no difficulty in showing to such as would listen that the boasted prosperity was not so real as it seemed. The little pamphlet, "Are We Prosperous?" by "A Boston Merchant" is a good example of the protests against accepting the specious appearances of activity in business as sufficient evidence of actual increase in well-being. The booklet begins by admitting that "labor is fully employed, . . . trade is active, . . . money plenty," and that everywhere "are heard rejoicings over our prosperity." But, runs the argument, if true prosperity consists "in the productive employment of labor," there is no great ground for congratulation. For nearly a million of men are engaged in the service of the government and nearly a million more are making materials of war. So far as the work of supplying the wants of the community is concerned, all these persons are "not only non-producers, but are destroyers and consumers of the capital of the country." The "enhanced activity" of trade and the full employment of labor mean only that the people left at home are working more than usually hard in the effort to supply these nonproducers as well as themselves with the requisites of life. The producers who sell to the government are receiving in exchange not products that are wealth, but evidences of debt. This unproductive employment of labor, consumption of capital without replacement, and rapid accumulation of debt, may quicken the pace of business, but it does not make true prosperity.[4]

From the present point of view it would be improper to enter at length upon the question in what degree the production and accumulation of wealth were retarded in the years from 1861 to 1865. Such a discussion would involve an attempt to gauge the relative importance of several indeterminate elements, such as the degree in which the labor force of the North was weakened by enlistments, how far the withdrawal of laborers into the army was compensated by the increased exertions of those who stayed at home, how far the introduction of labor-saving machinery in agriculture and other industries was promoted by the lack of hands, whether industry suffered from lack of capital because of the huge sums lent the government, etc. All these problems lie beyond the scope of the present inquiry. But it is pertinent to ask here: what influence did the greenback currency have as one of the many factors that affected the production of wealth? On this problem the preceding investigations throw some light.

In the first place, the paper standard was responsible in large measure for the feeling of "prosperity" that seems from all the evidence to have characterized the public's frame of mind. Almost every owner of property found that the price of his possessions had increased, and almost every wage-earner found that his pay was advanced. Strive as people may to emancipate themselves from the feeling that a dollar represents a fixed quantity of desirable things, it is very difficult for them to resist a pleasurable sensation when the money value of their property rises or their incomes increase. They are almost certain to feel cheerful over the larger sums that they can spend, even though the amount of commodities the larger sums will buy is decreased. Habit is too strong for arithmetic.

But, more than this, "business" in the common meaning of the word was unusually profitable during the war. The "residual claimant" . . . is in most enterprises the active businessman, and, as has been shown, his money income did as a rule rise more rapidly than the cost of living. Only in those cases where the advance of the product with which the given individual was concerned lagged so far behind the advance of those things that he wished to buy as to neutralize the gain which he made at the expense of his employees and creditors, was the businessman actually worse off. In other words, "business" was, in reality as well as in appearance, rendered more profitable by the greenbacks. There is therefore no error in saying that the business of the country enjoyed unwonted prosperity during the war. And it may be added that the active businessman is probably a more potent factor in determining the community's feeling about "good times" and "bad times" than is the workingman, the landlord, or the lending capitalist.

The effect of high profits, however, is not limited to producing a cheerful frame of mind among businessmen. Under ordinary circumstances one would say that when the great majority of men already in business are "making money" with more than usual rapidity they will be inclined to enlarge their operations, that others will be inclined to enter the field, and that thus the production of wealth will be stimulated. But the circumstances of the war period were not ordinary and this conclusion cannot be accepted without serious modifications.

1. It has been shown that businessmen realized the precariousness of all operations that depended for their success upon the future course of prices — and nearly all operations that involved any considerable time for their consummation were thus dependent. So far did this disposition prevail that it produced a marked curtailment in the use of credit. The prudent man might be willing to push his business as far as possible with the means at his own disposal, but he showed a disinclination to borrow for the purpose. Thus the uncertainty which all men felt about the future in a large measure counteracted the influence of high profits in increasing production.

2. The foregoing consideration of course weighed most heavily in the minds of cautious men. But not all businessmen are cautious.

Among many the chance of winning large profits in case of success is sufficient to induce them to undertake heavy risks of loss. On the whole, Americans seem to display a decided propensity toward speculative ventures and are not easily deterred by having to take chances. To men of this type it seems that the business opportunities offered by the fluctuating currency would make a strong appeal. But, while the force of this observation may be admitted, it does not necessitate a reconsideration of the conclusion that the instability of prices tended to diminish the production of wealth. For in a time of great price fluctuations the possibilities of making fortunes rapidly are much greater in trade than in agriculture, mining, or manufactures. Every rise and fall in quotations holds out an alluring promise of quick gain to the man who believes in his shrewdness and good fortune, and who does not hesitate to take chances. The probable profits of productive industry in the narrower sense might be larger than common, but this would not attract investors in large numbers if the probable profits of trading were larger yet; and such seems clearly to have been the case during the war when the paper currency offered such brilliant possibilities to fortunate speculators in gold, in stocks, or in commodities. Instead, then, of the greenbacks being credited with stimulating the production of wealth, they must be charged with offering inducements to abandon agriculture and manufactures for the more speculative forms of trade.

This tendency of the times did not escape observation. On the contrary, it was often remarked and lamented in terms that seem exaggerated. Hugh McCulloch, for instance, in his report as secretary of the treasury for 1865, said:

> There are no indications of real and permanent prosperity . . . in the splendid fortunes reported to be made by skilful manipulations at the gold room or the stock board; no evidences of increasing wealth in the facts that railroads and steamboats are crowded with passengers, and hotels with guests; that cities are full to overflowing, and rents and the necessities of life, as well as luxuries, are daily advancing. All these things prove rather . . . that the number of non-producers is increasing, and that productive industry is being diminished. There is no fact more manifest than that the plethora of paper money is not only undermining the morals of the people by encouraging waste and extravagance, but is striking at the root of our material prosperity by diminishing labor.[5]

More explicit was Mr. Wells's statement of the movement away from industry and toward speculative trading. In one of his reports as special commissioner of the revenue he said:

> During the last few years large numbers of our population, under the influence and example of high profits realized in

trading during the period of monetary expansion, have abandoned employments directly productive of national wealth, and sought employments connected with commerce, trading, or speculation. As a consequence we everywhere find large additions to the population of our commercial cities, an increase in the number and cost of the buildings devoted to banking, brokerage, insurance, commission business, and agencies of all kinds, the spirit of trading and speculating pervading the whole community, as distinguished from the spirit of production.[6]

Within the period under review, then, it seems very doubtful whether the high profits had their usual effect of leading to a larger production of raw materials or to an increase in manufactures. The prudent man hesitated to expand his undertakings because of the instability of the inflated level of prices; the man with a turn for speculative ventures found more alluring opportunities in trade.

No one can read contemporary comments on American social life of the later years of the war without being impressed by the charges of extravagance made against the people of the North. Newspapers and pulpits were at one in denouncing the sinful waste that, they declared, was increasing at a most alarming rate. The "shoddy aristocracy" with its ostentatious display of wealth became a stock subject for cartoonists at home, and earned a well-merited reputation for vulgarity abroad. So common are the comments on this subject that no specific references need be given; one has only to examine the files of newspapers and magazines, or to read published sermons or letters, to find how universally observers were impressed by the prevalance of extravagant expenditure.

In trying to account for this unpleasant phase of social development, men usually laid the blame upon the paper standard. High prices were said to make everyone feel suddenly richer and so to tempt everyone to adopt a more lavish style of living than his former wont. Thus the view gained general credence that the greenbacks were ultimately responsible for a great increase in the consumption of wealth.

The enormous profits of "residual claimants" [businessmen] made possible the rapid accumulation of an unusual number of fortunes, and the families thus lifted into sudden affluence enjoyed spending their money in the ostentatious fashion characteristic of the newly rich. It is therefore true that the monetary situation was largely responsible for the appearance of a considerable class of persons — of whom the fortunate speculator and the army contractor are typical — who plunged into the recklessly extravagant habits that called down upon their heads the condemnation of the popular moralist.

7

But if the greenbacks were in the last resort a chief cause of the increased consumption of articles of luxury by families whom they had aided in enriching, they were not less truly a cause of restricted consumption by a much larger class of humbler folk. The laboring man whose money wages increased but one-half, while the cost of living doubled, could not continue to provide for his family's wants so fully as before. He was forced to practice economies — to wear his old clothing longer, to use less coffee and less sugar, to substitute cheaper for better qualities in every line of expenditure where possible. Similar retrenchment of living expenses must have been practiced by the families of many owners of land and lenders of capital. In other words, the wartime fortunes resulted in a very large measure from the mere transfer of wealth from a wide circle of persons to the relatively small number of residual claimants to the proceeds of business enterprises. The enlarged consumption of wealth which the paper currency made possible for the fortunate few was therefore contrasted with a diminished consumption on the part of the unfortunate many on whose slender means the greenbacks levied contributions for the benefit of their employers.

That the diminished consumption of wealth by large numbers of poor people escaped general notice, while the extravagance of the newly rich attracted so much attention, need not shake one's confidence in the validity of these conclusions. The purchase of a fast trotting-horse by a government contractor, and the elaborateness of his wife's gowns and jewelry, are much more conspicuous facts than the petty economies practiced by his employees. The same trait that leads fortunate people to flaunt their material prosperity in the eyes of the world leads the unfortunate to conceal their small privations. Even an attentive observer may fail to notice that the wives of workingmen are still wearing their last year's dresses and that children are running barefoot longer than usual.

But though the newspapers were not full of comments on the enforced economies of the mass of the population, wholesale dealers in staple articles of food and clothing noticed a decrease in sales. In reviewing the trade situation in September, 1864, when real wages were near their lowest ebb, *Hunt's Merchants' Magazine* remarked that "the rise in the prices of commodities has . . . outrun the power of consumption and the fall trade has been almost at a stand. Those articles such as coffee, sugar, low grade goods, which [form] the staple products of the great mass of the people in moderate circumstances, has [sic] reached such high rates that the decline in consumption is very marked, amounting almost to a stagnation of the fall trade."[7]

It would be of exceeding interest to trace the temporary change in the character of the consumption of the people that resulted from the artificial alteration of the distribution of wealth by the greenback currency — to see, for example, how the consumption of tobacco and liquors was affected as compared with the consumption of sugar, coffee, flour, and woolen fabrics. But unfortunately there are no reliable data to serve as the basis of such an investigation. The Revenue Commission of 1865-66 made an attempt to estimate the decline in the consumption of cotton, tea, coffee, sugar, and molasses, but its figures are too largely the results of guesswork to possess much significance.[8] All that can be said with assurance is that the consumption of many articles of luxury increased very greatly, while the consumption of many staple articles declined. It is probable that in the first year or two of the war a spirit of economy pervaded nearly all classes of the people.[9] As the characteristic effects of the greenback standard began to make themselves felt, still more careful supervision of expenditures was forced upon wage-earners and small owners of land and lenders of capital, while [businessmen] began to find their profits uncommonly great. The great fall of prices in the first half of 1865, combined with the continued advance of money wages, alleviated the situation of the first class of persons, though it did not quite restore them to the situation that existed before the war. To [businessmen] it brought a reduction in profits that was in part merely nominal — the expression of their fortunes in fewer figures, but with a denominator of enhanced value — and in part real — the relative increase in the shares of the product that went to other cooperators in production and the increased value of the dollars in which whatever pecuniary obligations they had contracted must be paid. But, on the other hand, the fact that they had survived the sharp fall of prices that they had foreseen would come with the end of the war relieved their minds of a great source of anxiety, and put them in a position to enjoy the gains that they had saved. Consequently in 1865, consumption of goods of all kinds probably increased over that of 1864; of staple articles, because money wages had risen, while prices had fallen; of luxuries, because, though profits were less enormous, fortunes were felt to be less precarious.

[1] Spaulding, *Congressional Globe*, 37th Cong., 3d Sess., p. 288.
[2] *Ibid.*, p. 386.
[3] *Debt and Resources of the United States* (Philadelphia, June, 1863), pp. 21, 23, 24; cf. Wells, *Our Burden and Our Strength* (Troy, N. Y.), 1864; Blodget, *The Commercial and Financial Strength of the United States* (Philadelphia, 1864). Also see the series of letter published in London by Robert J. Walker, under the title *American Finances and Resources*, 1863 and 1864.
[4] *Is Our Prosperity a Delusion? Our National Debt and Currency*, by a Boston Merchant [A. W. STETSON], (Boston, 1864). The title on the cover is *The Age of Greenbacks*.
[5] P. 9.
[6] *Executive Document No. 27*, 41st Cong., 2d Sess., p. xxxi. Cf. Charles A. Mann, *Paper Money*, pp. 187-94. The opponents of the greenback party were

fond of pointing to the less rapid increase of national wealth between 1860 and 1870 than between 1850 and 1860, shown by the figures of the federal census, as an indication of the influence of the paper currency in discouraging production. Cf. Amasa Walker, *The National Currency* (New York, 1876), p. 44; *The Nation* (New York), Vol. XII, p. 286; Wells's fourth report, cited at the beginning of this note, p. xxxi. The imperfections of the Census of 1870, however, to say nothing of the unreliability of statistics of national wealth in all American censuses, make these data of slight value.

[7] Vol. LI, p. 243; cf. also pp. 370, 447.

[8] *H. R. Executive Document No. 34,* 39th Cong., 1st Sess., Special Reports Nos. 1-4.

[9] Cf., e. g., remarks of T. M. Parker, *Congressional Globe,* 37th Cong., 2d Sess., p. 885; "Report of the Bank Commissioners of the State of Maine," December, 1862, in *Executive Document No. 20,* 38th Cong., 1st Sess., p. 3.

Eugene Lerner's study of inflation in the Confederacy focuses on many of the same issues as Mitchell did for the North. Lerner shows that the slow deterioration of economic life in the South was accompanied by, and in part was a cause and symptom of, one of the grossest periods of price and monetary expansion in American economic history.

MONEY, PRICES, AND WAGES IN THE CONFEDERACY, 1861-65

By Eugene M. Lerner

THE MONEY SPENT by the Confederate government to purchase war supplies came largely from the printing press; tax collections and bond sales raised relatively small amounts. As the ratio of money to goods available increased, prices rose. Union armies continuously reduced the area in which Confederate notes were accepted as money, and southerners living in captured territory shipped large amounts of these notes to the sections where it still passed as currency. Like government deficits, the Confederate notes received from occupied territory increased the stock of money in areas still controlled by the Confederate government. The rising prices became, in effect, a tax on holding money; to avoid the tax, people spent their money more rapidly, driving prices still higher.

As the war continued, the real output of the Confederacy declined. Many of the most capable white workers left the labor force and joined the army. The northern blockade forced the South to become self-sufficient, isolated the Confederacy from the benefits of foreign trade, and compelled southern labor to be used where it formerly had the least comparative advantage. Worn-out or destroyed machinery was difficult to replace, and northern troops concentrated on razing railroad equipment and entire factories and on cutting the supply lines of raw materials. The increase in the stock of money, the rise in velocity, and the decline in real output in the Confederacy from 1861 to 1865 produced the worst inflation of our history since the Revolutionary War.

In Sections II and III of this paper, I construct money and price indexes for this period; in Sections IV, V, VI, and VII, I describe price movements in various parts of the South and the effect of the northern blockade; in Section VIII, I discuss the real value of money; in Sections IX, X, and XI, wage movements; and in Section XII, the popular response to the inflation.

TABLE I
Total Stock of Money in the South in Millions of Dollars

Date	Bank Notes and Deposits*	Confederate Government Notes	Total	Index: January, 1861 = 100
1861:				
January	$ 94.6	....	$ 94.6	100
April	121.8	....	121.8	130
June	119.3	$ 1.1	120.4	130
October	146.3	24.5	170.8	180
1862:				
January	165.2	74.6	239.8	250
April	151.1	131.0	282.1	300
June	142.9	166.1	309.0	330
October	181.5	287.3	468.8	500
1863:				
January	239.1	410.5	649.6	690
April	257.1	561.7	818.8	870
June	267.5	637.3	904.8	960
October	274.7	792.4	1,067.1	1130
1864:				
January	268.1	826.8	1,094.9	1160

*These figures are not adjusted for interbank deposits and are therefore biased upward.

II

The stock of paper money in the South consisted of Confederate issues, bank notes and deposits, state treasury notes,[1] shinplasters,[2] and legalized counterfeits. I estimated the amount of Confederate notes outstanding from the periodic reports of Secretaries Memminger and Trenholm; and I used United States Treasury figures, southern bank reports, and unpublished bank records to estimate the amount of bank credit issued.[3] State treasury notes, shinplasters, and legalized counterfeits were ignored, because their combined total value was insignificant compared with the amount of Confederate notes and bank credit issued.

My estimates indicate that the stock of money in the South increased approximately elevenfold in the three years from January, 1861, to January, 1864. In the light of the large amount of Confederate notes issued, this increase seems remarkably small. The rise in the stocks of money was thus limited because banks sharply increased their reserve ratios as the war continued.

Commercial banks had no central bank to support them during

crises. Southern bankers expected mass withdrawals whenever Union troops approached, and they protected themselves the only way they could — by limiting the amount of credit they created. Georgia banks had 47 per cent reserves in June, 1862, and 69 per cent in June, 1863; the Bank of Fayetteville had 21 per cent in May, 1861, and 46 per cent in November, 1863; the Bank of South Carolina had 5 per cent in January, 1861, and 30 per cent in October, 1863; the Bank of the Valley in Virginia had an average of 41.2 per cent in 1861, 56.5 per cent in 1862, 57.2 per cent in 1863, and 66.6 per cent in 1864.[4]

In the North during these war years, $1.49 was created by the banks per dollar printed by the government.[5] In the South, as of January, 1864, only $1.20 had been created by the banks per dollar printed by the government. The stock of money, and therefore prices, would have risen still more had southern bankers not increased their reserve ratios.

III

Abundant price quotations during the Civil War are available for the cities of Richmond, Virginia; Wilmington and Fayetteville, North Carolina; and Augusta, Georgia. Richmond, the capital of the Confederacy, was overcrowded and under frequent attack throughout the war. Wilmington was described as a veritable "fairy city" where boats that ran the blockade landed and sold their goods. Augusta became an important supply base for part of the southern army, and Fayetteville was a small, inland community. Because each of these cities had unique characteristics and because they were several hundred miles apart, any generalization that is valid for all four can probably be extended over a somewhat broader area without great error.

Wholesale prices are preferable to retail prices for a study of inflation, because they "govern" the retail level and are more uniform and homogenous than retail prices. To depict the price movements of commodities, regularly and systematically reported quotations are necessary. The wholesale-price quotations used in this study were taken from the local newspapers that reported regularly on market conditions.[6] These quotations are more readily available and much easier to use than the prices recorded in the best alternative source, the account books of firms.

From newspaper quotations, five unweighted arithmetic price indexes were constructed:[7] one for each of the four cities selected, and one averaging the commodity prices of all four cities.

Continuous price series were constructed[8] for 28 commodities in Richmond, 23 in Fayetteville, 34 in Augusta, and 25 in Wilmington.[9] The monthly price relatives of each commodity were calculated, using the commodity's average price during the first four months of 1861 as a base.[10] These price relatives were then averaged to form the price index for each city. The general price index for the entire eastern part of the Confederacy was prepared by averaging fifty-seven[11] different commodity price series taken from all four cities.[12] This index is presented in Figure 1 and Table 2.

IV

For 31 consecutive months, from October, 1861, to March, 1864, the general price index of the Confederacy rose at an almost constant rate of 10 per cent a month. As the real value of money fell, Confederate notes were no longer used as a store of value. Lenders refused to extend credit unless they were repaid in gold, leather, or some other commodity. When debtors tried to use the inflated currency to pay off obligations incurred before the war, creditors refused to accept payment. J. D. Davidson, an attorney in Lexington, Virginia, received numerous letters like the following: "Some time about the 1st of the present month, Mr. Jack Jordan again came to me when I refused to take the money [for his debt] owing to the condition of the currency."[13] Davidson's clients wanted to wait until the war was over and the price level lower before they accepted payment.

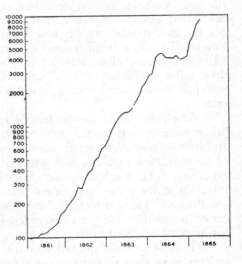

FIG. 1.—The general price index of the Confederacy. (First four months of 1861 = 100.)

As early as 1862 some firms stopped selling their produce for currency alone. Customers had to offer some commodity along with their Confederate notes to complete the purchase, a practice that became widespread during 1863. The Gregg Cotton Mills received numerous letters from other manufacturers requesting the exchange of products. One person wrote: "Money will buy little or nothing here and unless I can find some means of getting food for my work-men, I fear I shall lose them."[14]

As the war went on, money continued to fall in value. By April, 1865, the general price index had risen to 92 times its prewar base.

Changes in velocity, in the stock of money, and in the supply of goods determined price changes. Contrary to popular opinion, commodity price movements were not directly affected by military events.[15] On February 17, 1864, the Confederate Congress enacted a currency reform. All existing notes except small notes were to be exchanged for new currency at the ratio of three for two by April 1, 1864.[16] In anticipation of the reform, southerners began to spend

TABLE II

GENERAL PRICE INDEX OF THE EASTERN SECTION OF THE CONFEDERACY

(First Four Months of 1861 = 100)

Month	Year				
	1861	1862	1863	1864	1865
January	101	193	762	2,801	5,824
February	99	211	900	2,947	6,427
March	101	236	1,051	4,128	8,336
April	101	281	1,178	4,470	9,211
May	109	278	1,279	4,575	
June	109	331	1,308	4,198	
July	111	380	1,326	4,094	
August	120	419	1,428	4,097	
September	128	493	1,617	4,279	
October	136	526	1,879	4,001	
November	161	624	2,236	4,029	
December	172	686	2,464	4,285	

their old notes more rapidly. Prices rose immediately; the general price index rose 23 per cent from February to March, 1864. In May, 1864, the currency reform began to take hold. The general price index dropped dramatically and stayed low through December. This decline took place despite the invading Union armies, the reduction in foreign trade, the impending military defeat, and the low morale of the army. The currency reform was more significant than these powerful forces.

V

To compare the price rise of each city with the average price rise in the entire eastern section of the Confederacy, the index for each city was deflated by the general price index. The results are plotted on two graphs, Figures 2 and 3, to facilitate reading. Values

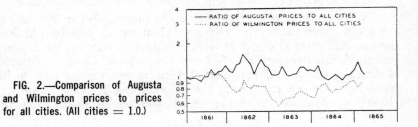

FIG. 2.—Comparison of Augusta and Wilmington prices to prices for all cities. (All cities = 1.0.)

greater than 1 indicate that prices rose more from the base period in the city in question than in all four cities; values less than 1 indicate that prices rose less.

Figure 2 compares Wilmington and Augusta, the two cities whose price indexes deviated most from the general price rise during the early years of the war. A large part of the difference between these two price series is explained by their composition. The index for Augusta contains five items not included in the Wilmington index: New Orleans whiskey, apple brandy, peach brandy, nails, and iron. The prices of these commodities increased considerably faster than an average of all prices. The output of spirits was restricted to save corn for consumption, and the demand for iron increased because of military needs. These commodities give the Augusta index a strong upward bias.

New indexes were constructed that eliminate this bias by including only items common to Augusta and Wilmington. When these new indexes were deflated by the general price index, the two series usually were closer together.[17] This suggests that, had the indexes of all four cities contained a still larger number of common items, the estimated price rises of the four cities would be even more uniform than Figures 2 and 3 indicate.

In Figure 3, Fayetteville and Richmond are compared. The most significant aspect of Figure 3 is the sudden and rapid rise in the Richmond series after January, 1864. This rise, indicating that prices rose faster in Richmond than in the general index, suggests the effectiveness of Union troops in cutting the city's supply lines. They confirm General Sherman's observation that in 1864 goods were scarcer in Richmond than in the Confederacy as a whole.

Figures 2 and 3 indicate that prices rose approximately the same amount from the base period in all four cities during the first three years of the war. Only Richmond prices broke away from the general

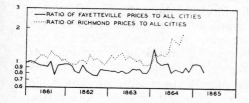

FIG. 3.—Comparison of Fayetteville and Richmond prices to prices
for all cities. (All cities = 1.0.)

price movement in 1864.[18] These statistics imply that communication and transportation facilities were not so deteriorated that traders
could no longer take advantage of large price differentials. Rather,
they imply that the businessmen of the South continued to ship
goods from one area to another throughout the war, making for
uniform price rises.[19]

VI

Since most commodities are substitutes for some others, a
student of price movements usually expects all commodity prices to
rise or fall at approximately the same rate. Although numerous
special circumstances affecting each product cause the rates of price
change to vary somewhat, an extremely strong force is necessary to
keep the price changes of different commodities radically different
over the short run.[20]

During the Civil War the blockade imposed by the North was
just such a force. The effect of the blockade was to shift to the right
the supply curves for the home market of goods formerly exported,
which tended to lower their prices, and to shift to the left those of
goods formerly imported, which tended to raise their prices.[21] The
more essential foreign markets or foreign producers were to a commodity, the greater was the shift in the product's supply schedule to
the home market and the more pronounced its price change.

The effect of the blockade on southern prices can be illustrated
by dividing the commodities that make up the general price index
into four mutually exclusive categories: imports, partly imported
goods, exports, and domestic products.[22] Partly imported goods are
those the Confederacy produced only in limited quantities; to satisfy
the demand, they were also imported. Domestic products are those
neither exported nor imported and therefore not directly affected by
the blockade. . . .

These figures show in striking fashion the distorted price movements in the Confederacy caused by the northern blockade that
closed southern ports. Instead of constantly crisscrossing, as in

17

"normal" times, the prices of these groups fall into four neat rows. Commodities entirely imported had their supply virtually cut off, and their prices rose the most. The blockade did not affect the home production of partly imported goods, and their prices rose less. The prices of domestic goods, which were not directly affected by the blockade, rose still less. The prices of goods formerly exported rose least of all: King Cotton was begging for buyers in southern markets.

These different price rises suggest the reason why blockade-runners carried "Yankee gee-gaws, silks and trinkets" rather than necessities: the price of wheat, corn, and other products produced in limited quantities in the Confederacy simply did not rise fast enough.

Differences in the rates of price rise among commodities caused changes in the income distribution of the Confederacy. The once wealthy planters, who derived the bulk of their income from crops normally exported, lost relative to all other classes. In an attempt to protect themselves from the effects of the blockade, planters demanded immediate government aid.[28] However, their pleas for subsidies were rejected. Mrs. Chestnut's well-known diary portrays in detail the plight of southern planters who tried to maintain their former living standards in the face of their reduced real income.

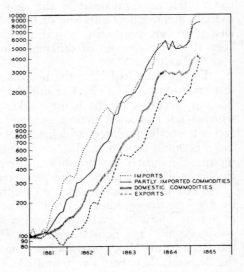

FIG. 4.—Price indexes of commodity groups. (First four months of 1861 = 100.)

VII

The blockade was felt in every corner of the southern economy. It not only distorted prices and changed the distribution of income; it also affected the food people ate and the goods they produced.

The ratio of the price index of imported goods to that of exported goods is shown for each month in Figure 5. This ratio rises very rapidly through November, 1861, indicating that the difference between the price rise of exports and that of imports widened during the early months of the war. Stocks of commodities normally exported accumulated, tending to lower their price;[24] and supplies of goods normally imported declined, tending to raise their price.[25]

The South's small industrial base made it difficult for her to begin producing commodities normally imported. The shift in output was further complicated by the "bottlenecks" caused by shifting production rapidly from peacetime to wartime goods. Like so many countries in Europe during World War I, the Confederacy hoarded manpower in its army and overmobilized. The army drained the economy of necessary laborers, and, as the war continued, troops had to be delegated to work in factories.

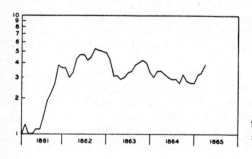

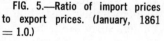

FIG. 5.—Ratio of import prices to export prices. (January, 1861 = 1.0.)

Nevertheless, the effect of the blockade was greatest in the short run. Gradually substitutes, though poor ones, were found for imported goods. Various roots and dried bark replaced coffee; wooden shoes were used instead of leather ones; sorghum took the place of sugar. Other imported goods, such as paper, were used more sparingly; letters were written on crude brown paper, sheets torn out of ledger books, and the insides of envelopes. A few formerly imported commodities, such as salt, were produced at home; it was not uncommon to see people wash and boil the ground under their smokehouses to salvage the salt drippings from animals slaughtered in earlier years. By these slow, often painful means, the demand for imports was gradually reduced, though until September, 1862, not as rapidly as their supply was falling.

Beginning in October, 1862, the ratio of import prices to export prices followed a downward trend. Planters shifted from growing cotton to growing products whose prices rose faster. "The cotton crop harvested in the fall of 1861 amounted to about 4,500,000 bales; the next year it dropped to about 1,500,000; in 1863 it was somewhat less than 50,000; and the next year it was about 300,000."[26] On the other hand, the demand for cotton rose as wool and other materials became more expensive. The decreased supply and increased demand made the price of cotton, like that of other exports, rise more rapidly.

VIII

The general price index of the Confederacy increased twenty-eightfold from the first quarter of 1861 to January 1864. During the same period the stock of money increased only elevenfold. The difference between these ratios is attributable to increases in the velocity of money and to decreases in the South's real output. Unfortunately, one cannot determine with strict accuracy from the statistical data now available the extent to which each of these forces changed. However, a measure of their combined strength is given by the real value of the stock of money.[27] This statistic increases if velocity falls or real income rises, and declines if velocity rises or real income falls.

Estimates of changes in the real value of Confederate cash balances are shown in Table III. Until June, 1862, the index of real value was greater than 100, the level of January, 1861. Instead of reducing their cash holdings immediately, southerners held notes longer, suggesting that they were slow to realize that inflation was under way. In October, 1862, when it was clear that more inflation was in store, the value of cash balances fell below the January, 1861, level. After this date, prices rose more than the stock of money increased.[28]

This pattern, in which the aggregate real value of cash balances first rises, then falls, has been found in every major inflation for which statistical data are available. Keynes, in describing the inflations of post-World War I in Europe, accounted for this repeated occurrence as follows:

> At first there may be a change of habit in the wrong direction, which actually facilitates the Government's operation [of collecting taxes by issuing notes]. The public is so much accustomed to thinking of money as the ultimate standard, that, when prices begin to rise, believing that the rise must be temporary they tend to hoard their money and to postpone

purchases, with the result that they hold in monetary form a larger aggregate of real value than before. . . . But sooner or later the second phase sets in. The public discovers that it is the holder of notes that suffer taxation and defray the expenses of government and they begin to change their habits and to economize in their holding of notes.[29]

TABLE III
The Real Value of Money

Date (1)	Increase in Stock of Money (Jan., 1861 = 100) (2)	Index of Commodity Prices (Jan., 1861 = 100) (3)	Real Value of the Stock of Money (Col. 2 ÷ Col. 3) (4)
1861:			
January	100	100	100
April	129	100	129
June	127	108	117
October	180	135	134
1862:			
January	253	191	133
April	298	279	107
June	337	328	102
October	496	522	95
1863:			
January	687	756	90
April	666	1,168	57
June	959	1,296	74
October	1,129	1,858	61
1864:			
January	1,159	2,776	42

On January 10, 1863, Secretary Memminger stated that velocity had fallen to two thirds of its prewar rate.[30] If the Secretary's estimate was correct, the real income of the South declined 40 per cent by January, 1863.[31] If he was correct only in that velocity fell, the decline in the real value of money by January, 1863, would still be attributable to the drop in the South's real output.

During the first two years of the war, the real income of the South fell because the Confederate army drained large numbers of white men from the labor force. General Clement A. Evans estimated that approximately 40 per cent of the white men of military age were in the army.[32] Colonel Thomas L. Livermore put the number still higher and thought that "substantially the entire military population of the Confederate States not exempted by law were enrolled in the army."[33] The jobs left vacant could not be filled immediately. Old men, women, slaves, or wounded veterans were the replacements for men called to service; these workers were not so productive as the men they replaced.

As war continued, the invading Union armies, the northern blockade, and the reallocation of southern labor tended to reduce output. These disturbing forces, however, were partly offset. Patriotism made workers become more efficient at their jobs, work longer hours, and discover "short cuts" in production. Large numbers of army privates receiving eleven dollars a month deserted to work on their farms back home. Like France during World War I, the Confederacy realized it was overmobilized and sent soldiers home to work in factories; this raised the South's real output. If the conflicting forces just described offset each other, the army's heavy drain on manpower caused a "once and for all" drop in real output,[34] a drop felt most seriously during the first two years of the war.

Though the fall in output was largely responsible for the decline in the real value of cash balances during the early years of the war, the rise in velocity caused its continuing decline. Taxing through printing money was as appealing to the Confederate government as it was to the Continental Congress in earlier years of American history and has been to so many governments since that time. Like all people who live through prolonged and rapid price rises, southerners came to realize that the only way to avoid the tax on holding money was to reduce their cash holdings. Some resorted to limited forms of barter and refused to accept cash alone for their products. Others adopted more stable currencies, such as northern greenbacks, or made their notes payable in commodities. Durable goods, land, precious metals, and jewelry were kept as ultimate reserves instead of notes or bank deposits. As velocity increased, prices rose still higher and the real value of cash balances declined.

IX

By curtailing foreign trade, the northern blockade compelled the Confederacy to manufacture most of its own war supplies. Undoubtedly, the rapid rise in commodity prices, so bitterly denounced by the people who suffered under it, aided the southern war effort by stimulating the output of war goods, the building of new plants, and the development of industrial processes.

Prices rose much faster than wages in the Confederacy, and southern businessmen made large profits. Describing the period from 1760 to 1800 in London, England, Professor Hamilton writes:

The high level of profits raised large incomes which have supplied practically all the savings in a capitalistic society. As J. M. Keynes has pointed out, savings without investment not only would have proved fruitless, but would have depressed business and thus limited savings. By keeping the normal rate of profits far above the prevailing rate of interest, the lag of wages behind prices stimulated the investment of savings as they took place.[35]

Businessmen in the Confederacy, like those in England a century earlier, responded to their higher profits by trying to build new equipment, expand their labor force, and produce more goods.

Victor S. Clark, after studying manufacturing in the Confederacy, concluded that the lack of competent metalworkers and machinists was never remedied; "It seems to have been the limiting factor in the production of arms and munitions up to the very close of the conflict."[36] The rise in prices had the effect of helping to offset the scarcity of labor. Since prices rose much faster than wages, real wages fell. Southern laborers tried to maintain their prewar living standards by working longer hours and holding down more than one job. In many cases wives and children entered the labor force for the first time to supplement the family income. This increase in the labor force reduced the most important "bottleneck" in southern production.

X

To study wage movements in the Confederacy, I took wage quotations from the account books of various southern firms.[37] Since the median is not affected by extreme values, it was the statistic used as typical of all wages in a trade[38] in any given month.[39] The first quotation listed in 1861 was taken as the base, and successive monthly medians were expressed as a percentage of this value. For some occupations quotations were not available for 1861. To utilize the quotations that were available for later years, I assumed that during 1861 wages increased in these trades as much as the average increase in all other trades.[40] The first quotation for these occupations in 1862 was therefore given the value of 1.085, a base in 1861 was determined, and the successive monthly quotations were expressed as a percentage of this base.[41] An unweighted average of these relatives was then struck. These values are presented in Table IV and plotted in Figure 6. They reveal that the average wage increased approximately ten times during the four years of the war, or at a rate of 4.6 per cent a month.

To determine the movement of real wages, the rise in money wages should be deflated by a price index weighted according to workers' expenditures. Unfortunately, no budget studies are currently available for the South during the Civil War.[42] However, the change in real wages may be approximated by deflating the rise in money wages by a wholesale price index of 21 domestic commodities.[43]

23

TABLE IV

Wage Index for the Confederacy
(January, 1861 = 100)

Month	Year				
	1861	1862	1863	1864	1865
January	100	121	201	397	784
February	100	112	207	381	884
March	99	118	212	462	987
April	101	119	237	402	
May	107	122	233	398	
June	105	127	241	372	
July	100	122	263	385	
August	100	136	296	394	
September	106	139	305	450	
October	101	160	341	527	
November	116	166	371	528	
December	114	177	349	521	

The most serious objection to deflating money wages by a wholesale price index of farm products and textiles is that it overstates the decline in the value of a worker's money wage by between 20 and 40 per cent.[44] The price index used to deflate money wages, plotted in Figure 6, reveals that wholesale domestic prices rose approximately

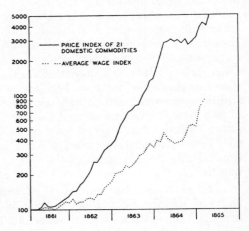

FIG. 6.—Index of prices of twenty-one domestic commodities compared with index of wages. (January, 1861 = 100.)

40 times by March, 1865, or at a rate of 9 per cent a month. If this index overstates the rise in the cost-of-living price index by, say 30 per cent, the cost of living rose approximately 30 times in the Confederacy. Since money wages rose only ten times during the war, real wages declined to approximately one third their prewar level.

In addition to money wages, workers received part of their wages in kind,[45] and this portion was not reduced by the rise in prices. In February, 1865, the Henry Garst Sawmill paid its help $90 and a barrel of flour for a month's labor.[46] Undoubtedly, some workers increased their take-home pay, but not their rate of real hourly wages, by working longer hours. Others worked night shifts and received about one-and-a-half times the day rate; still others must have supplemented their family incomes by growing food on their own small plots of land or having other members of their family take jobs also.

These various ameliorations were probably not very large. If they were equivalent to a 10 per cent increase in money wages, real wages in the Confederacy had declined to well under 40 per cent of their prewar level by March, 1865. Southern labor complained bitterly that its wages were "totally inadequate to afford us the merest necessities of life — plain food, shelter, fuel, and clothing. We are literally reduced to destitution."[47]

Physical productivity probably declined during the war. More people were employed in a fixed plant. For example, 21 people were employed by the Fries Mills in 1861 and 48 in December, 1864. Production was constantly interrupted by Confederate agents who impressed raw materials. The Fries Mill smuggled wool through the Union lines to make Confederate uniforms. When agents seized this wool because the import duty had not been paid, the mill was unable to replace it. The mill did not fulfil its government contract and temporarily halted production.[48] The conscription act also prevented steady and continuous production. The manager of a shoe factory in Montgomery, Alabama, reported:

It takes fully one half the time of my clerks and about as much of my own to attend to the detailing men. I no sooner have a man trained and somewhat efficient than he is ordered to report to camp, and then, after considerable delay, I have his services replaced by a new one and an invalid, in most cases, who is one half the time in the hospital and the other half not able to do much work.[49]

Machinery worn out through normal use was difficult to replace, and occasionally entire factories were destroyed by fire or northern troops. This happened, for example, to some of the furnaces of the Tredegar Mills. These events probably more than offset any increase in productivity caused by patriotically increased endeavor. They reduced the marginal physical product and offset in part the increases

TABLE V
RATIO OF MEAN SKILLED WAGE TO MEAN UNSKILLED WAGE

Date	Ratio	Date	Ratio
1861:		February	2.62
January	3.76	March	2.77
February	4.28	April	2.46
March	3.92	May	2.30
April	4.73	June	2.32
May	4.25	July	2.61
June	3.03	August	2.97
July	4.25	September	2.25
August	3.37	October	2.24
September	......	November	1.69
October	5.30	December	1.86
November	......	1864:	
December	......	January	2.96
1862:		February	2.23
January	3.38	March	2.21
February	3.38	April	3.15
March	3.98	May	2.57
April	4.02	June	2.84
May	3.72	July	2.81
June	3.09	August	2.59
July	3.15	September	3.21
August	3.38	October	3.21
September	3.00	November	3.05
October	2.30	December	1.39
November	2.49	1865:	
December	2.38	January	1.16
1863:		February	3.04
January	2.91	March	3.73

in marginal revenue product caused by inflation. They tended to lower wages by causing downward shifts in the demand schedule for labor.

XI

Changes in the dispersion of wages about the average monthly wage reveal that the labor force was undergoing a change during the war. As a measure of dispersion I took a ratio of the mean skilled wage to the mean unskilled wage.[50] These figures are recorded in Table V. They reveal a downward trend and indicate that the wages of unskilled workers in the South rose faster during the war than the wages of skilled workers. During both world wars and the succeeding inflationary periods there was a similar tendency for the wage spread between occupations to narrow.[51]

Even before Fort Sumter was fired upon, the South had a chronic shortage of skilled workers. The great majority of skilled immigrants coming to America during the 1840's and 1850's settled in the North. Free labor has traditionally feared the competition of slave labor, and the long distances between large southern communities limited the extent of the market that a skilled worker could serve. During the war, the persistent demands of the army reduced the small skilled labor force to such an extent that production was seriously impeded.

In May, 1862, the Quartermaster General wrote the Secretary of War:

> The supplies of this department are totally inadequate to fill the requisitions made upon it. It has been formally reported to me today that requisitions representing the complete outfit of 40,000 men are necessarily unfilled. . . . The deficiency has been occasioned in a great measure by the interference of the conscription act with the arrangements of manufacturers with whom contracts have been made. Under its operation they have been deprived of the service of their employees to such an extent that they have been rendered incapable of complying with the contracts made with this department for continued supplies of various articles absolutely essential for issue to the Army.[52]

A mill in Selma, Alabama, that would roll "iron enough for all our vessels and cast guns for all the batteries"[53] was scheduled for completion in the fall of 1863. In May, 1864, it was still unfinished for want of skilled mechanics. In May, 1864, it was reported that in Charlotte, North Carolina, "a number of our most important tools are idle a large portion of the time for want of mechanics to work them, and some of these tools, the steam-hammer for instance, are the only tools of their class in the Confederacy."[54] The commander of the Naval Ordnance Works at Atlanta, Georgia, complained that he was "unable to have forged the wrought iron bolts for the Brooke gun for the want of blacksmiths," and that "nearly all of the lathes are idle for want of hands."[55]

The *Richmond Enquirer* indignantly pointed out:

> Nearly the whole operation of this extensive establishment, the shoe bureau like the post office, is stopped now because of the absence of the operatives at the front, where, so far, they have done no work save eating up a certain quantity of bacon, pears, and cornmeal. . . . We understand there is an abundance of leather here, and if the shoemakers were not absent, many thousands of pairs of shoes might now be on hand to supply the present and prospective wants. Men in an army cannot march long without shoes.[56]

One week later the *Enquirer* reported that "considerable trouble" was caused in cotton and woolen mills by the conscripting of a few skilled hands. "Not only were women and children stopped from work, but the Government orders for cotton and cloth had to go unfilled."[57]

The shortage of skilled labor induced firms to raid their competitors' labor force. Banton Duncan, who received a contract from the Treasury Department to print Confederate notes, wrote Secretary Memminger that "Hoyer and Ludwig [another printing firm] has already seduced away two of my journeymen."[58] Two days later the Secretary received a letter from a different printing firm stating that "Mr. Duncan has planned the ruin of Mr. Ball and myself. He has already seduced away our workmen; arson has been tried to destroy our premises. Every other effort failing, he tries to scandalize my past life."[59] Letter followed letter, until the harassed Secretary ended the raiding of labor among his printers by making it official Treasury policy to cancel the contract of "any contractor, who by offers of higher wages, or in any way incites any person employed by any contractor to leave such service, or who employs anyone in the service of another contractor, even after he may have been discharged, without his written consent."[60]

The skilled workers of the South were essential to production and accounted for only a small fraction of a firm's total payroll. Under these conditions they could, and did, successfully press for large absolute wage increases.

To maintain output in the face of the large drain of manpower into the army and the shortage of skilled workers, new sources of labor had to be found. Women and children had to be attracted into the labor force and slaves redirected from the farms to factories.

Quartermaster supply depots were located in the larger towns. Many of the women in those areas had never worked in factories before, yet Ramsdell relates that "thousands of women and girls sought employment in the clothing shops."[61] Some women took jobs because it was now patriotic to work for "The Cause." Some wanted to augment the family income and took advantage of the ease of entry into the labor force. A large number, however, must have been attracted by the relatively high wages, for the wages of the unskilled workers in the South during the Civil War rose more than those of skilled workers already in the labor force.

Before the war, slaves were not widely used in manufacturing.[62] Rather, it was the growing of cotton more than anything else that led to the spread of slavery through the South. Typically, all forced labor has required costly supervision to offset its carelessness, wasteful idling, and willful destruction. Cotton-growing, however, had several characteristics that made it adaptable to slave labor.[63]

Many slaves, of course, were highly skilled, and some of the more

28

famous southern buildings, such as the old Vicksburg Courthouse, were built by slaves. The wages of Negro and white bricklayers working on the Statehouse of South Carolina reflect this skill: Negro help systematically received 25 cents less per day than white labor. In May, 1863, white labor received $3.25 per day and Negroes $3.00; in February, 1864, whites received $5.00 and Negroes $4.75; in July, 1864, whites received $6.00 and Negroes $5.75.[64] Since the employment of Negro help cost more than that of white help (because of wages for guards and other expenses) and since the wages of slave and free labor, percentage-wise, came closer together as war continued, these quotations suggest that slaves were more skilled than the whites remaining at home.

Before the war, slaveowners generally preferred to keep their slaves on their own plantations. Slaves were not hired out to factories, "because high wages were not adequate compensation for the liability to contagious and other diseases, demoralization, and the checking of the birth rate caused by the separation of husbands and wives."[65] The firms, in turn, preferred free labor because the factories were forced to assume responsibility for a slave's accident.[66] Southern management also recognized that white workers did not work well side by side with slaves. For example, in 1838,[67] white laborers had protested the hiring of Negro carpenters.[68]

The war may not have changed personal attitudes, but it did alter the established pattern of slave usage. Cotton production declined, and the demand for slaves on plantations fell off correspondingly. Plantation owners and their sons, as well as overseers, were in the army, and the women left at home could not organize or direct their field hands. Firms needed labor and advertised widely for Negro help. "The Macon Armory advertised for 100; the Tredegar Iron Works want 1000; the Naval Gun Foundry and Ordnance Works at Selma wanted 200; the salt works in Clarke County, Alabama, advertised for 500. Almost every industry was competing for Negro labor."[69] Attracted by relatively high returns, more and more slaves were placed on the labor market and were rented to mills, factories, and railroads.

XII

Most southerners who suffered through this inflation believed it was caused by speculators or government impressment agents. Consequently, they tried to combat inflation largely by denouncing these groups, prohibiting goods from crossing state lines, and instituting price control. Southerners confused the forces that actually instigated inflation — the increase in the stock of money and the decrease in real output — with the process through which these forces operated.

They did not concentrate on the basic causes of inflation, and they were unable to formulate a program of reform that might have mitigated some of their hardships.

"The band of harpies preying upon the vitals of the Confederacy,"[70] the speculators and extortioners, was the most widely alleged cause of the inflation. Governor Vance of North Carolina found that, because of extortion and speculation, "it will be impossible to clothe or shoe our troops this winter."[71] One writer in the *Wilmington Journal* claimed that "the speculators have caused the present high prices, and they are determined to make money even if one-half of the people starve."[72] This view was also presented to government officials. Secretary Memminger was told that "the high prices are owing to the wicked spirit that infests so many persons to make money upon the downfall of others, overbidding, overreaching, when we are struggling for our most sacred liberty and independence."[73] Two days later another person wrote the Secretary: "The cause of the high prices lies in the bull and bear games carried on by unprincipled speculators who would sacrifice the whole of the South to enrich themselves."[74]

The number of speculators was reputed to be legion.[75] However, a critic of this position pointed out that everyone with products to sell — farmers, merchants, and manufacturers alike — was accused of being a speculator.[76] Another critic suggested that blockade-runners could not justly be called extortioners. "Their operations certainly bring goods into the country and thus tend to relieve prices — they certainly cannot increase scarcity."[77] But these calm voices went unheard; instead, southerners enjoyed the vicarious thrill of concocting suitable punishments for speculators. One could think of no worse punishment for a speculator than placing him "in the ranks of the army and make him live on half rations of raw, stinking, beef, and black bread."[78] The less imaginative felt that the speculators simply "ought to be hung until dead by the side of traitors and tories."[79]

Poor transportation facilities,[80] droughts,[81] Union armies,[82] and the blockade[83] were also accused of causing the inflation. However, these accusations were neither as bitter nor as frequent as those levied against the agents of the Confederate government who were in daily contact with the public. Except for speculators, these agents were held responsible for high prices more frequently than any other single group or event.

The military authorities, for security reasons, were stringent in granting passports to enter and leave cities. As a result, it was reported that, in Wilmington, "no carts came in with produce. Nothing is brought to market. Nobody comes in to buy or sell."[84] The same events were reported in Richmond.[85]

The specific government agents most despised were the impressment officers.

[If] prices are inconveniently high for poor folks . . . it must be expected so long as the necessities of life are impressed on their way to market by Government agents, who are too lazy to go through the country in search of supplies. Half of the troubles of the army and nearly all of the troubles of the people are due to the existence of the pestiferous commissaries.[86]

Part of this thorough condemnation came because large quantities of impressed goods were never used. They had rotted and decayed.[87] Part also came because commodities were impressed largely from the immediate vicinity of the stationed army.[88] The decreased supply of commodities raised prices to civilians in the area. When it was rumored that impressment officers were near Richmond in 1864, "the people having become alarmed by the interferences of government agents with the sources of supply, cleared the market of flour and produced a heavy advance in the price of that article."[89]

In direct response to the public protests of high prices, "caused" by speculators, extortioners, and impressment agents, the government enacted price control.[90] Secretary of the Treasury George Trenholm, addressing the Commissioners of Prices, said: "In the function conferred upon you by Congress . . . resides . . . the only power capable of interposing a check on the progress of depreciation [of the currency]."[91]

The price commissioners were constantly harassed by the public to lower their ceiling prices.[92] Secretary Trenholm told Governor Bonham of South Carolina that, when he arrived in Richmond, he found

the commissioners of prices had fixed the schedule rate of wheat and corn at $30 and $24 per bushel, respectively, for the months of August and September. . . . Public meetings were held . . . and resolutions adopted patriotically insisting upon a reduction of the standard rates, and their establishment upon a basis sufficiently low to inspire confidence in the currency. The result was that the commissioners reassembled and reduced the schedule prices to $7.50 for wheat for the month of August and $5 for the month of September. A wiser and more patriotic course was never pursued by any people.[93]

The price ceilings imposed by the Confederate government became more and more unrealistic as time passed. In June, 1863, the ceiling prices were, on the average, only 66 per cent of the going market price. By July, 1864, the ceiling prices were only 53.3 per cent, and in October, 1864, only 37.3 per cent of the true market price. The extent to which legal ceilings were flaunted by the public is indicated by the large numbers of newspapers that regularly published a commodity's going market price and its legal ceiling price side by side.

Despite Secretary Trenholm's belief that low price ceilings were essential for the success of the government, the commissioners realistically raised their ceilings when it was urgent that the army procure commodities.[94] When this procedure took too long, the army simply ignored the ceiling rates and paid the full market price.[95]

The controls the South imposed were ad hoc measures designed to placate an outraged citizenry. Aggregate spending was not effectively curbed, and every expectation of higher prices was realized in fact. Under these conditions the Confederate controls completely collapsed.

The people of the South did not focus their attention on the basic cause of the rise in prices that plagued their country. Like the people of other countries during every age, they attempted to correct only the abuses of high prices. Had southerners attacked the most basic cause — the increase in the stock of money per unit of real income — with more vigor and understanding, they might have mitigated some of their hardships.

[1]These were issued in Alabama, Florida, Georgia, Louisiana, Mississippi, and North Carolina (John C. Schwab, *The Confederate States of America*, 1861-1865 [New York: Charles Scribner's Sons, 1901], pp. 149-51).

[2]This was the name given to notes with a face value of less than one dollar issued by cities, railroads, turnpike companies, factories, insurance companies, savings banks, and other southern businesses.

[3]Scattered bank reports are available for five southern states during the war. Georgia figures can be found in the annual reports of the controller-general. Figures for the Bank of the State of South Carolina are available in South Carolina state documents. Virginia bank figures are available in the *Richmond Enquirer* for January 1, 1861; October 1, 1861; April 1, 1862; January 1, 1863; and January 4, 1864. (Since the same banks are not always included in these reports, link relatives were used to determine percentage increases in notes and deposits.) Figures for Louisiana are available in her state documents, but unfortunately this series ends with the capture of the state. North Carolina figures, available in several documents, are of limited utility, because each bank reported on a different date. In addition to these sources, complete bank records for some banks are available in manuscript form at Duke University, the University of Virginia, and the North Carolina State Archives.

From these sources I calculated the number of times by which bank credit expanded in each of these states during the war. The banks of Florida and Alabama were assumed to have behaved like those of the neighboring state of Georgia, Tennessee banks were assumed to have behaved like those of Louisiana, because both states were occupied by Union forces at approximately the same time. Banks in Mississippi, Arkansas, and Texas were omitted for lack of data.

The amount of notes and deposits outstanding in southern states on January 1, 1861, was taken from the United States Treasury figures. Unfortunately, no figures are available for Texas, Arkansas, or Mississippi.

By multiplying the number of times bank credit expanded in each state by the number of notes and deposits outstanding in each state on January 1, 1861,

I estimated the amount of notes and deposits outstanding during the war. These estimates were added to the amount of Confederate notes issued. They are presented in Table I.

[4]During the summer of 1864, bank reserves in some areas declined. In Georgia the reserves were 63.5 per cent in June, 1864. This decline occurred because of the large amount of cash lost by withdrawals for the currency reform of February 17, 1864. The record books of the Bank of the Valley reflect these withdrawals as follows:

Date	Total Deposits
Feb. 3, 1864	$416,593.24
Feb. 15, 1864	345,566.62
Feb. 29, 1864	318,616.56
Mar. 14, 1864	264,379.57
Mar. 31, 1864	17,934.34
Apr. 30, 1864	3,747.27

These withdrawals indicate the public's reluctance to deposit money in banks (i.e., to save in this form) after the currency reform.

[5]Milton Friedman, "Price, Income, and Monetary Changes in Three Wartime Periods," *American Economic Review*, vol. XLII (May, 1952), p. 635.

[6]I used the *Richmond Enquirer, Richmond Whig, Richmond Dispatch, Richmond Sentinel, Wilmington Journal, Fayetteville Observer, North Carolinian, North Carolina Presbyterian, Daily Chronicle and Sentinel* (of Augusta), and *Daily Constitution* (of Augusta).

[7]A simple average of relatives gives equal weight to each item; in measuring the rate of rise of prices, Mitchell felt this was the best kind of index to use when the price rise was caused by an increase in the money supply (Wesley C. Mitchell, *The Making and Using of Index Numbers* [Bureau of Labor Statistics Bull. 656 (Washington, D.C.: Government Printing Office, 1938], p. 8).

[8]To construct these price series, the quotations for each item continuously listed in the newspapers were recorded. (About three times as many quotations were collected from these sources as could be used. Discontinuous series were rejected.) When only one quotation was available for a commodity in a given month, as occasionally happened, this figure was taken as typical of the commodity's price during that month. More often, two or three quotations were available. When I had two quotations for a given month, I took their simple average as typical of the price for the month. When I had three quotations, I gave equal weight to both the beginning and end of the month. (If I had quotations for, say, the first, fifteenth, and thirty-first, I averaged all three quotations. If I had quotations for the first, twenty-fifth, and twenty-eighth, I rejected the twenty-eighth and used only the figures for the first and twenty-fifth.) In most cases, however, at least one quotation a week was available, and the four quotations for the month were averaged.

[9]The complete list of commodities for each city is:

Richmond — corn, rye, red wheat, flaxseed, hay, oats, cotton, tobacco, bacon, butter, lard, cornmeal, family flour, extrafine flour, superfine flour, Irish potatoes, rice, salt, sugar, coffee, molasses, tallow candles, adamantine candles, whiskey, sole leather, upper leather, beeswax, lime.

Fayetteville — corn, rye, wheat, flaxseed, cotton, wool, bacon, lard, family flour, peas, molasses, New Orleans sugar, salt, tallow, iron, nails, peach brandy, apple brandy, cotton yarn, sheeting, green hides, beeswax, spirits of turpentine.

Augusta — corn, wheat, hay, cotton, bacon, butter, eggs, chickens, lard, cornmeal, family flour, peas, rice, coffee, molasses, sugar, pork, salt, tea, beef, bagging, 4/4 sheeting, cotton yarn, 7/8 shirting, osnaburgs (defined in n. 43 below), 3/4 shirting, cotton rope, New Orleans whiskey, apple brandy, peach brandy, nails, iron, dry hides, starch.

Wilmington — corn, hay, cotton, bacon, beef, butter, eggs, chickens, live turkeys, dead turkeys, pork, lard, cornmeal, superfine flour, peanuts, sheeting, wool yarn, beeswax.

[10] Since the Confederacy did not reach full strength until May, 1861, when all eleven states had seceded, this base seemed reasonable to me when I constructed these indexes. At the suggestion of Professor Earl J. Hamilton, I investigated the possibility that prices were already inflated by the first quarter of 1861 because southerners had anticipated war and hoarded goods. The best available price study for the South prior to the Civil War, Professor George Taylor's thirteen-commodity index for Charleston, was used. The quarterly figures for 1858 and 1859 were taken as a base. Professor Taylor's index reveals the following rise in prices:

| | Price Index |
Date	(1858-59 = 100)
Jan., 1861	109.6
Feb., 1861	111.1
Mar., 1861	110.9
Apr., 1861	110.2

These figures suggest that during the first quarter of 1861 prices were 10 per cent above the 1858 and 1859 average and indicate that the 1858-59 period would have been a more suitable base.

[11] The items in this index are: wool, corn, cotton, flaxseed, hay, oats, rye, tobacco, wheat, bacon, beef, butter, chickens, cornmeal, coffee, eggs, extrafine flour, family flour, superfine flour, lard, molasses, peanuts, peas, pork, Irish potatoes, sweet potatoes, rice, salt, sugar, tea, dead turkeys, live turkeys, adamantine candles, tallow candles, bagging, cotton rope, osnaburgs, 4/4 sheeting, 3/4 shirting, 7/8 shirting, cotton yarn, wool yarn, iron, nails, apple brandy, peach brandy, New Orleans whiskey, hides, soles, upper leather, beeswax, lime, spirits of turpentine, starch.

[12] If the same commodity appeared in two or more cities, its average price relatives were recorded. Where a commodity appeared in only one city, that series alone was recorded. These figures were then averaged to form the general price index.

[13] University of Wisconsin Historical Society, McCormic Collection, Special Davidson Collection, Charles Aenentrout to James D. Davidson, March 13, 1864, Fol. Jan., 1863-65.

[14] Letter from J. Ralph Smith, general supervisor of the State Works of South Carolina, to William Gregg, Sept. 4, 1863 (Raphael P. Thian [ed.], *Appendix* [Washington, D.C., 1878], vol. II, p. 140).

[15] The single exception that I found was the siege of Richmond during 1864. This will be treated in greater detail later.

[16] For a more complete discussion of this act, see my article in the *Journal of Political Economy*, vol. XLII (Dec., 1954), pp. 521-22.

[17] The new indexes were farther apart in only four months: April, 1861; July, 1861; April, 1864; and October, 1864.

[18] These figures suggest a picture different from the one held by some historians (E. Merton Coulter, *The Confederate States of America, 1861-1865* [Baton Rouge: Louisiana State University Press, 1950], p. 220, and Charles Ramsdell, *Behind the Lines in the Southern Confederacy* [Baton Rouge: Louisiana State University Press, 1944], *passim*).

[19] A hypothesis accounting for these figures is that horses and wagons, not railroads, were the most important form of transportation in the South, and these simple facilities could be repaired or replaced more readily when destroyed than railroad equipment.

[20] Rapid technological advance in the production of one commodity, for

instance, could account for different rates of price rise. It is assumed throughout this section that great technological gains were not made in the South during the war.

[21] Legislation passed by both sides to prevent trading with the enemy had the same effect.

[22] These categories include: *imports* — wool, molasses, sugar, coffee, tea, and salt; *exports* — tobacco, cotton, peanuts, peas, rice; *part imported* — bagging, cotton rope, 4/4 sheeting, 3/4 shirting, 7/8 shirting, cotton yarn, wool yarn, iron, cut nails, soles, uppers; *domestic* — corn, flaxseed, hay, rye, wheat, bacon, beef, butter, chickens, cornmeal, eggs, family flour, extrafine flour, superfine flour, lard, Irish potatoes, sweet potatoes, dead turkeys, live turkeys, tallow, osnaburgs. See Fig. 4.

[23] In Danville, Virginia, it was reported to the Treasury Department that "there seems to be a strong desire generally to place almost the entire crop under the control of the government. This sentiment is not slight. A general and strong desire prevails that this course is absolutely necessary" (letter from Almanzon Huston to Memminger, June 16, 1861 [Thian (ed.) *Appendix*, vol. I, p 140].)

In a letter to the editor of the *New Orleans Delta*, the alternative to government subsidiaries to planters was ominously suggested: "If the planters are prohibited from sending their cotton to market until the blockade is raised, and they are to receive no money in the meantime, how are they to get along? Their negroes must have shoes and winter clothing; their families must have something; their country store debts must be paid, else the country merchants cannot pay their debts to the wholesale city merchants. Therefore, they can get no goods, and the whole business of the country is completely broken up" (Oct. 3, 1861 [*ibid.*, p. 358]).

Other letters to the Secretary of the Treasury pointed out that, because the blockade lowered the price of cotton and tobacco, planters were unable to buy Confederate bonds or to pay their taxes (letter from F. S. Lyon to C. J. McRaie, May 13, 1861 [*ibid.*, p. 98]; letter from C. T. Lowndes to Memminger, June 13, 1861 [*ibid.*, p. 133]; letter from James F. White and J. W. Drake to Jefferson Davis, July 13, 1861 [*ibid.*, p. 211]; and many others).

[24] Since the southerners tried to coerce European countries into recognizing the Confederacy in 1861, some voluntarily withheld their cotton from the European trade.

[25] Ramsdell also attributed much of the rapid rise in the price of cloth in 1861 to the depletion of stocks (Charles Ramsdell, "The Control of Manufacturing by the Confederate Government," *Mississippi Valley Historical Review*, vol. VIII [Dec., 1921], p. 234).

[26] Coulter, *The Confederate States*, p. 242. These figures appear to me to be extreme. However, they are suggestive of the change in production that went on during this period.

[27] Since $MV = PY$, $M/P = Y/V$, where M is the stock of money; P, the price level; Y, real income; and V, income velocity.

[28] This study ends in Jan. 1864, the last date for which I was able to obtain figures on the quantity of money in circulation in the South. I believe that the real value of the stock of money continued to decline until the end of the war.

[29] John M. Keynes, *A Tract on Monetary Reform* (New York: Harcourt, Brace & Co., 1924), pp. 50-51.

[30] Secretary Memminger's full statement is as follows: "In a former report it was shown that the circulation of the Confederate States before the war might be estimated at $100 million. [My estimate of the quantity of money outstanding in the South before the war is very close to that of the Secretary of the Treasury. Mine is $94.5 million; his, $100 million.] In the existing state of things, it is probable that a larger amount of currency is required. In time of peace **money**

passes rapidly from hand to hand, and the same money in a single day will discharge many obligations. A large portion, too, of the operations of business is performed by bills of exchange and bank checks. In the present stagnation of commerce and intercourse, larger amounts of ready money are kept on hand by each individual, and the Confederate Treasury Notes and Call Certificates are used as substitutes for bills and drafts to a considerable extent. If this view be just, we may venture to add as much as 50 per cent to the usual amount of currency, and this would raise the sum total at which it might stand to $150 millions. The difference between this sum and the actual circulation will show the redundancy (Memminger, "Report of January 10, 1863" [Thian (ed), Appendix, vol. III, p. 102]).

[31]The real value of cash balances had declined to 0.9 by January, 1863. If velocity fell to two-thirds, real income must have been only 60 per cent of its January, 1861, amount.

[32]General Evans found 318,000 men enrolled in the army on Jan. 1, 1862; 465,584 on Jan. 1, 1863; 472,781 on Jan. 1, 1864 and 439,675 on Jan. 1, 1865 (Clement A. Evans, Confederate Military History [Atlanta: Confederate Publishing Co., 1899], vol. VII, p. 500).

[33]Livermore is quoted with approval by Rhodes: "The number of men in the Confederate army was 1,082,119" (James Ford Rhodes, History of the Civil War [New York: Macmillan Co., 1904], vol. V, p. 186). Since "the total number of all white males who came within the final limits of military age was probably under 1,150,000" (Chester Wright, Economic History of the United States [2d ed.; New York: McGraw-Hill Book Co., 1949], p. 434), Livermore's estimates must surely be too high.

[34]According to General Evans' figures, the number of men in the army stayed at roughly their January, 1863, level. This means the effect of mobilization was to reduce suddenly the number of people in the labor force.

[35]Earl J. Hamilton, "Profit Inflation and the Industrial Revolution, 1751-1800," in Enterprise and Secular Change, ed. Frederic C. Lane and Jelle C. Riemersma (Homewood, Ill.: Richard D. Irwin, Inc., 1953), p. 328.

[36]History of Manufacturers in the United States: 1607-1928 (New York: McGraw-Hill Book Co., 1928), vol. II, p. 51.

[37]The most fruitful source of quotations was the Tredegar Iron Works. Their account books have recently been opened to the public and are now available in the Virginia State Library. The payroll book for 1863 and 1864 is complete. However, the payroll book for 1861-62 was lost or destroyed. Some wage quotations for this earlier period can be gotten from the firm's daily journal. Quotations for foundry and forge workers, pattern-makers, carpenters, blacksmiths, boilermakers, machinists, turners, and fitters are available. The University of North Carolina has the account book of the Henry Garst Flour and Saw Mill and the John Judge Sock and Yarn Factory. These include quotations for farm hands, butchers, and general labor. In the Moravian Archives at Winston Salem, North Carolina, the account books of the Fries Cotton and Wool Company are available. Only the total payroll and the number of people employed are listed. From this source the average take-home pay was recorded. The timebook of the Atlanta, Georgia, arsenal, available at the National Archives in Washington, revealed figures for 1863 and 1864 for guards, machinists, carpenters, cartridge-makers, and superintendents. The accounts of the Central Laboratory of Georgia, also located in the National Archives, give data for 1863, 1864, and 1865 on carpenters, watchmen, overseers, bricklayers, brick-burners, and painters. In the Historical Commission of Columbia, South Carolina, the records for the building of the statehouse are available and reveal the figures for quarrymen, assistant quarrymen, blacksmiths, engineers, watchmen, carpenters, hostlers, architects, and railroad inspectors in 1862-63. The Graham Robinson Iron and Steel Works account

books at the University of Virginia reveal the wages paid to several workers in the mills, not classified by profession, throughout the war.

[38] In the case of pattern-makers the high wage, rather than the median, was used because for the years 1861-62 it was the only quotation available.

[39] The mode was rejected because some series were bimodal or trimodal, while others had no mode.

[40] There were 16 cases for which figures were available in both 1861 and 1862. These include forge-workers, pattern-makers, sawmill help, turners, fitters, watchmen, four individuals in the Graham Robinson Mill, foundry help, boiler-makers, carpenters, and the help in the Fries Cotton and Wool Company Mill. The average of the first quotation in 1862 to the first quotation in 1861 for these 16 cases was 1.085.

[41] If figures were available only for 1863, the trades were not used.

[42] The earliest systematic reports for family living in the United States that have been located are for the years 1816-17 and 1835. The next study available is for the 1870's (see Faith M. Williams and Carle C. Zimmerman, *Studies of Family Living in the United States and Other Countries* [U.S. Department of Agriculture Misc. Publication 223 (Washington, D.C.: Government Printing Office, 1935)], p. 7).

[43] This index includes corn, hay, rye, wheat, bacon, beef, butter, chickens, flaxseed, cornmeal, eggs, superfine flour, family flour, extrafine flour, lard, Irish potatoes, sweet potatoes, live turkeys, tallow, and osnaburgs.

As we have seen, the northern blockade curtailed the supply of imported commodities but increased the supply of exported commodities to the home market. It made import prices rise more and export prices rise less than an average of all commodity prices. The prices of farm products and textiles were not directly affected by the blockade. (The supply of wool and cotton, of course, was affected by the blockade. The textile included in my index is osnaburgs, the type of cloth worn by Negroes and manufactured in the South.) The prices of farm products and textiles rose as a result of the increase in the quantity of money and the decrease in real output. By deflating money wages by their average price rise, one approximates the way in which these forces alone affected the value of a worker's income.

[44] I assume that prices in the South behaved like prices in the North during the Civil War and in the United States during the two world wars. In the Civil War an average of textile and farm prices rose 19 per cent more than the cost-of-living index; in World War I, 21 per cent more; in World War II, 40 per cent more.

[45] Some workers received part of their wages in kind before 1861, just as some do today. During the Civil War this practice intensified.

[46] University of North Carolina, Southern Historical Collection, "Henry Garst Payroll Book, 1860-1866," p. 30.

[47] Letter from Taylor to Memminger, Oct. 14, 1863 (Thian [ed.], *Appendix*, vol. II, p. 153).

[48] See Moravian Archives (Winston-Salem, N.C.), "Fries Letter Books" (MSS), 1863.

[49] Quoted in Ramsdell, "The Control of Manufacturing by the Confederate Government," p. 248.

[50] I classified the following trades as skilled: engineers, bricklayers, machinists, foremen, boilermakers, pattern-makers, carpenters, blacksmiths, and the highest figure found in a month for foundry and quarry help. As unskilled trades I classified sawmill help, butchers, farm help, watchmen, overseers, yarn-and-sock-factory help, isolated individuals in steel mills, and railroad inspectors.

[51] Philip W. Bell, "Cyclical Variations and Trend in Occupational Wage

Differentials in American Industry since 1914," *Review of Economics and Statistics*, vol. XXXIII (Nov., 1951), p. 331.

[52] Letter from A. C. Meyers to H. G. Randolph, May 23, 1863 (U.S. War Department, *The War of the Rebellion*, Series IV [Washington, D.C.: Government Printing Office, 1880-1901], vol. I, p. 1127).

[53] Letter from C. Jones to J. M. Brooke (*ibid.*, vol. III, p. 523).

[54] Letter from H. Ashton Ramsay, chief engineer, to Commander J. M. Brooke, chief, Bureau of Ordnance and Hydrography, May 5, 1864 (*ibid.*, p .521).

[55] Letter from D. M. McCorkle to J. M. Brooke (*ibid.*, p. 522).

[56] June 16, 1864.

[57] June 21, 1864.

[58] Letter from Duncan to Memminger, Oct. 21, 1862 (Thian [ed.], *Appendix*, vol. I, p. 656).

[59] Letter from E. Ketzinge to Memminger, Oct. 23, 1862 (*ibid.*, p. 657).

[60] Correspondence of the Treasury, April 23, 1863 (*ibid.*, vol. III, p. 444).

[61] "The Control of Manufacturing by the Confederate Government," p. 223.

[62] Ulrich B. Phillips, *American Negro Slavery* (New York: D. Appleton-Century Co., 1918), p. 380.

[63] The work involved was simple and routine in character, since only plain tools were used; supervision was relatively easy because more labor was used per acre than for many other crops; at the peak of the labor demand in picking, practically the whole slave family, young and old, could be employed; though the methods employed exhausted the soil and so necessitated either a more careful and varied agriculture, for which slave labor was less adapted, or else resort to new fertile land, this latter alternative was always available, for the rich alluvial soil of the Mississippi Valley was more fertile than that of the older cotton-growing states, and the limit of expansion had not been reached in 1860 (Wright, *Economic History of the U.S.*, p. 303).

[64] South Carolina State Archives, account book for the South Carolina Statehouse.

[65] Phillips, *American Negro Slavery*, p. 380.

[66] *Ibid.*, p. 379.

[67] J. R. Commons and Ulrich B. Phillips (eds.), *Documentary History of American Industrial Society* (Cleveland: A. H. Clark Co., 1910-11), vol. II, p. 360.

[68] In 1858 Frederick L. Olmsted stated that, in a mining camp, a group of 20 or 30 white laborers came up to a newly hired white Englishman and told him "they would allow him 15 minutes to get out of sight, and if they ever saw him in those parts again, they would give him hell." The reason given to Olmsted for this action was that the Englishman was "too free-like with the niggers and they thought he'd make 'em think too much of themselves" (*ibid.*, p. 170).

[69] Coulter, *The Confederate States*, p. 258.

[70] *Wilmington Journal*, Oct. 9, 1862.

[71] Letter from Z. B. Vance to Weldon N. Edwards, Sept. 18, 1862 (U.S. War Department, *The War of the Rebellion*, vol. I, p. 85).

[72] July 6, 1862.

[73] Letter from Joseph Newman to Memminger, March 20, 1863 (Thian [ed.], *Appendix*, vol. II, p. 57).

[74] Letter from George F. Gerding to Memminger, March 22, 1863 (*ibid.*, p. 62).

[75] "On Thursday last, our town was full to overflowing with the merchants and speculators, Jews and Gentiles, men from East and West, North and South, who came to attend the advertised auction sale of goods" (*Wilmington Journal*, Aug. 30, 1862).

[76] *Ibid.*, July 10, 1863.

---

[77] *Ibid.*, Sept. 29, 1864.

[78] *Ibid.*, July 6, 1862.

[79] Nov. 20, 1862.

[80] Jan. 4, 1862; *Richmond Enquirer*, March 20, 1863; *Richmond Whig*, June 13, 1864.

[81] Letter from Ruffin to Northrop. Nov. 3, 1862 (U.S. War Department, *The War of the Rebellion*, vol. II, p. 159); *Richmond Whig*, August 15, 1864.

[82] *Richmond Whig*, June 13, 1864; *Wilmington Journal*, June 14, 1862.

[83] *Wilmington Journal*, March 31, 1864; *Richmond Whig*, Aug. 23, 1864.

[84] *Wilmington Journal*, Jan. 24, 1863.

[85] "The owners of a number of country carts that used to bring supplies to this market have of late ceased to come, though the markets are destitute of vegetables common to the season. As many carts as formerly start for the city, but many now stop before reaching their destination, haul up at some convenient place by the roadside, sell their goods and put for home instantly. The market men allege, with show of justice, we presume, that when they come into the city, they are bothered half out of their wits to get out again. When applying for a passport, they have to produce somebody who knows them, as a voucher, a thing not always easy to do. Then, again they say they are stopped on every corner of the street and subjected to cross questioning by the military guard whose importunities are not always to be resisted" (*Richmond Enquirer*, June 15, 1864).

[86] *Richmond Whig*, Oct. 21, 1864. The *Richmond Whig* of May 2, 1864, reflected public sentiment in its short news item on the impressment of horses: "The horse impressment business seems to have died out. The long legged, white hatted men, with their negroes and bailers, were nowhere to be seen on Saturday. The number of animals secured by impressment in Richmond is said to have been ridiculously small — so many had to be liberated as belonging to Government officers. . . . An attempt was made to seize the President's horse while standing with his carriage in front of his office."

[87] "Last year the country was filled with Government agents impressing the wheat and grinding it before it was dry. The result was thousands of bushels were either bulked up or ground damp and destroyed. The agents were warned of the result, but they were too wise to take advice. Most of them were impudent young men who ought to have been in the ranks. They knew nothing about business and were insulting wherever they went" (*ibid.*, July 19, 1864).

[88] *Richmond Enquirer*, March 13, 1863. (This newspaper is misdated March 13, 1862.)

[89] *Richmond Whig*, Sept. 2, 1864.

[90] Ramsdell has shown that, by controlling the number of conscripts allowed to work in specific factories, the government was able to influence the price of the commodities produced. Early in the war this control extended only to the goods the government purchased for its own use. However, by the end of the war, Ramsdell concluded that the army attempted to regulate the price of commodities going to the consumer as well ("Control of Manufacturing by the Confederate Government," p. 239).

[91] Speech delivered in Montgomery, Alabama, Sept. 3, 1864; reported in the *Richmond Whig*, Oct. 12, 1864.

[92] "What do the Confederate Commissioners mean by fixing the prices of wheat and corn at the figures they have? . . . Is it the intention of the Commissioners purposely to increase the price of provisions? . . . It is well known that producers will always demand higher prices from private purchasers than that fixed by schedule, and if the Government attempts to keep up with and outbid the market in this way, by the expiration of the year, prices will have reached a point beyond that which imagination can follow them" (*ibid.*, July 19, 1864).

[93] Letter from Trenholm to Governor Bonham, August 5, 1864 (Thian [ed.], *Appendix*, vol. IV, p. 378).

[94] "Having readopted the schedules for May and June last, in accordance with the clearly manifested wishes of the people, we have thought it advisable and proper to stimulate the sales and delivery of small grain, etc. now so much needed as to be indispensable by advancing the price of wheat, flour, corn, meat, oats, and hay delivered in the month of August" ("Report of the Price Commissioners," in the *Richmond Enquirer*, Aug. 2, 1864).

[95] Letter from the Commissioner of Prices in Virginia to Secretary of War Seddon, Aug. 1, 1864, reprinted in the *Richmond Enquirer*, Aug. 2, 1864.

This article by Victor Clark is a remarkable piece of work. Clark had studied the history of manufacturing in the United States from earliest times to the period just after World War I. He thus brought a perspective to Civil War economic history which few scholars since have had. He stressed the importance of technology in stimulating economic growth but concluded that the War did not "revolutionize" manufacturing methods and production. Is this conclusion justified?

MANUFACTURING DEVELOPMENT DURING THE CIVIL WAR

By Victor S. Clark

THE DRAMATIC INCIDENTS of history so focus our attention, that they subordinate unduly attendant circumstances of first importance, and present themselves as the creators of the very conditions that gave them birth. Not improbably we and our successors for years to come shall interpret the present world war as the origin of a social and economic, as well as a political revolution, of which it is only an intermediate — though indeed a critical and tragic phase. In a like manner we are still inclined to attribute to the stress of the Civil War the beginning of our transition from a planting to a manufacturing nation, although that struggle of itself changed no existing economic tendency in America, and like a whirlpool in a river neither contributed to the volume of our production nor permanently diverted its direction.

During the decade that preceded 1860 the country had made the most remarkable industrial progress in its history. Railways had extended until they began to form a truly national system of communication; settlement had spread rapidly through the prairie states and upon the Pacific Coast; our foreign commerce was unprecedented; immigration was increasing; and new mineral resources — not only the precious metals of the West, but copper and iron from Lake Superior — were developed. In spite of the financial crisis of 1857, the nation was prospering and growing as seldom before when the War broke out.

No form of production had responded more promptly or more fully to the encouragement afforded by these conditions than manufacturing. During these ten years our iron and textile industries had grown two thirds. Although premonitory symptoms appeared before 1860 of the coming decline of our merchant marine, American shipyards at that time built — not sporadically, but as a regular business — commercial and war vessels for other countries, and equipped them with all the appliances of steam navigation. Our locomotive works sent a substantial share of their output to Europe. We were probably in advance of any other nation in the use of interchangeable mechanism and the application of automatic machinery to producing standard parts. A commission sent by the British government to America soon after the Crystal Palace exhibition, to study our machinery, reported that more than 100 different automatic power tools were used to shape the parts of a Springfield rifle. The Colt Arms Works, at Hartford, was probably the finest private establishment of the kind in the world. Before the War we made both military rifles and the machinery to manufacture them for the British and other foreign governments, and, even in the midst of hostilities, New England makers produced equipment for European arsenals.

We had applied factory methods of mechanical production not only to making firearms, but also to the manufacture of clocks, and watches, sewing machines, and agricultural and textile machinery. In a word, the factories and workshops of New England and the central states were already prepared to equip armies and to replace the waste of modern war. We did not have to create these establishments when hostilities began, but only to transform them to military uses. Indeed until currency inflation unsettled foreign exchange and domestic prices, even our heavy engineering industries, which were relatively less advanced than light metal-working, produced a surplus above both military and civilian needs, although the latter embraced railway equipment and development machinery for the West. While hostilities were in progress our works continued to build steamships, locomotives, mills, and power tools for South America and Europe.

If the War did not create new manufactures, neither did it revolutionize industrial labor in the northern states. For fifteen years or more English-speaking and German immigrants had been crowding into our factories and workshops. British and Irish operatives already predominated in the cotton factories of Rhode Island, and Welsh and Scotch ironmakers manned the furnaces and rolling mills of Pennsylvania.

In the South the War, instead of stimulating the infant manufactures already in existence, interrupted their normal growth; so that for a decade thereafter they made no appreciable progress. The only important engineering works in the Confederacy in 1861 were at Richmond. These have survived; but other works erected or extended for war purposes proved unimportant in the subsequent history of southern ironmaking. When North Carolina seceded, the state government compiled a list of 40 cotton mills and 8 woolen mills within its jurisdiction. There were factories of greater individual importance in Virginia, South Carolina, and Georgia, and small establishments existed in Alabama and Tennessee. But the total number of cotton spindles in the seceding states was less than those in the single city of Lowell, and their number soon declined from lack of normal replacement and through the destruction wrought by northern troops.

Although the Civil War did not, like the period of international disturbance that culminated with the War of 1812, create new forms of domestic industry in America or modify radically methods of production, it was the immediate occasion of a far-reaching change in the attitude of our government towards manufacturing. We hardly need to recall that our second war with England was followed by a high tariff era, whose rising tide of protection did not culminate until 1828. Still it is an interesting instance of those repetitions that so often occur in economic history, that the war of the rebellion was like its predecesssor in inaugurating a second cycle of high protection, which, starting from purely fiscal motives, expanded into an avowed attempt to shape by governmental forces the forms of national production. The fact that the secession of the South and its subsequent political impotence left the manufacturing states in control of federal policies, affected the subsequent organization, and what we might term the political history, of American industry. During the War itself, high duties helped northern factory owners to control the domestic market in spite of heavy internal taxes, and this practical monopoly compensated them for the temporary loss of their southern customers. But the high tariff policy then inaugurated was a post-bellum influence so far as it had permanent effect upon the growth of our manufactures.

Neither did the War prove a stimulus to technical development, beyond what might be expected in times of peace. Although the Bessemer process of making steel was in practical operation in England when our heaviest demands for ordnance and armor arose, it was not introduced into the United States until 1865. During this period we continued to import from England most of the high-grade iron used by our arsenals for rifle barrels, though we drew increasingly upon domestic sources for this material as the War progressed. At a time when the Krupps were making successful heavy artillery of steel, American makers were experimenting with wrought-iron cannon. All our heavy ordnance in actual service was of cast iron, and our field guns were of iron or brass. The Confederates manufactured howitzers of an Austrian alloy, which was thought to be a stronger metal than was used by the North. Shortly before the attack on Fort Sumter, army engineers had cast at Pittsburgh, by the Rodman process, a 15-inch coast gun weighing 25 tons and throwing a 337-pound shot; four years later 20-inch guns weighing 50 tons and throwing 1000-pound shot were cast at the same foundry. Although English and European works were rolling armor plates 12 inches thick, the largest mills in America so recently as 1863 refused John Ericson's orders for 1½-inch plates because their shears were not heavy enough to trim them. It was not until the close of the War that 5-inch plates were tendered to the government by American makers. The plank-like heavy armor of the Confederate ironclads and rams was forged; and the armor of the monitor turrets was built up of successive layers of thin rolled plates. Though Ericson even defended the latter method of construction, practice proved it to be inferior and it was discarded as soon as heavier armor could be procured. Foundry and rolling-mill practice made quantitative progress during the War — bigger masses of metal could be produced and handled than before — but there was no marked improvement in processes and principles. In fact, American metallurgy then stood at the boundary between two eras, that of iron and that of steel; and in ironmaking alone we made little technical advance between the middle 1850's and the introduction of the Bessemer process.

Shortage of labor and a sudden demand for large quantities of standard goods extended the use of machinery. It is a familiar incident of our economic history that the enlistment of thousands of country boys in the army and navy forced American farmers to adopt such novelties as mowers and reapers, which had but recently been perfected, and which under different circumstances might have been slow to overcome rural prejudice. This change from hand to animal cultivation greatly stimulated the manufacture of farm machinery, especially in the West. The introduction of sewing machines was going on apace when the War began, and the urgent demand for uniforms caused them to be almost at once universally employed in the clothing industry. Their use increased so rapidly in boot and shoe-making that they forced the invention of other machinery to perform correlated operations, and hastened the transition of this industry from a domestic to a factory organization. Yet in all such instances, the effect of the War was to accelerate existing tendencies, not to change their direction; and the question arises whether this abnormal acceleration for a short interval really affected the average rate of technical progress over a longer period.

Although inventors kept the patent office busy, no epoch-making improvement, like the steamboat, the powerloom, the harvester, the sewing machine, the telegraph, or the Goodyear rubber process, marked the war era. Even in the field of military devices the government accepted but tardily any idea that had the taint of novelty! Breechloading firearms were already manufactured in America, and machine guns were soon tendered to the army; but four years of repeated successful tests hardly induced our military authorities to adopt them. Indeed Gatling guns were never used except in a few subordinate operations. The naval authorities showed more enterprise than the army heads in utilizing inventions. They were the first to test armored vessels against other ships of war, and they introduced the revolving turret. Both the North and the South employed submarine mines and fixed torpedoes. Meantime, private inventors experimented with firing artillery under water and constructed submersible vessels.

Although this period contributed no outstanding improvement to the technical equipment of American industry, hostilities did not halt progress in the arts of peace. Steam engineering, textile manufacturing, photography, printing, paper-making, glass-making, and other branches of manufacture continued their uninterrupted technical advance.

Half a century ago war made lighter requisitions upon the productive forces of a country than at present. Man's powers of destruction were comparatively undeveloped, and his powers of creation were correspondingly less exerted. Except in 1864 our furnaces did not during any war year make materially more iron than in 1860, and the increase of their average output was less than the normal growth in times of peace. As early as 1870, American pig-iron production was nearly double that of the war era. The North experienced little dearth of any raw material except cotton. Michigan and the Far West furnished copper, and Missouri and Wisconsin supplied part of our demand for lead. A temporary shortage of coal occurred in the East, and there was some talk of converting locomotives into wood burners; but no such embarrassment as exists today confronted our industries from lack of fuel. For a short time paper stock was wanting, but a rise in the price of rags drew out such a large supply that speculators in these materials lost money. At the same time, wood pulp began to be used for print paper. Coal-tar colors already had been discovered, and their manufacture began on Long Island in 1865. But vegetable indigo was used to dye uniforms of the boys in blue. A temporary shortage of this material was overcome, and the North was soon able to provide itself with all requisites for the domestic manufacture of both army and civilian clothing.

During the uncertain months before the South seceded, New England manufacturers acquired large stocks of cotton. These supplies, with some foreign importations, with cotton procured in southern territories occupied by northern troops, and with the crop of southern Indiana, Illinois, and other northern and border states, kept our spindles partly employed throughout the war. Several new mills were built, others were enlarged, and the cotton thread industry was finally established. Yet 50 per cent of the cotton machinery of the country was idle, and our consumption decreased to about one half what it was in 1860. Manufacturers of coarse goods suffered most. Consequently the Merrimack mills felt the shortage of cotton more than those of southern Massachusetts and Rhode Island. Indeed the War roughly marks the date when the primacy of spindles in America began to swing from Lowell to Fall River. No substitute for cotton was discovered, though hopeful efforts were made to adapt flax fibre to this requirement. Homespun manufactures increased in some sections of the North, and extended in the South until they supplied clothing for the common people and for no small portion of the Confederate troops.

During this period of partial idleness, some New England cotton companies made firearms for the government, and others undertook to manufacture woolens. Indeed the latter industry grew as rapidly as the cotton industry declined. Before the outbreak of the War the whole United States consumed in domestic manufacturing about 100,000,000 pounds of wool annually; by 1865 the North alone used double this amount. The South had relatively less wool than the North had cotton, and lacked machinery to manufacture this meagre quantity. Though many northern mills made cloth exclusively for the army, so that in 1862 the government was actually oversupplied from domestic sources and tried to cancel contracts, the diversification of the industry in response to civilian demands was an equally marked feature of the period. At this time the manufacture of fine worsted dress goods became established in this country, and the national colors were first made of domestic bunting.

The manufactures established in the South during the Confederacy were largely of an emergency character. Arsenals, cannon foundries, armor forges, and powder works were erected, only to be destroyed by northern raiders after a year or two of service. A few cotton mills survived the waste of war, principally in the vicinity of Augusta. The Confederate and state governments directly promoted and superintended manufacturing. Virginia and Georgia imported textile machinery on public account, and North Carolina disbursed through a manufacturing board many millions in paper currency. The product of cotton mills in that state was impressed by the authorities at 75 per cent advance upon the cost of making, as reported by the mill owners themselves. Even then the state had to use its control over transportation and raw materials to prevent an evasion of these requirements.

Manufacturing profits in both sections of the country were very high, partly on account of the steady rise in prices that accompanied currency inflation. The mill owners who lost money were those who gambled on an early peace. Even industries purveying to luxury, such

46

as the manufacture of cut glass, decorated porcelain, silks, and fine dress goods, throve beyond example. Nor was this prosperity supported entirely by shoddy contractors and legitimate profiteers. The ordinary returns of our growing grain and provision exports, the enormous winnings of our petroleum pioneers, and the general stimulus of active demand in a country with more natural resources than it could utilize, combined to make this an era of profitable trade, high wages, and remunerative investment. Even the fictitious gains of inflation must have affected the popular imagination. According to the state census, between 1860 and 1865 Rhode Island increased the value of its cotton goods from $15,000,000 to $55,000,000, in spite of lessened output; the value of woolen cloth produced rose from $4,000,000 to nearly $11,000,000; and the value of iron manufactures increased from $1,750,000 to $4,500,000. Between 1862 and 1864 inclusive, threescore factories were built annually in the city of Philadelphia. At the close of the War one of the most competent observers in the South wrote after a trip through the North:

"Currently with the enormous and unexampled expenditure of men, money, and materials which the Federal States were subjected to for five years, every one of them increased its production and added to its wealth. And this increase of wealth was permanent and visible. It is to be seen in new furnaces, mills, factories, tanneries; in new mines of iron, coal, copper, lead, and zinc; in new railroads and countless oil wells; in the multiplication of machinery and the establishment of new industries; in the vast number of new vessels on lakes, rivers, and canals; in the extraordinary increase of elegant and costly dwellings in country and town."

Allowing for the fact that the contrast between the wasted South and the intact and growing resources of the North must have struck with peculiar vividness the vision and imagination of a war-worn visitor from the former section, nevertheless the facts themselves were indubitable. However, the question still remains: were these improvements the creation, or even indirectly the outcome, of a carnival of economic waste, that like a wound in the body of the state incited an abnormal production of new tissue to heal its losses? Or were they rather the victory of economic forces rallying from the depression of 1857, that carried us happily through the stress of war on a tide of trade prosperity — a tide that continued to rise through all the unsettling circumstances of hostilities, peace, and reconstruction, until it ebbed in the breakers of another crisis in 1873? If the War was the controlling factor in manufacturing conditions between 1861 and 1865, is it not remarkable that its effect should to such a considerable degree coincide with the results of normal peace influences during other interpanic intervals of our history?

In this article, E. D. Fite surveys the performance of the agricultural sector of the economy. He starts from the premise that agricultural development was on the upsurge well before the onset of War. The enormous demands of War and the economic readjustments it created contributed, in Fite's judgment, to a fundamental redirection in agricultural methods and production.

THE AGRICULTURAL DEVELOPMENT OF THE WEST DURING THE CIVIL WAR

By Emerson D. Fite

O NE OF THE MOST remarkable features of the industrial and commercial conditions in the North during the Civil War was the steady growth of the agricultural states of the West. The passionate excitement of war and the deep interest in politics, which the present generation is wont to consider the only prominent characteristics of the time, after all absorbed but a part of the country's attention. There was a peaceful expansion westward, an agricultural development in those states comparable to that of the previous decade, which added enormously to the nation's resources and contributed largely to the final success of the North. Without the War this development might, indeed, have been greater; but its extent, in spite of the War, was marvelous.

The leading agricultural states — Indiana, Illinois, Wisconsin, and Iowa — were in the midst of great development when the year 1861 opened. Notwithstanding the check caused by the panic of 1857, the advance of their farming interests in the previous decade had been conspicuous, their agricultural area having increased 80 per cent and the value of their farms 270 per cent (from $277,000,000 to $1,027,000,000). Their combined wheat crop rose from 21,000,000 bushels in 1849 to 63,000,000 bushels in 1859, that of corn from 120,000,000 bushels to 230,000,000 bushels, and that of oats from 20,000,000 to 38,000,000 bushels. This growth, more rapid than agricultural growth had ever been in any other section of the North, was in strong contrast to the gradually decreasing crops of the East.

During the years of fighting there was continued advance. Large crops in 1860 and 1861 were succeeded in 1862 by the largest crops in the history of the country up to that time, when in the four states under consideration the wheat crop of 83,000,000 bushels was 33⅓ per cent more than in 1859, that of corn 290,000,000 bushels, 25 per cent more than in 1859, that of oats 43,000,000 bushels, an advance of 15 per cent. With the exception of the corn crop of 1863, which was damaged by frosts, and the wheat crop of 1864, these figures were maintained, and in some respects surpassed, in 1863, 1864, and 1865. The same is true also for the North as a whole, according to the estimates of the Department of Agriculture.[1]

In no way, perhaps, is the steady progress better illustrated than by the grain shipments from the city of Chicago. The record of this city is marvelous. Starting in 1838 with a shipment of 78 bushels of wheat, and each year thereafter increasing her shipments, but never before 1860 sending out over 10,000,000 bushels of wheat and wheat flour, this new city for each year of the War shipped, on the average, 20,000,000 bushels of wheat and wheat flour. Her yearly corn exports, before 1860 never above 11,000,000 bushels, averaged during the War 25,000,000 bushels. Of all kinds of grain her shipments in 1860 were the largest to that date — 31,000,000 bushels. But in 1861 these mounted up to 50,000,000 bushels; to 56,000,000 bushels in 1862; 54,000,000 bushels in 1863; 46,000,000 bushels in 1864; and 52,-000,000 bushels in 1865. So it was also for Milwaukee, Detroit, Toledo, and other lake ports, and for Cincinnati, though with no such phenomenal advances.[2] The commerce of the Great Lakes, by which route over 90 per cent of this grain was transported to Buffalo and other eastern lake ports, was also very large, nearly twice as large as before 1861, while the grain receipts of Buffalo and New York and the business of the New York railroads and canals showed equal progress.

The lake ports, especially Chicago, were undoubtedly profiting by the closing of the Mississippi River to New Orleans, for they gained most of the shipments from the interior which usually went to the southern port, so that the increased shipments of northern cities and the increased traffic of the northern transportation routes do not exactly measure the growth of the crops. From 1850 to 1860 New Orleans received on the average approximately 10,000,000 bushels of grain each year.[3] If we say that all of this trade was diverted to the one city of Chicago — an unreasonable assumption — we see that it constituted only from one third to one half of the increase of Chicago's trade. The opening of the river in 1863 had no appreciable effect in starting traffic again southward, because marauders on both banks continued to make the route unsafe, and because the westerners had come to appreciate the speed and directness of the northern routes.

It was a striking coincidence that the greater harvests and the loss of the river route southward were so fully anticipated by the railroad construction of the previous decade. In 1850 Indiana had 225 miles of railroads, Illinois 110 miles, Wisconsin 20 miles, and Iowa none. In 1860 the four states together had over 6,990 miles of road ready to accomplish the heavy tasks to be imposed upon them. Whatever might be the increase of the crops, although the river was closed, there were ample facilities to take them to market. Seven new trunk lines from the South, West, and North centered in Chicago, whence three other trunk lines and the lakes led eastward. This city, which in 1850 celebrated the arrival of its first train, was entered during the last part of the war by 90 trains daily. Better preparation in these sections for the strain of war could hardly have been devised.

At the beginning of the War many feared molestation of the crops; but, when with each succeeding year plenty filled the land, boastings and congratulations were universal. That we were a great agricultural nation in a time of war few public teachers, speakers, or newspapers, allowed the people to forget. It was fortunate that the source of our food supply was within our own borders, and not in the Confederacy, and that it was never included within the theatre of war. With food plenty, the doubts and fears that so easily lend themselves to discontent in a time of public crisis had little place.

Another effect of the abundant food supply, which has never yet been adequately set forth, but which, nevertheless, was very important, was its influence on foreign countries. We were a granary for Great Britain, and to a small extent for the Continent, from which countries the Confederate States were endeavoring to win recognition by pointing with pride to the fact that they were the largest source of the world's cotton supply. From 1850 to 1860 the production of American cotton had increased 120 per cent — from 2,450,000 bales to not quite 5,400,000 bales — that of wheat by less than 75 per cent — i.e., from 100,000,000 bushels to 170,000,000 bushels. Furthermore, while the export of wheat was practically stationary in the period, that of cotton rapidly increased.[4] The cotton-consuming countries of the world were so far dependent on the southern staple that over 80 per cent of the cotton consumed in Great Britain from 1851 to 1860 came from the United States; in 1860, 75 per cent of that consumed on the Continent also came from America. But in the same period the dependence on American grain was very much less, since we shipped almost none at all to the Continent, and in almost every year were outstripped by Russia in shipments to Great Britain.

What would be the effects of the War on these relations at once became a leading question in Europe, and it was generally assumed that there would be a great decrease in the receipts of both American staples, of grain as well as of cotton.

With the declaration of the blockade of the southern ports by the United States one part of the expectation was fulfilled. The foreign factories could get little or no American cotton, and began to shut down or run part time. The 2,580,700 bales received in Great Britain from America in 1860 fell to 1,841,600 bales in 1861; 72,000 bales in 1862; 132,000 bales in 1863; 198,000 bales in 1864; and 462,000 bales in 1865; but, on account of the enlarged importations from other fields — Brazil, Egypt, West India, East India, China, Japan, Turkey, and Asia Minor — the yearly consumption did not fall off as much as did the American imports. The familiar story of the distress among the unemployed British operatives need not here be retold. In the consumption of cotton on the Continent, France took the lead, consuming about one quarter as much as Great Britain. Germany was second, wih Russia, Holland, Spain, and the other minor countries and ports following.[5] In 1860, as has just been stated, three fourths of this cotton came from America, to disappear practically with the opening of the War; but here again, as in the case of Great Britain, on account of increased importations from other countries, the yearly consumption did not fall off equally with the American importations. Roughly speaking, the different Continental countries succeeded throughout the War in getting for use 50 per cent of the usual amount. There was distress among the French operatives, as in England, but not to so great an extent.

Great Britain's wheat crop (exclusive of the crop of the islands of the British Seas), which in 1858 and 1859 averaged 16,000,000 quarters annually, in 1860 fell to 13,135,124 quarters; in 1861 to 11,078,948 quarters; in 1862 to 12,271,546 quarters; in 1863 to 13,-957,554 quarters. In 1864 it rose to 17,922,048 quarters.[6] The average yearly price per quarter in 1860, 1861, and 1862 rose to 53s. 3d., 55s. 4d., and 55s. 5d., respectively, but in 1863 fell to 44s. 9d., and in 1864 to 40s. 5d.[7] For three successive years the country's grain crops were failures, and she was forced to import twice as much grain as usual. In the emergency it was the United States, at war, that supplied the new demand — the same United States that had cut off the cotton. Great Britain was astonished. In 1861, the year when American cotton ceased to arrive in Great Britain, the British imports of American wheat and wheat flour were 36,000,000 bushels, three times more than ever before; in 1862, 37,000,000 bushels. The lowest point during the War was in 1864 — 20,000,000 bushels.[8] Russia and Germany were the other great granaries of Great Britain, but the shipments of wheat and wheat flour from the one country to Great Britain actually fell off in 1861, 1862, and 1863; while those of the other increased, and that but slightly, only in one year — 1862.[9]

French importations to Great Britain in wheat and wheat flour, usually ranking next after those from Germany and Russia, in the first three years of the war fell off enormously, being only 25 per cent of what they were in 1860, for the sufficient reason that France also, along with Great Britain and all of southern Europe, suffered crop reverses in 1861. The French crop in this year was 25,765,000 quarters, as compared with an average yearly crop of 32,000,000 quarters in 1858, 1859, and 1860. Importations, which in 1858, 1859, and 1860 had averaged about 400,000 quarters, suddenly rose to almost 5,400,000 quarters in 1861.[10] Of these increased importations from one third to one half came from the United States. The American shipments to France before 1861 were practically nothing; but in the year following the poor harvests they were 10,000,000 bushels of wheat and wheat flour, 5,000,000 bushels the next year.[11]

Our northern press and the public watched with keen interest these foreign shipments of grain. They noted that, when the British and Continental crops were poor, our own chanced to be unprecedentedly abundant; and they universally believed that these shipments played a large part in preventing foreign recognition of the Confederacy. The reasoning was most frequently applied to Great Britain, inasmuch as American in general were well acquainted with the situation there. American grain was more important to the British than American cotton, reasoned the northerners. If Great Britain attempted to secure more of the latter by breaking the blockade, her receipts of the former would be materially lessened by the resulting war with the United States. This deficiency other nations were not in a position to make up any more quickly than that in cotton; and the resulting very high prices of food, going far beyond the prevailing high prices of 1862, and involving the whole kingdom, would be far more serious than a partial loss of work in a single district. Our large American harvests, therefore, were peculiarly fortunate, for, in addition to supplying our wants at home, they affected powerfully our international relations.[12]

The same considerations apply to our relations with France, though not so forcibly. The French crops, in the first place, were poor but in a single year, not, as in Great Britain, for three years. The French importations were not nearly so large as the British, and prices in France did not go so high. Moreover, the cotton industry in France, one quarter as large as in Great Britain, occupied a comparatively small position in the nation. But, in this connection, we must not consider France by herself: she was a member of a combination, more or less strong, desirous of recognizing the Confederacy; and this combination, as a whole, could not dispense with American grain.

The shipments abroad had a pronounced reaction, also, on this country; for in the early part of the War, when we were producing more than was necessary for our own wants, and when, therefore, our home markets would naturally have been overstocked and prices for the farmers very low, the strong foreign demand tended to remove the surplus, and prevent that disappointing result.

The other leading activities of the western farmers — hog, cattle, and sheep raising — were also flourishing. According to the Cincinnati *Price Current*, the number of hogs packed in all the West, which never before the War had been above 2,500,000, in 1862-63 rose to 4,000,000 and in 1863-64 was 3,000,000. This increase was represented most graphically by the record of Chicago, where the number jumped from 151,339 in 1859-60 to 970,264 in 1863-64, and to a less degree by that of Cincinnati, St. Louis, and other cities. In 1862 Chicago outstripped Cincinnati, and wrested from her the title "Porkopolis of the West." Most of the packing was done in the cities, where the industry was fast becoming centralized, but a part of it was still done in the small towns and in the country. Despite the progress of packing, however, we are informed by the statisticians of the time that the number of hogs raised each year was no greater than in 1860.[13] The change is to be explained rather by the fact that the farmers sent to the market more of their stock than usual. Cattle raising was normal, and cattle packing was in its infancy.

In the nation at large the progress of sheep raising was most remarkable, inasmuch as wool was the most important substitute for cotton. The production of wool increased gradually from 1860, when it amounted to 60,000,000 pounds, to 1865, when the total production was 140,000,000 pounds; while in the latter year there were 32,000,000 sheep in the North, double the number of 1860. The western states shared the progress along with all the North. Illinois, the leading agricultural state, in four years more than trebled her number of sheep. Ohio, the leading wool state, doubled hers. "No branch of business increased more rapidly than the domestic wool trade"[14]: it grew with "gigantic strides." Everywhere the wool-growers were very energetic. Their conventions, new associations, and jealous rivalry with the wool manufacturers over the tariff are characteristic features of the times. In 1865 the National Wool-growers' Association was formed.[15]

So far as crops and herds and flocks are concerned, the evidences of great material prosperity in the West are unmistakable. There was unusual activity in all branches of agriculture, and, on the whole, unusually large crops and large herds and flocks. Other factors, such as prices and freight rates, the growing use of agricultural machinery, the prosperity of agricultural fairs, increase in population, the occupation of new lands, and public agitation in favor of increased transportation facilities furnished testimony to the same effect. But in the very beginning of the War two contrary factors were very strong, the crash of the wildcat banks and high freight rates.

Many banks in Illinois, Wisconsin, and Indiana had, as the only security of their circulating notes, the bonds of the border and slave states. These bonds secession sent on a wild career of decline, which grew worse and worse after the opening of actual hostilities. Deprived in this way of the means of redeeming their notes, many of the western banks, especially the small ones in the country, closed their doors; and the bonds were sold at auction for the benefit of the note-holders. If we say that, on the average, these were sold for $0.80 on the dollar, which is a high estimate, the loss to the people of Illinois, where the bank-note circulation was $12,000,000, was over $2,000,000. Eighty-nine of the 110 banks of the state were ruined; 39 in Wisconsin; 27 in Indiana. These failures of the small country banks fell heavily on the farmers.

The losses occasioned by high freight rates were just as widespread as those due to poor banking. The enormous grain shipments of 1861, accompanied by the closing of so many routes seaward — the Mississippi River, the Baltimore & Ohio Railroad, and, with the coming of the winter, the Great Lakes — found the railroads and other transportation lines unprepared. They were new, and had never handled heavy traffic. Much freight had to be turned away, and freight rates went up with a bound. The aggregate freight rate from Chicago to New York via Buffalo, by lake and canal, for a bushel of wheat rose suddenly from $0.1725 in July until it reached $0.3894 in October of the same year — over 100 per cent increase, whereas in the corresponding three months of 1860 the customary rise in the autumn had been but a little over 66-2/3 per cent. The West was frantic, but helpless before the transportation lines; for, while the freight rates advanced so very fast, the price of spring wheat in New York in the same time — July to October — went only from 72 cents to $1.15 — 50 per cent increase in the wholesale price paid to farmers, to be set over against the 100 per cent increase in freight rates. Press and public and state legislatures were loud in complaint. Large crops were of no avail to farmers if transportation lines took all the profits.

The sequel is important. In October, 1864, after the depreciation of paper money had been constantly raising prices in general for almost three years, the freight on a bushel of wheat Chicago to New York by Buffalo, via lake and canal, was only $0.27, almost $0.12 less than in October, 1861, and in not a single month from 1861 to 1864 was the figure of October, 1861, again reached. On the other hand, the price of a bushel of spring wheat in New York in the same interval, October, 1861, to October, 1864, jumped from $1.15 to $2.35 in July, 1864, $1.85 in October, and $2.28 in January, 1865. Similarly, between the same two points over the same route, the freight on a bushel of corn increased, July to October, 1861, from $0.1581 to $0.3563; while the price per bushel of corn in New York advanced

54

only from $0.46 to $0.54. But in October, 1864, the same freight was $0.2381; while the price per bushel was $1.56 in July, 1864; $1.58 in October; $1.86 in January, 1865. Again, in the fall of 1861 the highest price paid for a live-stock car, Chicago to Buffalo, was $95; in the fall of 1864 only $130 for the largest cars, $105 for smaller ones. But the price of live cattle in the latter year was 100 per cent more than in 1861, and of live hogs 200 per cent more. Thus we arrive at a most interesting and important result: the prices of agricultural products in 1864 and the first part of 1865 were 100 per cent to 200 per cent more than in 1861, while freight rates for grain were less than in 1861, and those for live stock advanced but slightly. This rise in farm products was greater, and lasted much longer, than the rise in freight rates. Never had the products of the farm so great a cash value. For their crops the farmers were getting not only the increased nominal value which an inflated currency produced, but in addition the part of this increase, and more, which naturally would have been added to the freight rates. This remarkable result, following two good years in 1862 and 1863, was rich recompense for the losses of agriculture in 1861, and a cause of great buoyancy and prosperity.[16] The amount of debts and farm mortgages paid off during the War was vast.[17]

The use of labor-saving machinery on the farms had already begun when the War opened, but was largely extended during the struggle. Mowers and reapers were yet new: only on the largest farms of the West were they common. The wheat drill was not common in any section. As soon, however, as men began to go to war, the increasing use of new labor-saving machinery was as striking a feature of farming as were the large harvests. The new devices were necessary to make up for the scarcity of laborers. But for them, so we are assured from many sources, a large part of the crops could not have been gathered.[18] In 1864 over 70,000 mowers and reapers were manufactured, twice as many as in 1862, and many more than in any year before. The manufacturers could not supply the demand. But a small proportion of these were sold out of the United States.[19] The horse-rake was likewise recognized as an efficient labor-saving device, and its use was rapidly extended. Many new harrows, grain drills, corn planters, and steam threshers were put on the market. At the agricultural fairs, both state and county, which, with some diminution in 1861, were held throughout the War, attended by the usual crowds, and meeting with the usual successes and failures, the exhibitions of the new machinery afforded the chief attraction, and aroused the greatest possible interest. Only one exhibit compared with them in popularity — another comparatively new labor-saving device — the sewing machine.[20]

There was definite increase of population in all the agricultural states, as shown by the census and by the school statistics. Illinois, by the United States census in 1860, contained 1,711,915 people; in 1865, by the state census, 2,141,510 — a gain of 430,000.[21] The number of scholars of school age rose from 472,000 to 580,000, the number of teachers increased by 2,500.[22] Wisconsin in the five years gained 90,000 population, 47,000 children of school age and 460 teachers. Minnesota, the newest state, gained 78,000 people, and showed an increase of 900 teachers. Iowa gained 180,000 people; Kansas 35,000; and Nebraska 30,000. Aside from natural increase, one source of the increase in population was foreign immigration, attracted partly through the active personal efforts of agents in Europe, sent out by states, railroads, and private individuals, partly through descriptive pamphlets, which were sent broadcast. From 1861 to 1865 some 45,000 immigrants, on landing in New York, continued their journey to Illinois; 23,000 to Wisconsin; 7,000 to Iowa; and 5,000 to Minnesota.[23] There were many refugees from the border and slave states, especially in Illinois. Although it is impossible to measure this movement, numerous references in the press and in the reports of railroad presidents leave no doubt that it was strong.[24] In 1863 it was reported that one third of the land sales of the Illinois Central Railroad were to these southern settlers.

Then there was immigration from other states, especially from the East, where there was a pronounced tendency toward depopulation of country districts and small towns. In New York State, out of a total of 948 cities and towns, there were 505 that decreased in population from 1860 to 1865, 463 of which had shown an increase in 1860 over 1855. In Massachusetts, out of a total of 385 cities and towns, 197 showed a decrease in 1865 over 1860, and 102 of these 197 had shown an increase in 1860 over 1855. The same conditions existed in Rhode Island.[25] Some of this drift of population away from these rural districts of the eastern states was westward. The Secretary of State of the state of New York, impressed by the shifting population of that state, sent out circulars inquiring into the probable causes of the changes; and in about 230 replies received we find that 65 towns attributed their loss to emigration, chiefly to the West.[26] Newspapers and railroad reports add their testimony to the same effect. St. Paul, Minnesota, a typical town of 13,000 in the growing sections of Minnesota, in the five years from 1861 to 1865 received 2,200 persons from other states.[27]

Another strong indication of the growth of population in the agricultural West was the constant occupation of new lands in every year of war. The Illinois Central Railroad, in the counties bordering along its lines, in 1860 sold 53,841.70 acres; in 1861, 102,247 acres; in 1862, 87,599 acres; in 1863, 221,578 acres; in 1864, 264,422 acres; in 1865, 154,252 acres.[28] These heavy sales were, moreover, not to

56

speculators in large amounts, but to a large number of holders in small amounts. In 1862 and 1863 approximately 6,000 buyers, many of them from the southern and border states, took an average of less than 60 acres each. During the whole War the counties along the line of the railroad grew in population 430,000. In other states — for example, in Minnesota — the railroads were actively disposing of their lands.

The state and government lands were also filling up. Wisconsin sold 340,000 acres of school lands, swamp lands, and university lands; Minnesota 155,000 acres of school lands.[29] Under the Homestead Act, by the terms of which the general government gave away to actual settlers, not to speculators, for a nominal fee, farms of 160 acres each, 140,988 acres were taken up in the various states and territories from January 1 to July 1, 1863; 1,261,592.61 acres from July 1, 1863, to July 1, 1864; and 1,160,532.32 acres from July 1, 1864, to July 1, 1865 — more than 21,600 farms occupied in two-and-a-half years by permanent settlers. Of these homesteads 7,864 were in Minnesota; 2,211 in Wisconsin; 711 in Iowa; 1,755 in Nebraska; 3,115 in Michigan; 2,067 in Kansas; and a smaller number in several other states and territories. The government disposed of much land in other ways. There were cash sales amounting to one half of the homestead entries, large gifts to the veterans of the Revolutionary War, the War of 1812, and the Mexican War, and gifts to various railroads and to agricultural colleges.[30]

Two contrary movements, tending to reduce population in the West, must not be overlooked — a further migration to the newly opened mines west of the Missouri River and the formation of armies. In every year of the War there was overland travel across the plains to Colorado, where gold was discovered in 1858, to Nevada, where silver was discovered in 1860, and to Idaho, where gold was discovered in 1863. The excitement in 1863 and 1864 in Iowa, Missouri, and Illinois, over the discoveries in Idaho may be taken as typical. Maps, suggested routes, and descriptive articles abounded in the newspapers of St. Louis, Chicago, and other cities; and, when the spring of 1864 opened, hundreds of prairie schooners started overland westward and scores of boats ascended the Missouri River. On a single day in the early summer, 420 wagons were observed to cross the Missouri River at four different points in Nebraska. This represented 2,000 people. In a letter from Denver, the readers of the Boston *Journal* were informed that 10,000 people were on the road between the Missouri River and Denver, all bound for Idaho. A certain judge, journeying from Fort Kearney to St. Joseph, declared that on no day was he out of sight of wagons; on one day he met 400 wagons.[31] It was certainly a strong movement, but there were special reasons for it aside from the gold fever: first, the disturbed conditions in Missouri, torn as the state was by the fierce struggles of radicals and conservatives, and harassed by bushwhackers; and, second, the approach of the draft. It is significant that the governor of Iowa assumed by proclamation to prohibit any leaving that state until after the draft. The rush to Colorado and Nevada earlier was similar. In 1860, one year after the excitement in Colorado began, the census-takers found 32,227 people in the territory. Her estimated population in 1864 was 75,000. Nothing accurate measures the migration to Nevada, although it was roughly estimated that 30,000 went there in 1861. Thus through the War there was a continued migration away from the leading farming sections.

All the states and territories we are considering furnished men for the armies. Up to December 1, 1864, Illinois raised 197,000 soldiers; Iowa 70,000 up to December 31, 1864; Wisconsin 75,000 up to December 31, 1864.

And yet, despite this drain of men, the West grew. Statistics of population, immigration, and the sale of new lands furnish a body of evidence that cannot be gainsaid. They show the arrival of new people, the making of new farms, a continued progress in western agriculture while war was raging in the South. It was the new settlers, aided in part by labor-saving machinery, who reaped the usual crops and the annual increase thereto, and clinched the prosperity of the West.

A further illustration of the growth of the West is to be seen in the sway of the western markets over the rival commercial cities of the East. The chief aim of the seaboard cities, in their attempts to extend their trade, was to secure improved transportation facilities westward. New York, by the construction of the Atlantic & Great Western Railroad, secured new connections with the lake route at Cleveland, and also with Cincinnati and the Southwest. In a great ship canal convention, attended by 2,000 people and presided over by the Vice President of the United States, New York joined her interests with Chicago in memorializing Congress to improve, for military and commercial reasons, the Illinois and New York canals. This she was led to do by Chicago's threat to send her grain seaward over the Canadian and St. Lawrence route. Philadelphia completed a new railroad to Erie, to compete with the new Atlantic & Great Western, and, in opposition to the Chicago-New York canal schemes, favored the improvement of the Ohio River. She also secured new connections with Cincinnati and Chicago. Boston, with only one road to the West, endeavored to divert the terminus of the Grand Trunk from Portland to herself, to tap that road at Ogdensburg, New York, to divert the Erie Canal traffic at Albany by completing the Hoosac Tunnel, and to build a new road to the terminus of the Erie at Newburgh, New York. The obvious explanation of the great public interest in these and similar transportation projects is that the West appealed to all as a valuable market. There was, of course, the desire to find a new market to take the place of the lost southern trade, but in this search the transportation lines would not have been so eager as they were to reach out to the West if the West had not been prosperous.[32]

To this survey there is but one possible conclusion. In the middle and last part of the War, western farmers enjoyed vigorous prosperity; there was steady progress in the size of the crops, in the extent of the cultivated area, and in population; profits were normal in the middle of the struggle, and in the last part of it extraordinarily high. The westerners themselves claimed prosperity for their section, and the business interests of the East, in their endeavors to expand, recorded their belief in the same prosperity.[33]

[1] For elaborate statistics of the crops see the Annual Report of the New York Chamber of Commerce for 1873-74, pp. 326-345. For the whole country the crops were (in million bushels) :—

	Wheat	Corn
1839	84.8	377.5
1849	100.2	591.6
1859	170.2	827.1
1862	186.8	564.6
1863	190.9	451.1
1864	160.7	530.4
1865	148.5	704.4

The Confederate States produced in 1859 31,000,000 bushels of wheat, 280,000,000 bushels of corn; hence the decline in the total corn crop recorded in 1862.

[2] The figures given are from the Report of the Chicago Board of Trade for 1888, p. 86. (A barrel of flour equals 4½ bushels of wheat.) In 1862 Milwaukee exported 15,000,000 bushels of wheat, three times as much as in any year before the war; so also for flour. (*Hunt's Merchants' Magazine*, June, 1867.) Cincinnati in both 1862 and 1863 shipped 1,000,000 bushels of wheat, 75 per cent more than in any year since 1857. (See Annual Review of the Commerce of Cincinnati for 1870, p. 113.) Before 1860 Buffalo had never received over 26,000,000 bushels of grain, including flour. In 1862 she received 72,000,000 bushels. (See Board of Trade Statement of the Trade and Commerce of Buffalo for 1865, pp. 27, 28.) The Erie and Champlain Canals delivered at tidewater in 1862, 32,000,000 bushels of wheat, almost three times more than ever before in any single year. (Annual Report of New York Produce Exchange for 1872-73, p. 285.)

[3] One fourth of this was shipped to foreign ports. For the yearly imports at

New Orleans from the interior see the Board of Trade Annual Statement of the Trade and Commerce of Buffalo for 1865, pp. 26, 27.

⁴ In 1850 we exported 635,381,604 pounds of cotton; in 1860, 1,767,686,338 pounds, the increase being gradual. (Ninth Annual Report of the Boston Board of Trade, p. 91.) The largest exportation of wheat and wheat flour, 1850-60, was, in 1857, 31,000,000 bushels. The average for the decade was about 20,000,000 bushels a year. In 1860 it was 16,000,000 bushels. (Report on the Internal Commerce of the United States, 1879, p. 116.)

⁵ There were 33,000,000 cotton spindles in Great Britain, 12,000,000 on the Continent, and 5,000,000 in the United States. Great Britain in 1860 consumed 2,633,000 bales; France, 621,000 bales; Germany, 307,000 bales; Russia and minor ports, 324,000 bales; Holland, 117,000 bales; Spain, 106,000 bales. (Report of the United States Revenue Commission, 1865-66, pp. 131, 134.)

⁶ See Report of the New York Produce Exchange, 1875-76, p. 324. From 1856 to 1859 the total imports of wheat into the United Kingdom averaged 16,000,000 cwt.; in 1860 they were 25,000,000 cwt.; in 1861, 29,000,000 cwt.; in 1862, 41,000,000 cwt.; in 1863, 24,000,000 cwt.; in 1864, 23,000,000 cwt. In these years the imports of American wheat were, respectively (in cwt.), 6,497,335, 10,866,891, 16,140,670, 8,704,401, and 7,895,015. Those who attribute our increased exports solely to the fact that the price of wheat here did not rise as fast as that of gold, and that, therefore, it was cheaper to buy grain with which to pay our English debts than it was to pay them in gold, overlook the failure of the English and Continental crops. The commercial column of the Chicago *Tribune* for 1861 and 1862 contains frequent extracts from the London *Mark Lane Express*, the leading English agricultural paper, upon the condition of the English and Continental crops.

⁷ See Report of New York Produce Exchange, 1876-77, p. 320.

⁸ The Report of the New York Chamber of Commerce, 1864-65, p. 101, gives a full table of exports of breadstuffs from the United States to Great Britain and Ireland from 1847 to 1865.

⁹ See Report of New York Produce Exchange for 1878, p. 327.

¹⁰ Prices per quarter were as follows: 1858, 38s.; 1859, 38s. 9d.; 1860, 35s. 7d.; 1861, 42s. 2d.; 1862, 40s. 5d.; 1863, 34s. 4d.; 1864, 30s. 6d.; 1865, 28s. 8d. See Report of New York Produce Exchange for 1875-76, p. 336.

¹¹ See Report on Internal Commerce of the United States, 1879, p. 243, Appendix.

¹² Rhodes, in his elaborate discussion of the recognition question, does not mention the American grain imports into Great Britain, although the matter was so fundamental, and was prominently recognized as such in the newspapers of the time.

¹³ The Report of the New York Produce Exchange for 1873-74 and the Report of the Commissioner of Agriculture for 1865 give full statistics for hog and cattle raising during the War.

¹⁴ From the Boston *Shipping List*. Jan. 4, 1865. The Statistical Abstract of the United States, 1902, p. 350, gives full statistics for the growth in the production and importation of wool. Ohio in 1854 had 4,845,189 sheep, 3,368,174 in 1860, 6,305,796 in 1864. The number of sheep in Pennsylvania, 1850-60, fell off 12 per cent: from 1860 to 1864 it increased 76 per cent. In Illinois, 1850-60, it fell off 14 per cent: from 1861 to 1864 there was an increase of almost 300 per cent. See Report of the Ohio Commissioner of Statistics for 1865, p. 23, and also An Address before the National Association of Wool Manufacturers at the first Annual Meeting in Philadelphia, Sept. 6, 1865, by John L. Hayes, Secretary.

¹⁵ Indiana and Illinois attempted to raise cotton in their borders, despite the northern frosts. Much publicity was given to these trials, and scant success was magnified into large achievement; but practically nothing was accomplished.

In all the western states the cultivation of sorghum, the Chinese sugar cane, introduced before 1860, was greatly extended, with a view to securing a succssful substitute for the sugar made in Louisiana, upon which they had been dependent up to the opening of the War, for regularly one half of the southern sugar had been consumed there. For example, in 1852 the sugar crop of Louisiana was 321,931 hogsheads, of which 206,000 hogsheads were exported to the western states. In 1858 the total crop was 362,296 hogsheads, of which the western states received 187,339 hogsheads. (See Hunt's Merchants' Magazine, Feb., 1860.) The conventions of the sorghum-growers rivaled those of the wool-growers in number and popular interest; but, despite the most persistent experiments, the new cane producd only syrup, no sugar at all. Ohio and other states attemped to introduce sugar beets as a new source of sugar, the Ohio Board of Agriculture even going so far as to offer a prize of $5,000 for the successful production of the beet sugar. All the attempts failed. By 1864 in the West sugar was a luxury. Both in the East and in the West prices were high. In Cincinnati the average price per pound, which in 1860 and 1861 was $0.06, became $0.20 in 1864 and 1865. Molasses in the same period rose from $0.33½ per gallon to $1.35 — for many people prohibitive prices, as we may see from the decline in the general consumption of sugar per capita from 30½ pounds in 1860 to 17 and 18 pounds in 1863-64. In 1861 the consumption of cane sugar in the United States, excluding the Pacific coast, was 296,950 tons of foreign sugar and 118,331 tons of domestic sugar: in 1865 the figures were 345,809 tons of foreign sugar and 5,000 tons of domestic sugar. (See the Report of the New York Chamber of Commerce for 1862-63 and for 1865-66.)

[16] Lest any think that, in the matter of freight rates, I have been deceived into accepting gold quotations in 1864 for quotations in paper, I would call attention to the fact that the rates for cattle cars are contemporary rates, taken from the successive reports of the Chicago Board of Trade. Such contemporary quotations were not in gold, but in paper. The grain rates were published in 1873, but are substantiated by the contemporary rates as given in the reports of the Chicago Board of Trade.

For the grain freight rates see the Reports of the New York Chamber of Commerce for 1872-73, p. 392; for the rates for live-stock cars see the Report of the Chicago Board of Trade for 1861, p. 57, and for 1864, p. 68. For the prices of wheat, corn, cattle, and hogs see the Aldrich Report of 1893. I have been unable to find the quotations for hogs and cattle in Buffalo. The relative advance is shown by the prices in other cities. Beefs, good to prime, live weight, in New York rose from $4.90 for 100 pounds in October, 1861, to $11.76 in April, 1865; hogs, good to prime, light weight, in New York rose from $3.75 and $4.12½ in October, 1861, to $13.00 and $14.50 in Jan., 1865.

[17] Recent Financial, Industrial, and Commercial Experiences of the United States, by David A. Wells (New York, 1872), p. 25.

[18] See Report of Ohio Commissioner of Statistics for 1865, p. 9; Scientific American, July 4, 1863.

[19] The Genesee Farmer, June, 1864, gave a list of over 190 companies making agricultural machines — 75 in New York State, 25 in Illinois, 25 in Ohio, 25 in Pennsylvania, and many scattering. For the extent of these manufactories see Scientific American, Feb. 13, 1864; Country Gentleman, May 19, 1864; Railroad Record, May 11, 1865. See also the introduction to the volume on Agriculture in United States Census of 1860. The value of the exports of agricultural implements, all kinds, and not only mowers and reapers, was as follows: $611,152 in 1863-64; $1,385,274 in 1864-65; $1,373,004 in 1865-66; $936,210 in 1866-67. (From tables in Commerce and Navigation of the United States for the various years.) The Scientific American, Feb. 13, 1864, states that at that time the average price of mowers and reapers was $130. This would be $9,100,000 for

70,000 machines. The exports of all kinds of machinery in 1863-64 and 1864-65 were worth but $1,000,000, average of two years. The mowers and reapers exported must have been but a part of this. I have drawn on the files of the *American Agriculturist*, *Ohio Farmer*, *Country Gentleman*, and *Genesee Farmer*.

[20] The state fairs, also, after 1861 were maintained as usual. I have in my possession a mass of material to show the continuation of the fairs, both county and state. The files of the Springfield *Republican*, *New York Tribune*, and *Chicago Tribune* are valuable on this subject as well as the agricultural papers. In almost every account of the exhibits, mention is made of the interest in the agricultural machinery and sewing machines. The agricultural press was flourishing in the middle and the end of the War. By the end of 1864, the *American Agriculturist* had a circulation of 100,000 — an increase of 100 per cent over 1861. See the *Ohio Farmer*, Jan. 30, 1864, for the general prosperity of farmers' papers.

[21] Chicago's population increased from 109,260 in 1860 to 178,539 in 1865.

[22] The growth of the schools was very marked, and a common cause of boasting. The figures given are from the reports of the State Superintendent of Education in the various states. The erection of new school buildings in Illinois was as follows, in 1859, 679 new buildings; 1860, 557; 1861, 382; 1862, 321; 1863, 349; 1864, 528; 1865, 510; 1866, 612 — thus practically normal activity in this respect in 1864 and 1865.

[23] These figures have been compiled from tables given in the Annual Reports of the Commissioners of Emigration of the State of New York, 1861-65. The work of the Mormon missionaries was systematically carried on in Europe throughout the War; and the foreign immigration to Utah was quite strong — 1,941 in 1861; 3,418 in 1862; 3,561 in 1863; 1,694 in 1864; 1,092 in 1865.

[24] See Annual Reports of the President of the Illinois Central Railroad, 1861-65.

[25] These figures have been compiled from the New York State Census for 1865 and from the Census of Massachusetts, 1895, vol. i. Most of the decadent towns were very small. Of the 505 in New York, 393 were under 3,000; 112 between 3,000 and 10,000; and only 2 over 19,000. In Massachusetts 169 of the 197 decadent towns were under 3,000; 28 between 3,000 and 10,000; and only 4 over 10,000. The Rhode Island Registrar's Reports for 1865 show that, in that state, 18 of the 31 towns decreased in population in 1865 as compared with 1860, of which only 7 decreased in 1860 as compared with 1850.

[26] See a small pamphlet entitled Preliminary Report on the Census of the State of New York for 1865. (Boston Public Library.)

[27] See McClung's St. Paul Directory and Statistical Record for 1866, St. Paul, 1866.

[28] The figures are taken from the Annual Reports of the Illinois Central Railroad, Land Department. The *Railroad Journal*, each year, published abstracts of the annual reports of all the principal railroads.

[29] See the Annual Reports of the Commissioners of School and University Lands, Wisconsin, 1861-65 also the Report of the Auditor of the State of Minnesota for 1865. McClung's St. Paul Directory for 1866 shows that, in 1861, 326,749 acres of public lands weer taken up in Minnesota in various ways; 109,526 acres in 1862; 303,669 acres in 1863; 676,234 acres in 1864; 794,425 acres in 1865.

[30] See the Annual Reports of the Commissioner of the General Land Office, 1861-65, for the government sales and gifts.

[31] The shipping columns of the St. Louis papers are the basis of the statement as to steamers on the Missouri. For the overland movement see the *Chicago Tribune*, June 17, 1864; the *Boston Journal*, June 17, 1864; and the *Daily Missouri Republican*, June 10, 1864. The record of wagons across the river in

Nebraska was: at Omaha, 156 wagons; Nebraska City, 131; Plattsmouth, 90; Brownville, 45 — 422 in all.

[32] This phase of the subject can be treated in only the very briefest form. It would be a large task to develop it and to give all the references. The interest of the commercial world in the Western trade and in transportation westward was very great.

[33] Great credit must be given to the national government for its wise and far-seeing legislation in favor of western interests. In 1862 the Department of Agriculture was taken way from the jurisdiction of the Patent Office, where it was pinched and inefficient, and set up as an independent bureau. There were the Homestead Act and the Agricultural Land Grant Act, and an act in encouragement of immigration. Colorado, Arizona, Dakota, Nevada, Idaho, and Montana were organized as territories, and Kansas and Nevada were set up as states. Colorado and Nebraska refused statehood. Rich government subsidies were guaranteed to the Union Pacific Railroad, with its branches in Kansas and Nebraska, and also to the Northern Pacific. In every year of the War, armed forces gave protection from the Indians.

Mitchell, *History of the Greenbacks*, p. 388, says, "It is safe to conclude from these figures that the farmers of the loyal States were among the unfortunate producers whose products rose in price less than the majority of other articles, and that from this standpoint they were losers rather than gainers by the paper currency. . . . It seems very doubtful whether farmers, as a whole, did not lose more than they gained because of the price disturbances." This view is based on a study of but a single factor, and certainly must be changed by study of the other factors bearing on the situation.

PART TWO

Monetary and Physical
Costs of the War

The use of the printing press by both the northern and Confederate governments affected seriously the money cost directly and indirectly incurred in the prosecution of the War. This topic was pioneered by Wesley Mitchell in his study of the Greenbacks and in the excerpt reprinted here. Recent studies by Milton Friedman and his students at the University of Chicago have not discredited Mitchell's work but indeed have made it appear all the more pioneering.

The chaotic condition of Confederate monetary statistics makes a calculation of the monetary costs of the War and the magnitude of the War effort virtually impossible. It has been estimated, however, that nearly 60 per cent of all the money received by the Confederacy was created by fiat; taxes provided 5 per cent of government revenue; nearly 30 per cent of government money to prosecute the War was obtained from bond sale to banks, other institutions, and private persons; the remainder came from miscellaneous sources. Compared to the North, southern financial costs appear even greater.

The physical cost of the War was especially heavy on the South. To be sure, physical and human capital losses in the North were heavy. But the magnitude of the damage compared to the economy's ability to absorb it made southern losses even more burdensome. In the following selection, Professor Sellers attempts to isolate the over all physical cost of the War in the South by geographic region. It is a curious and neglected article and one which shows quite clearly the great gaps in data which existed at the time Sellers made his study (1927).

Eugene Lerner's article traces essentially the same ground. Lerner's thesis is that agricultural capacity was decimated by the War and that postwar economic conditions only aggravated further the readjustments necessitated by recovery. Moreover, Lerner states that manufacturing capacity was least affected in the postwar periods by losses incurred during the War and consequently was in a position to grow more rapidly than agriculture.

Taken together, the three selections in this unit dramatize quite clearly that in either purely monetary or more prosaic economic terms, nations (or regions) that engage in large-scale war suffer costs and consequences that go well beyond what can be seen by the naked eye or the unambiguous statistic.

FOR FURTHER READING

There are three scholarly articles especially which may be read in conjunction with the selections of this unit.

Milton Friendman, "Price, Income, and Monetary Changes in Three Wartime Periods," American Economic Association, Papers and Proceedings, vol. XLII (May 1952), pp. 612-625.

Marshall A. Robinson, "Federal Debt Management: Civil War, World War I, and World War II," ibid., vol. XLV (May 1955), pp. 388-401.

Eugene M. Lerner, "The Monetary and Fiscal Programs of the Confederate Government, 1861-65," Journal of Political Economy, vol. LXII (Dec. 1954), pp. 506-522.

Works of a more general nature that also have good summaries of Civil War monetary experience are:

Herman Krooss, American Economic Development (New York: Prentice-Hall, 1955), especially Chapter 14.

Seymour Harris (ed.), American Economic History (New York: McGraw-Hill Book Company, 1961), especially Chapter 8.

In this excerpt from the monumental study of the Greenbacks, Wesley Mitchell carefully calculates what effect the Greenback had upon the amount of government expenditures incurred by the Union in the prosecution of the War. One of the central questions examined is the extent of financial burdens of the War upon different income groups.

THE GREENBACKS AND THE COST
OF THE CIVIL WAR
By Wesley C. Mitchell

THE PROBLEM AND THE METHOD OF SOLUTION

Discussion of the consequences of the legal-tender acts has so far been confined to the economic relations between individuals. There is, however, another phase of the subject to be considered. The reader who turns back to the account of the debates upon the legal-tender bills will find that most of the unfortunate consequences that followed their enactment were foretold in Congress—the decline of real wages, the injury done creditors, the uncertainty of prices that hampered legitimate business and fostered speculation. But a majority of this Congress were ready to subject the community to such ills because they believed that the relief of the treasury from its embarrassments was of more importance than the maintenance of a relatively stable monetary standard. There was little of that confusion between economic and fiscal considerations that has frequently been held responsible for the attempts of government to use its power over the currency as a financial resource. Rather, there was a conscious subordination of the interest of the community in a stable monetary standard to the interest of the government in obtaining funds to carry on the War. It is therefore incumbent upon one who would judge the policy from the standpoint of its sponsors to inquire into the financial effects which to them seemed most important as well as into the effects on the distribution of wealth.

This topic has two aspects — one of which has already been discussed. Power to issue Greenbacks formed a quickly available financial resource from which the treasury was able to meet large amounts of indebtedness already accumulated when the legal-tender acts were passed. But while such issues relieved immediate needs, their ultimate effect was to increase the future demands on the treasury. The first of these consequences has been dealt with in the historical chapters of Part I, where an attempt was made to show how much immediate help the Greenbacks afforded Mr. Chase. It remains for the present chapter to treat the larger question: What effect had the Greenbacks upon the amount of expenditures incurred?

Few questions raised by the legal-tender acts have attracted more attention than this last. Even while the first legal-tender bill was being considered, its critics declared that if made a law it would increase the cost of waging the War by causing an advance in the prices of articles that the government had to buy.[1] As the War went on, the soundness of this view became apparent. Simon Newcomb, writing early in 1865, estimated that by the end of 1864 the Greenbacks had increased the amount of indebtedness incurred by the federal government $180,000,000 beyond the amount that would have been incurred had the specie standard been maintained. Even if the War should end in 1865, he prophesied, $300,000,000 more would be added to this needless augmentation of the debt.[2]

When the War was over and the divers reasons that had deterred many men from criticizing the financial policy of the government were removed, competent writers began to express similar views with freedom. For example, Mr. H. R. Hulburd, comptroller of the currency, said in his report for 1867: "Probably not less than 33 per cent of the present indebtedness of the United States is owing to the high prices paid by the government while its disbursements were heaviest."[3] Mr. C. P. Williams put the increase of debt at one third to two fifths; C. A. Mann, at one fourth; S. T. Spear, at a billion dollars; L. H. Courtney, an English critic, at nearly $900,000,000.[4] Of later discussions that of Professor H. C. Adams has attracted the most attention. He estimated that of the gross receipts from debts created between January 1, 1862, and September 30, 1865, amounting to $2,565,000,000, the gold value was but $1,695,000,000 — a difference of $870,000,000 between value received and obligations incurred.[5]

All of these estimates seem to rest either upon guesses or upon reduction of sums borrowed in currency to specie value. The former method of arriving at the result inspires little confidence even when the guesses are made by men intimately familiar with the federal finances, and the latter method assumes that all government expenditures rose in proportion to the decline in the specie value of the Greenback dollar, and that all revenues remained what they would have been on a special basis — assumptions subject to important exceptions.[6] The problem of ascertaining the financial consequences of the Greenback issues is much too complex to be solved by methods so crude. Some branches of expenditure were much affected by the depreciation of the currency, other branches but little. The effect of the paper currency on the receipts of the government is quite as important a part of the problem as the effect on expenditures, and examination shows that here as there different items were affected in very different degrees. Finally, the Greenbacks were themselves a "loan without interest" though, on the other hand, they increased the volume of the interest-bearing debt by augmenting expenditures. These three topics, then — the influence of the paper-money standard on ordinary expenditures and receipts, and on interest — must all be examined by anyone who hopes to frame an adequate estimate of the net effect of the Greenbacks on the cost of the War. As will appear, however, examination of these topics is beset by serious difficulties.

GREENBACKS AND EXPENDITURES

It is a familiar remark of writers on public finance that all things required by government fall into one or two categories — commodities and services. If the conclusions of the preceding chapters on prices and wages are well founded, it follows that this elementary distinction regarding the objects of government expenditure is of very great importance for the present problem. For, since prices advanced in much greater ratio than wages, it is clear that the Greenback issues must have increased the sums paid for commodities more than the sums paid for labor. Indeed, this difference between increase in cost of commodities and of labor seems to have been much wider in the case of the government than in the case of private persons; for, as was shown . . . , the wages of federal employees were advanced on the average considerably less than the wages of other persons. Clearly, then, the first step in any estimate of the effect of the legal-tender act upon the expenditures incurred by government during the War should be a careful separation of expenditures for commodities from expenditures for services.

Accordingly, it is a very serious obstacle that one encounters in finding that such a separation cannot readily be made. A statement of the expenditures of the preceding fiscal year is published in each annual report of the Secretary of the Treasury. But in these statements the items are arranged rather according to the department of government through or for which the specified sums were spent, than according to the object of expenditure. For example, the first general division of expenditures is placed under the caption "Civil," and under this caption the first three items are "For Congress, including books"; "For executive"; "For judiciary." It is obvious that each of these items must include payments for both commodities and services; but there is no way of separating the two classes of payments.

A more detailed statement is given in the annual *Account of* the Receipts and Expenditures of the United States rendered by the register of the treasury. But even these bulky documents do not make possible such a division of expenditures as is desired. A careful examination of the register's accounts for the fiscal years 1863-65 shows that about one third of the total expenditures each year consists of items which appear to include payments for both labor and commodities in unknown proportions. Such, for example, are expenditures upon fortifications, armories, and hospitals, repairs of ships, construction of buildings, incidental expenses of various bureaus, and the like. The best that can be done with these accounts to to divide the items into three classes: (1) expenditures for salaries and the like, most of which appear to have been little affected by the paper currency; (2) expenditures for commodities; (3) expenditures that include payments for both commodities and labor. Even with such a scheme of classification it is sometimes difficult to decide where certain items should be placed.

If this division of expenditures be accepted, the next step is to determine in what ratio the expenditures falling within each of the three classes shall be assumed to have been increased. In the first class the largest items are the pay of the regular and volunteer armies. As was shown . . . , the wages of private soldiers were increased from $13 to $16 per month after May 1, 1864. Since this increase was made with the avowed object of compensating soldiers in some measure for the decline in the purchasing power of the paper money, one must consider three sixteenths of the pay of the army after that time as an addition to the money cost of the War. It is not improbable also that, had the specie standard been maintained, it would have been unnecessary to grant such lavish bounties to stimulate enlistments. If so, a part at least of the large sums reported as paid in bounties should be added to the increase in the cost of the War. To be on the safe side, however, this item will be neglected. As for other employees of the government besides the soldiers, it appears that in few cases were the money salaries increased beyond the scale prevailing before suspension. No doubt it was largely from motives of patriotism that so many men in humble as well as in conspicuous positions remained in the service of the government at wages they would have accepted from no private employer. Their self-sacrifice lessened the effect of the Greenbacks upon the cost of the War in dollars and cents. But from any other than the narrowest fiscal point of view, it was one of the most unfortunate consequences of the paper-money régime that the men who were serving the country faithfully were compelled to submit to a great decrease in their real incomes.

With respect to the second of the above-described classes of expenditures, the question of interest is whether the depreciation of the currency affected the prices paid by the government for commodities as much as it did prices paid by private purchasers at wholesale. Reference to the tables . . . will show that the statistical material gleaned from the *Aldrich Report* indicates that public contractors did not advance their prices quite as rapidly as other dealers. But it must be remembered that the two series there brought into comparison are not constructed in the same fashion — one series gives the averages of four relative prices each year; the other gives the relative average prices of twelve months in some cases and of prices for unstated dates in others. Moreover, many of the government series are based on prices for 1861 instead of for 1860, and in the former year the government seems to have been paying rather higher prices than in the latter. Still further the whole number of articles included in the government list is not great, and about half belong to a single and financially unimportant group — drugs and chemicals. Finally, it is not improbable that there were changes in the qualities of some articles accepted from contractors that account for a relatively slight increase in price. For these various reasons, the divergence between the two series possesses little significance.

Much greater weight should be attached to the general conclusion . . . that the dominant factor in determining prices during the War was the fluctuating valuation of the currency. There is no reason why knowledge that he would be paid in Greenbacks should affect in different degrees the prices that a dealer would ask from the government and from private men. Since, then, the fairly satisfactory wholesale-price data show a rather close parallelism between prices of commodities and of gold, it seems fair to infer that the sums asked of the government for identical goods also rose and fell in rough agreement with the premium. True, prices seem not to have advanced so quickly as did the gold quotation, but neither did they fall so quickly. Everything considered, then, the most trustworthy index of the increase in the sums expended by the government upon commodities is probably found in the average premium upon gold in the several fiscal years.

An even larger element of conjecture enters into the estimate of the increase in the expenditures of the third class, which includes payments for both commodities and labor. So far as commodities are concerned it is as fair here as in Class II to apply the average premium upon gold as an index of the increase. But with reference to labor a new problem arises. The salaries of most persons in the regular service of the government, aside from soldiers, were not increased at all. But the titles of the items grouped in Class III as they appear in the register's accounts seem to indicate that the great mass of the labor was not that of officials, but that of workmen employed on a strictly commercial basis. In constructing fortifications, erecting

TABLE I

ESTIMATED INCREASE IN THE ORDINARY EXPENDITURES OF THE
FEDERAL GOVERNMENT CAUSED BY THE GREENBACKS
(*In millions of dollars*)

	FISCAL YEARS				
	1862 Six Months	1863	1864	1865	1866 Two Months
Expenditures: a					
Class I, salaries, etc.	92	242	259	408	45
Class II, commodities	82	214	258	402	43
Class III both labor and commodities	89	238	294	405	44
Assumed ratio of increase:					
Class II b	3%	37%	56%	102%	43%
Class III c	3%	27%	44%	77%	49%
Estimated actual increase:					
Class I, increase in pay of soldiers d	—	—	6	62	20
Class II	2	58	93	203	13
Class III	3	51	90	176	14
Total estimated increase each year	5	109	189	441	47

a The figures for the fiscal years 1863-65 are obtained from the annual reports on "Receipts and Expenditures." For the second half of the fiscal year 1862 the ordinary expenditures were estimated on the basis of the "Treasurer's Accounts" (H. R. Ex. Doc. No. 4, 38th Cong., 1st Sess.), and these expenditures were divided among the three classes according to the proportions given by the computations for 1863. Similarly, the expenditures for the months of July and August, 1865, are assumed to be two thirds of the total for the quarter July to September and are divided among the three classes in the same ratio as the expenditures for the fiscal year 1865.

b Average premium upon gold . . . .

c Average of premium on gold and increase in money wages according to system of variable weights . . . . For wages in each fiscal year I have taken the index number for January of the corresponding calendar year.

d Three sixteenths of pay of army (except bounties) after May 1, 1864, as the pay is reported in "Receipts and Expenditures." For the months of July and August, 1865, the increase is computed on one half the sum stated by the paymaster-general as paid to the army between June 30 and October 31. (Ex. Doc. No. 1, Part II, p. 898, 39th Cong., 1st Sess.)

and repairing public buildings, etc., it is probable that the government or its contractors paid as much for the labor hired as a private employer would have done. If so, it follows that the best index of the increased expenditure on the labor included in this class . . . shows the average relative wages for all employes for whom data are given in Table XII of the *Aldrich Report*. Assuming so much, we have two ratios of increase in expenditure for this class — one applicable to the prices of commodities, the other to the wages of labor. Since there is no way of distinguishing between expenditure for goods and labor it is necessary to make some purely arbitrary assumption regarding their relative amounts. The simplest assumption is that the increase in the total expenditures of Class III was midway between the average premium upon gold and the average increase in money wages. Perhaps this assumption may be accepted as well as any other, for, if no definite reason can be assigned for it, neither can any reason be assigned in favor of any rival assumption.

In accordance with the preceding plan, Table I has been constructed to show the probable increase in the expenditure of the government caused by the issues of paper money between the date of suspension and August 31, 1865, when the public debt reached its maximum amount[7]. The total increase for the whole period is $791,000,000. After all that has been said of the elements that enter into the problem it is hardly necessary to insist strenuously that this total is but a very rough estimate.

THE GREENBACKS AND RECEIPTS

Almost all the writers who have discussed the financial consequences of the legal-tender acts have confined their attention to the increase of expenditures. This procedure is perhaps natural for ardent critics of the paper-money policy, but a little consideration shows that it is unfair. The reports of the Secretary of the Treasury give the government revenue under five heads — customs, sales of public lands, direct tax, miscellaneous sources, and internal revenue. Of these receipts some were and some were not affected by the Greenback issues. In accordance with the provisions of the first legal-tender act, customs duties were paid in gold, and the ad valorem duties were assessed on the foreign specie valuation of goods. The receipts from this source therefore remained on substantially the same footing as if specie payments had been maintained. During the War receipts from the sales of public lands were an item of little importance — less than $1,000,000 per year — despite the decline in the value of the currency that might be paid by the purchaser of lands. The receipts from direct taxes were all collected under one law passed six months before suspension. This law fixed the total amount of the tax at $20,000,000 and determined the precise amount to be raised by each state.[8] Accordingly, the legal-tender acts had no effect upon this item — except that the states were enabled to pay their quotas in Greenbacks instead of in gold. The revenue derived from miscellaneous sources includes a considerable number of small items. Of these, some were doubtless increased by depreciation, e.g., pro-

72

ceeds of sales of captured and abandoned property. Other items were unaffected, e.g., receipts of fees by American consuls abroad. Premiums on sales of gold coin among these miscellaneous receipts may be set down from the present point of view as clear gain.

The last of the enumerated government receipts remains, the internal-revenue duties. This system of taxation was inaugurated by an elaborate law passed July 1, 1862, which imposed certain duties, partly *ad valorem*, partly specific, upon a great variety of manufactured articles; imposed a tax upon the gross receipts of canals, railroads, theaters, etc.; taxed auction and brokers' sales; required licenses for practicing professions; levied an income and a legacy tax, and placed certain taxes upon articles of luxury, such as carriages, pianos and plate.[9] This law was superseded two years later by another internal-revenue act which raised the rates of taxation, and increased the number of articles made to pay duties.[10]

At the time the first law was passed, the depreciation of the currency was not great, and probably the rates of taxation imposed do not differ much from what they would have been upon a specie basis. But without any modification of the terms of the law, the progressive rise of prices must have caused an increase of the revenue from *ad valorem* duties, and from taxes on gross receipts and upon incomes. Receipts from specific duties, licenses, etc., however, probably did not increase except as changes were made in the law or in its administration. While, then, the yield of this most important of the sources of federal revenue was materially affected by the legal-tender acts, it would be too much to argue, as was done with reference to expenditures for commodities, that it was increased in the ratio indicated by the premium on gold. Some arbitrary assumption, however, must be made regarding the ratio of increase if any estimate is to be had. Again, it is perhaps best to adopt the simplest expedient, and count the increase of receipts from internal taxes at the full amount indicated by the premium, but, on the other hand, take no account of the increase of receipts from miscellaneous sources. Since the latter sums are relatively small, it is probable that an estimate thus made will err rather on the side of overstating, than of understating, the increase of revenue.

The total increase of receipts shown by this method as applied in Table II is $174,000,000. Again the caution is hardly necessary that the result is to be accepted subject to a wide margin of error.

So far the discussion of the increase both of expenditures and of revenues has proceeded as if the paper currency had exerted none but simple and direct effects. There were other financial consequences of the shift from the specie to the paper standard, however, that were not unimportant, though they were indirect and difficult to gauge. Three of the most prominent must be indicated.

TABLE II

Estimated Increase in the Ordinary Receipts of the Federal Government Caused by the Greenbacks

(In millions of dollars)

	Fiscal Year 1862 (Six Months)	Fiscal Year 1863	Fiscal Year 1864	Fiscal Year 1865	Fiscal Year 1866 (Two Months)
Current receipts: a					
From customs	33.5	69.1	102.3	84.9	31.3
From sales of public lands	.1	.2	.6	1.0	.1
From direct tax	1.8	1.5	.5	1.2	.0
From miscellaneous sources	.5	3.0	47.5	33.0	12.3
From internal revenue	—	37.6	109.7	209.5	64.4
	35.9	111.4	260.6	329.6	108.1
Assumed ratio of increase	3%	37%	56%	102%	43%
Estimated actual increase	0	10	39	106	19

a As given by the annual statements of the register of the treasury (see "Finance Reports," 1862, p. 37; 1863, pp. 34, 35; 1864, p. 33; 1865, pp. 44, 45, 48). For 1862 the receipts of the last two quarters of the year are given; for 1866 two thirds of the receipts for the first quarter.

1. It is probable that not a little of the lavishness with which public funds were appropriated by Congress during the War can be traced to the paper-money policy. At least such was the opinion of a man so well placed to observe the operation of the treasury as Hugh McCulloch. In his report of 1867 he said: "As long as notes could be issued and bonds could be sold at a premium or at par, for what the statute made money, there was a constant temptation to liberal, if not unnecessary, expenditures. Had the specie standard been maintained, and bonds been sold at a discount for real money, there would have been an economy in all branches of the public service which unfortunately was not witnessed."[11]

2. If the paper currency tempted the government to reckless expenditures, it also predisposed the people to submit more willingly to heavy taxation. It has been remarked several times that the advance of money wages and of money prices made most people feel wealthier, and, feeling wealthier, they were less inclined to grumble over the taxes.

3. But while the feeling of prosperity may have been instrumental in procuring a cheerful acceptance of war taxes, it is very

74

doubtful whether the net effect of the paper-money system was favorable to revenue. It was pointed out in the last chapter that the lagging of money wages behind money prices necessarily diminished the consumption of wealth among wage-earners. In so far as this diminution affected the consumption of articles that paid either an import or an excise duty — and there were but few articles exempt from taxation by one of these methods — the fall of real wages must have lessened the tax receipts. Much the same must have been true, although in less degree, of the indirect taxes collected from the consumption of the great agricultural class, if the conclusion . . . is true, that farmers were injured rather than benefited by the price fluctuations. On the other hand, the extravagance of the fortunate families enriched by the receipt of high profits tended to increase the revenue for the time being; but it is improbable that the increase of receipts from the enlarged consumption of this limited class offset the decrease of receipts from the enforced economies of wage-earners and farmers.

While, then, these indirect effects of the paper currency on expenditures and receipts could not by any system of bookkeeping be brought to definite quantitative statement, it is probable that their net result was unfavorable to the treasury.

THE GREENBACKS AND THE PUBLIC DEBT

It may seem that in a discussion of the financial consequences of the legal-tender acts, account should be taken of the effect of the desertion of the specie standard upon the terms on which the government could borrow. The resort to a legal-tender paper currency, one may argue, is a confession of acute financial distress and as such must depress the market for bonds. Therefore, to the financial loss caused by the increase of expenditures should be added a second loss from the unfavorable terms to which the government had to submit in selling its securities.

Of course, it is true that the secretaries of the treasury in their efforts to borrow money were obliged to agree to some very hard bargains. There was little ground for exultation over the sale at par of bonds bearing interest at 5 or 6 per cent in gold when the currency received from purchasers was worth in specie but 50 per cent of its face value. But this loss arising from the difference in value between the paper dollars received by the treasury for bonds and the specie dollars which the treasury contracted to pay bondholders after a term of years is not a further loss in addition to the losses discussed in the preceding sections, but rather these same losses looked at from another point of view. For the estimate of the increase of expenditures above receipts, and therefore of debt contracted, rests precisely upon the decline in the value of the paper dollar from the specie standard. One may arrive at an estimate of the loss either by computing the increase in the number of dollars that had to be borrowed in paper money to be repaid in gold, or by estimating the decline in the specie value of the paper money raised by the sale of bonds; but to make estimates by both of these methods would be to include two guesses at the same item.

It is, of course, true that, had gold bonds been sold largely at less than par for paper money, a second loss would have been incurred from the discount in addition to the loss from the smaller purchasing power of the currency received. But, as a matter of fact, the deviations from par in the subscription prices for bonds were not of great importance. The prices of government securities did not fluctuate very widely during the War, for the very good reason that these prices showed merely the value of one set of government promises to pay, viz., bonds — in terms of another set — viz., Greenbacks. Most factors that affected the credit of the government would affect the specie value of all its promises in much the same manner, and therefore would not alter materially the ratio of one to another.

It remains only to say a word about the effect of the legal-tender acts upon the interest charge borne by the government. The great financial argument in favor of the Greenbacks has always been that they constitute a "loan without interest." However many millions the depreciation of this currency added to the principal of the public debt, the Greenbacks should be credited with whatever sum was really saved in this fashion. But against the saving of interest effected by issuing Greenbacks instead of selling bonds should be put down the loss of interest on the increase of debt arising from the augmentation of expenditures. If the rate of interest be taken at 6 per cent, a simple calculation shows that the interest saved by the Greenbacks up to August 31, 1865, was but $28,000,000 greater than the interest lost through the excess of increase of expenditures over the increase of receipts as shown by Tables I and II. By the end of this period the augmentation of debt caused by the Greenbacks had apparently become greater than the volume of Greenbacks in circulation, so that from this time forward the annual loss of interest probably exceeded the gain.

CONCLUSION

The public debt reached its maximum amount August 31, 1865, when it stood at $2,846,000,000.[12] Of this immense debt the preceding estimates indicate that some $589,000,000, or rather more than a fifth of the whole amount, was due to the substitution of United States notes for metallic money. Little as these estimates can pretend to accuracy, it seems safe at least to accept the conclusion that the Greenbacks increased the debt incurred during the War by a sum running into the hundreds of millions. If so, it follows that, even from the narrowly financial point of view of their sponsors, the legal-tender acts had singularly unfortunate consequences.

The present chapter, to agree with its predecessors, must end with the Civil War. But it may be pointed out that the financial effects of the legal-tender acts, like the economic effects, did not cease with the return to peace. No additional discussion is required to show that the varying depreciation of the currency continued to affect the volume of both receipts and expenditures until resumption of specie payments in January, 1879, restored the Greenbacks to equality with gold. It is equally clear that the United States notes continued to be a "loan without interest," and that, on the other hand, the government continued to pay interest on the unnecessary debt created during the War. But there is another phase of the subject that deserves special remark, because it is frequently overlooked. A considerable portion of the immense public debt in existence August 31, 1865, consisted of obligations expressly payable in "lawful money." Insofar as the government was able to pay these debts out of revenue before the Greenbacks had appreciated to par, it effected a saving.[13] But all such topics — the continued effect of depreciation on government expenditures and revenue, the annual loss or gain of interest, the cost at which the "lawful money" debt was paid, the expense at which specie payments were resumed, and the difficulties encountered in maintaining the convertibility of the paper money into specie — belong to a later period in the history of the Greenbacks. It is probable, however, that were a careful study made of these topics the indictment brought against the Greenbacks on financial grounds would be rendered yet more serious.

[1] See Mitchell, *History of the Greenbacks*, Part I, chap. ii, p. 57.

[2] Simon Newcomb, *Critical Examination of our Financial Policy* (New York, 1865), pp. 171, 172.

[3] *Finance Report*, 1867, p. 15.

[4] See L. H. Courtney, *A Review of the Financial Situation of Our Country* (Albany, 1868), p. 7; *Paper Money* (New York, 1873), p. 184; *The Legal-Tender Acts* (New York, 1875), p. 78; *Journal of the Royal Statistical Society*, vol. XXXI, p. 204.

[5] *Public Debts*, p. 131.

[6] Professor Adams is free from this reproach, for he is careful not to say that his figures represent the difference made by the Greenback policy in the cost of the War. This latter interpretation, however, has been commonly put upon the passage. E. g., see H. White, *Money and Banking* (1st ed.; Boston, 1896), p. 162.

[7] *Report of the Secretary of the Treasury*, 1866, p. 6.

[8] Act of August 6, 1861; 12 *Statutes at Large*, p. 294.

[9] 12 *Statutes at Large*, pp. 432-489. The amendments to this act were not such as to increase the total revenue derived from it. See acts of July 17, 1862 (12 *Statutes*, p. 627); March 3, 1863 (*ibid.*, pp. 713-731); and March 7, 1864 (13 *Statutes*, p. 14).

77

[10] Act of June 30, 1864, 13 *Statutes at Large*, pp. 223-306; amended by act of March 3, 1865 (*ibid.*, pp. 469-487).

[11] *Report of the Secretary of the Treasury*, Nov. 30, 1867, p. xi.

[12] *Report of the Secretary of the Treasury*, 1866, p. 6.

[13] Of course, when the lawful money debt was paid by refunding operations — that is, out of the proceeds of new loans themselves payable in gold — no such savings resulted, unless the new bonds were sold at a premium. An estimate of the saving actually effected may be found in the *Journal of Political Economy*, vol. V, pp. 146-149. The total arrived at is $72,000,000. If this sum be deducted from the above estimate of the increase in debt, the net loss to the government caused by the Greenbacks during the War will still appear to have been over a half a billion in gold.

Utilizing for the most part Census data, Professor Sellers analyzes the physical costs of the War on the southern economy. The picture he paints of the South's economic ability to effect a speedy recovery from the devastation of War was quite a gloomy one.

THE ECONOMIC INCIDENCE OF THE CIVIL WAR IN THE SOUTH

By James L. Sellers

"I CAN MAKE THE MARCH and make Georgia howl," wrote General Sherman to General Grant on October 9, 1864.[1] Whether General Grant agreed with this blunt assertion or not makes little difference; later historians have been impressed with the accuracy of Sherman's remark. Sherman was a staunch advocate of the potency of economic compression as a military policy. His march to the sea was the best, but not the only application of such a policy during the Civil War.

In discussing the rights of invaders, Sherman contended that the present War is a war between peoples and the invading army is entitled to all it can get from the people of the invaded territory.[2] This theory of conqueror's rights was given ample expression in his general order of November 9, 1864. The order provided that "the army will forage liberally upon the country during the march."[3] Although there were regulations prescribing the methods of foraging and restricting the properties to be appropriated, the evidence indicates a lax observance of the limitations.[4]

Historians are familiar, in a general way, with the destruction which took place. The livestock was driven before the army. The cavalry, artillery, and commissary were expected to keep themselves well supplied with good horses, equipment and provisions. Warehouses, mills, and ginhouses, the contents of which could not be appropriated, were to be destroyed. Depots, railroads, and deserted dwellings (assumed to be homes of rebels), as well as government buildings and property, were also on the condemned list.[5]

The helpless rage of the owner can well be imagined. I had a noble field of corn, not yet harvested. Old Sherman came along, and turned his droves of cattle right into it, and in the morning there was no more corn than there is on the back of my hand. His devils robbed me of all my flour and bacon and corn meal. They took all the pillowslips, ladies' dresses, drawers, chemises, sheets, and bed-quilts they could find in the house, to tie up the plunder in. . . . I sunk a cask of molasses in a hog-wallow; that I think I could have saved, but a nigger boy the rascals had with 'em said he 'lowed there was something hid there; and so he went to feeling with a stick, and found the molasses. Then they just robbed my house of every pail, cup, dish and what-not that they could carry molasses off to their camping-ground in.[6]

The general spirit of the order, without much regard to the protecting reservation, seems to have been followed by the soldiers. "One could track the line of Sherman's march all through Georgia and South Carolina by the fires upon the horizon," testified a not unbiased witness.[7] A northern colonel admitted that in nine cases out of every ten the mansions of the South Carolina slave-holders along the line of march were burned.[8]

Virginia was the battle-ground of the armies of Virginia and of the Potomac. It was consequently overrun to an unusual degree by hostile troops. On October 5, 1864, General Sheridan reported that the whole country from the Blue Ridge to North Mountain had been made utterly untenable for a rebel army. He had burned 2,000 barns filled with grain and hay and 70 mills stored with wheat.[9] General Lee testified to the completeness of the destruction within the state. In a communication to Secretary Seddon, January 11, 1865, he wrote, "There is nothing within reach of this army to be impressed; the country is swept clean. . . . We have only two days' rations."[10]

Wanton destruction was widespread in Alabama. Four years after the War, much of the country was pictured as desolate and deserted.[11] In Louisiana, General Butler ordered sequestered the property of all rebels west of the Mississippi.[12] The heavy losses reported for the state would indicate that this was no mere paper threat.[13]

The reports of travelers and inhabitants reveal a very great destruction of property throughout the South. Even in the uninvaded districts, property had been neglected and had depreciated in value. Such descriptions are convincing as to the general facts but they lack the precision of measurement which alone can satisfy the scientific students.

The exact extent to which war wastage had reduced the wealth of the South in 1865, is a fact of first importance in the understanding of the problems of economic reconstruction. Absolute accuracy

80

on a problem of this character is not to be expected; nor can one get an exact picture of actual conditions from a study of statistics. Statistical studies for large areas reveal only an average condition which, after all, is an imaginary concept. Despite this limitation, the average condition concept will give us that proportion of the prewar resources of a whole state or whole section which remained at the conclusion of the struggle.

Statistics for establishing this fact are not wholly satisfactory. The census reports and the agricultural reports are the standard sources. These are supplemented by the reports of congressional committees. The agricultural reports appeared annually, but their statistics were fragmentary, and frequently were omitted altogether. The decennial reports of the census do not afford material for the short-period comparisons which one would like to make.

Statistics of values are frequently misleading. The standard of value changed during the War and fluctuated in the years that followed.[14] As late as 1870 gold was exchanged for currency at a premium of 20 per cent.[15] In the South the influence of cheaper currency upon prices was probably offset to a considerable degree by the pessimism of defeat and the scarcity of currency. Because of these fluctuating factors in the statistics of evaluation, quantitative statistics afford a better index to actual changes and whenever they are available they have been used in this study.

Occasionally, duplicating statistics are shown. Because the agricultural statistics are more timely and the census statistics are more complete, it seemed that the evidence from both sources should be cited. The duplication at first may seem confusing, but in the end should be more satisfying to the reader.

The nucleus of this study is an examination of the losses of the South with a view to ascertaining what portion of the property remained at the close of the War and how the losses were distributed among the states. The war losses are, however, less important than the reduced relative productivity of the South. It is the relation between the war losses and the reduced productivity that makes the former so important. The geographic coincidence of heavy losses and reduced productivity furnishes the proof of their relationship.

The total assessed property evaluation of the 11 seceded states in 1860, was $4,363,030,367.[16] At the end of the War, the estimated wealth of these states was $1,603,402,429.[17] Of this vast decrease in evaluation, $1,634,105,341 is accounted for by the emancipation of slaves.[18] The remaining reduction of $1,125,522,577 is explainable only by losses or reduced values. There were changes in the prices of property. Real estate, especially, showed a marked decline in value. Nevertheless, quantitative statistics show a considerable decrease in the amount of actual property. This fact indicates that war consumption, destruction, and decay were important elements in the reduction.

From the above figures of evaluation it is evident that, exclusive of slaves, the southern wealth in 1860 had shrunk in value at the end of the War by 43 per cent. The census of 1870 assessed the property of the seceded states at $2,141,834,788. In comparison with the estimated statistics of 1865, this figure gives the large increase of half a billion dollars. Nevertheless, the total wealth of the South remained considerably below the figures shown by the previous census. The corrected returns given as "true evaluation" show a decrease of $713,700,000.[19] This amount does not take account of changes in the value of currency, which in 1870 was depreciated by 20 per cent. Including the computed correction for this difference in currency values, the wealth of the South, in 1860, exceeded that of 1870 by $1,231,500,000.[20] This computation shows that at the end of the war decade the wealth of the South was decreased by 30 per cent, and to recover the evaluation of 1860 would require an increase of 43 per cent upon the amount of wealth reported in 1870. In contrast to this loss of 30 per cent in the South, the North, during the same decade, had increased its wealth by approximately 50 per cent.[21]

An analysis of the statistics reveals that a large part of the decline was due to the fall in prices of southern real estate. Travelers and local journalists reported sales of farms for reduced prices varying from one half to one twentieth of their prewar values.[22] A single issue of the Milledgeville Southern Recorder advertised 21 executors' sales.[23] A number of these were large estates. The agricultural report for 1867 recorded average declines in the value of real property throughout the South varying from 18 per cent in Tennessee to 70 per cent in Louisiana.[24]

Comparison of the census reports of 1860 and 1870 shows that the assessed value of southern real estate declined 48 per cent during the decade, whereas in the North it had increased 73 per cent.[25] This decline for the former section is due to a variety of causes. Some of the best improvements had been destroyed. There had been no attention to upkeep and repair during the War. Replacements, likewise, had been neglected. The state of tillage had declined during the War from lack of supervision and working capital. There was also considerably less land under cultivation than there had been before the War. The decline in cultivated area was 18 per cent for the South as a whole.[26] South Carolina had lost one third of her cultivated land, and Louisiana and Virginia had suffered but slightly less; whereas Florida, Texas, and Tennessee showed increases in the cultivated area.[27]

The reduction in the value of real estate showed a decline paralleling the decline in cultivated area but in a more marked degree.

Louisiana and South Carolina again head the list with land evaluations at less than one third of their 1860 assessment.[28] The localiza-
tion of such extreme losses in value point to a local causation of a
more definite character. Further analysis of economic conditions
may throw additional light upon these facts.

The South was primarily an agricultural section. Next to her
land her agricultural capital was her most productive and most indispensable resource. The effect of the War upon the agricultural capital of the South is a question of first importance in considering the
economic result of that struggle. The amount and condition of agricultural capital set very definite and inescapable limits upon the
production of the area.

The livestock of the South was very seriously depleted during
the contest. The figures collected in 1866 show that the South was
short as compared with the numbers of 1860: 32 per cent in horses,
30 per cent in mules, 35 per cent in cattle, 20 per cent in sheep, and
42 per cent in swine.[29] Four years later the census reported a deficiency of 454,644 horses; 207,146 mules; 1,063,776 cattle; 1,354,380
sheep; and 6,330,696 swine.[30]

The problem of restocking southern farms in 1870 was a difficult
one. The increases necessary to restore the number of food and work
animals on hand in 1860 were very large in a number of the seceded
states. South Carolina, as compared with her sister states, had the
greatest shortage in almost every item. A 70 per cent increase in
horses, 76 per cent in cattle, 91 per cent in sheep, and 145 per cent
in swine would have been required in 1870 to restore the livestock of
the Old South state. Louisiana, Alabama, Georgia, and Virginia had
deficiencies varying from 20 per cent to 100 per cent in the various
items.[31]

The effect of this shortage upon agriculture is the more apparent
when the change in ratio of livestock to population is examined.
For every hundred of her population in 1860, South Carolina had 23
milch cows; in 1870 there were 13. The ratio for horses was reduced
from 11 to 6; for swine, from 137 to 56. South Carolina affords the
extreme example in this connection, but the figures for Arkansas,
Florida, and Georgia are scarcely less striking.[32]

The restocking of the southern farms was an especially slow
process. In 1880, Alabama, Georgia, Mississippi, North Carolina,
South Carolina, and Virginia had numerically less livestock than in
1860.[33] The value of livestock throughout the states of the Confederacy, excepting only Arkansas, Florida, and Texas, had not, in a
single instance, attained its prewar value during the 40 years following the contest.[34] However, the figures for 1900 show a close approximation to those of 1860, and by 1910 all of the states had attained a
new high mark in value of farm animals.[35]

The causes of this tardy restoration of livestock are not difficult to discover. The local quantity was wholly inadequate for food and work purposes, and there was no surplus wealth with which to purchase stock from outside areas. The indispensable utilization for food and work purposes left little surplus for breeding. As a consequence, the natural increase was very slow, and the period of recovery was especially long.[36]

In marked contrast to this condition in the South, a group of seven representative older states of the North showed an almost constant increase in the number of their livestock.[37] Although statistics of evaluation did not reflect this development completely, this is due to market conditions.[38] However, by the end of the century the increased number and improved quality had produced a great gain in value.[39] Whereas in 1900 the South had scarcely recovered its livestock development of 1860, these seven representative northern states had increased their quantity of livestock by 25 per cent and there had been an accretion of value of 76 per cent.

The War wrought havoc with farm implements and machinery. For the quantity of machinery we are compelled to rely upon statistics of value. In 1870 the assessed value of farm implements for the South was 55 per cent of the amount that it had been at the beginning of the decade.[40] South Carolina was again the greatest loser, having only one third of her prewar quota; Louisiana came second with two fifths, and Alabama was third with four ninths. In five other states (Arkansas, Florida, Mississippi, Texas, and Virginia) there were losses ranging between 40 and 50 per cent; while in only three states (Georgia, North Carolina, and Tennessee) did it fall below 40 per cent.[41]

The very slow recovery of the South is indicated by the changes in both the value of farms and the value of farm products. The value of farm products in the eight older states of the Confederacy showed but slight changes from 1870 to 1890. However, there was an increase of 17 per cent during the last decade of the century.[42] The value of farms in these same eight states declined from $1,427,000,000 in 1860, to $866,000,000 in 1870, and while it had attained a value of $1,554,000,000 in 1890, there was a slight drop in the following decade.[43] Thus, at the end of the century the total value of farm property in these states was practically the same as it had been 40 years previously. This is in marked contrast to the northern states, where farm values had more than doubled in the same period.[44]

The War affected every phase of economic life. Industry could not escape. In 1870 the nominal value of the products of manufacturies had increased over the amount of 1860 by 40 per cent.[45] This increase, however, was more than offset by the difference in prices at the two dates.[46] It is significant to note that the portion of the national production of manufacturies produced in the South had declined from 7.2 per cent in 1860 to 4.7 per cent in 1870; while the longitudinal line locating the center of manufacturing had shifted north from 40° and 33' to 40° and 47'.[47] Even in 1900 the central line was located at 40° and 36', but the southern portion of the national output was again 7.2 per cent.

Financial and business institutions suffered an almost complete collapse. "Mercantile capital and bank and insurance stock were consumed as in a furnace."[49] The credit situation in South Carolina was described in the following terms: "Four-fifths of all property of the deceased . . . were invested in Confederate securities and are therefore valueless. In like manner the funds of churches, colleges, charitable institutions, $15,000,000 in bank stock, and nearly all the funds of private individuals which were available have been almost entirely sunk."[50]

The banks of the South, which had never been adequate for the needs of their section, could not be restored immediately. The banking capital, which aggregated $61,000,000 in 1860, totaled only $17,000,000 ten years later.[51] The currency of the section was reduced from $51,000,000 to $15,000,000. With such a scarcity of banking and credit facilities, interest rates mounted to unbelievable heights.[52] The insurance business grew rapidly after the War, and the slowly accumulating premiums for investment supplemented the inadequate credit afforded by the banks.

Conditions were most inauspicious for the merchants. The situation was aptly described by a Mobile furniture dealer who had closed his store. "Everybody," he said, "wanted to buy and nobody had any money. . . ." If he refused credit he would make all of his old customers enemies; if he gave credit, he would go bankrupt.[53] The old merchants could not offer the credit needed by their customers and were compelled to go out of business or go over to a cash basis.[54] This made an opening for outsiders with more capital to come in and establish themselves. However, the credit accommodations of the newcomers were obtainable only at a high cost.[55]

In this description of southern conditions we have before us a series of economic facts. There was a shortage in agricultural capital, a reduced area under cultivation, diminished agricultural production, depreciated land value, stifled industry, demoralized commerce, totally inadequate banking and currency facilities with a correspondingly high rate of interest. These were all the results of war wastage which had produced a deficiency in fundamental capital for the essential productive industries.

The shortage of agricultural capital is the logical head of this concatenation of conditions. Agriculture was beyond all comparison the most important of the productive pursuits of the South. The loss of every third horse or mule throughout the communities of the South and the reduction of agricultural machinery by almost one half were inescapable economic facts. Two horses could not do the work of three, nor could one plow turn as many furrows as two. The cultivated area had to be reduced, and although the reduction was not in proportion to the deficit in agricultural capital, the neglected tillage absorbed the difference.

The contracted condition of husbandry due to inadequate capital was further aggravated by problems of labor. The transition from slave to free labor was not without its costs. While it is admitted that free labor generally requires less capital than slave labor, it is also true that it requires more working capital to run plantations with free labor than it takes to run plantations already supplied with slaves. The transition after the War was from plantations already supplied with slaves to free laborers. Wages were probably more than the mere keep of the worker, and moreover, the Negro lost his value as a credit asset. The Negroes were temporarily less productive as free laborers than they had been as slaves. They were not only less reliable, but they also frequently refused the disagreeable hand work which had been exacted of slaves.[56] This latter fact made an increased quantity of machinery and work animals necessary to keep up the old output.

Economic recovery in the South was retarded by other causes also. Channels of trade were dislocated by the War. The Mississippi was completely displaced by the railroads as an important artery of commerce between the East and the West. The instability of social and political conditions aggravated the economic disorder. The strained feelings between the sections did not promote business relations. There was little to offer as security to invite investors. The South could not compete in the money markets with regions more attractive to capital.

The financial policy of the federal government placed a heavy additional burden upon the southern states. Their share of the northern war debt and federal pensions, little or none of which returned to the southern states, constituted an unavoidable indemnity of at least a billion dollars.[57]

In the absence of assistance in any adequate quantity from without, the people of the South were compelled to create and accumulate their own productive capital. The accumulation of productive capital is a slow process. The South was set back to a mere subsistence basis. It is the initial accumulation that is most difficult, for capital begets capital and thereby assists in the accumulating process. It is a significant fact that southern agricultural capital and agricultural production at the end of the century had scarcely surpassed the development of 1860. There had been no corollary development of industry to absorb productive capital such as had taken place in the industry of the northeastern states.[58]

Geographically, one can fix in a general way the economic incidence of the Civil War in the South.[59] The complexity of the problem and the danger of dogmatic assertions is apparent from a brief study of the data accumulated in the course of making the present study. In the light of these statistics, it is evident that the heavier losses fell upon the older states of the Cotton South and Virginia. South Carolina was apparently singled out for special punishment.[60] The treatment meted out seems successfully to have eradicated her leadership and left her prostrate for generations to come.

The immediate poverty following the War was felt by all classes. Even the Negroes supplied by Freedman Bureau commissaries were probably not as well fed as they had been upon many of the plantations. However, it was the plantation owners who suffered most, for they who had most, had most to lose. But the professional classes and overseers who depended upon the prosperity of the planters suffered also. While their work was even more necessary during reconstruction than in the period before the War, their pay was seldom obtainable. The whole economic structure rested upon the planters and they no longer had the means to sustain it.

Chronologically, the economic incidence of the War did not fall upon one generation. Just as in northern England, where the economic destruction wrought by William the Conqueror was visible until the industrial revolution,[61] so the evidences of the devastation produced by the Civil War still remain in the economic life of the South. The census of 1900 showed that after the lapse of a full generation the South had hardly recovered the economic development of 1860. This once prosperous section, yielding almost half of the nation's produce, had become a region of minor importance which produced only about 10 per cent of the nation's wealth.[62] It seems that the marked decline in the proportion of the nation's production is a permanent condition resulting, at least in part, from the War. The poverty of the South has been reflected in the social life and leadership of the section, and this exhibits a sad contrast to its prewar glamour. To insist that this condition will be permanent is a harsh and perhaps an unhistorical position to take.

[1] *War of the Rebellion, A Compilation of the Official Records of Union and Confederate Armies* (Washington, 1880-1901), vol. 39, pt. III, p. 162. This will be cited henceforth as *Rebellion Records*.

[2] W. L. Fleming, *Civil War and Reconstruction in Alabama* (New York, 1905), p. 76.

[3] *Rebellion Records*, vol. 39, part III, p. 713.

[4] J. F. Rhodes, *History of the United States* (New York, 1892-1919), vol. V, p. 20; *Milledgeville Southern Recorder*, July 7, 1867.

[5] *Rebellion Records*, vol. 38, part III, p. 714.

[6] J. T. Trowbridge, *The South* (Hartford, 1866), p. 476.

[7] *Ibid.*, p. 475.

[8] Rhodes, *History of the U. S.*, vol. V, p, 88. (Quoted from C. F. Morse, *Memoirs*, vol. II, p. 254.)

[9] *Rebellion Records*, vol. 43, pt. I, pp. 37, 59, 443, 529.

[10] *Ibid.*, vol. 46, part II, pp. 1035, 1143.

[11] Fleming, *Civil War and Reconstruction*, p. 73; Trowbridge, *The South*, p. 440. General Wilson reported the destruction of his raid in March and April, 1865, to include 7 iron works, 2 rolling mills, 5 collieries, 3 factories, 4 niter plants, 1 military university, 1 navy yard, 5 steamboats, 35 locomotives, 565 cars, and 3 railroad bridges. During 28 days he had covered 525 miles. *Rebellion Records*, vol. 49, part I, p. 365.

[12] Jefferson Davis, *Rise and Fall of the Confederate Government* (New York, 1881), vol. II, p. 288.

[13] Compare the property statistics of Louisiana in the *Eighth* and *Ninth Census*. The losses are illustrated by the statistics cited in the following pages.

[14] *Review of Economic Statistics*, July, 1920, Supplement II, p. 5; D. R. Dewey, *Financial History of the United States* (New York, 1903), p. 293.

[15] *Ninth Census*, vol. III, p. 8; Dewey, *Financial History of the U. S.*, p. 376.

[16] *Ninth Census*, vol. III, p. 16.

[17] *Senate Report* No. 41, 42 Cong., 2d Sess., p. 214.

[18] *Ibid.*; *Eighth Census*, vol. IV, p. 337.

[19] *Eighth Census*, vol. IV, p. 337; *Ninth Census*, vol. III, p. 10.

[20] Based upon statistics cited in note 19. This does not agree with statistics cited in *Senate Report* No. 41, 42d Cong., 2d Sess., pp. 215, 237-238.

[21] *Ninth Census*, vol. III, p. 22.

[22] *Milledgeville Southern Recorder*, June 13, 1865; Jan. 29, 1867; Jan. 23, 1868; Trowbridge, *The South*, p. 181; Fleming, *Civil War and Reconstruction*, p. 258.

[23] Issue of Nov. 20, 1866.

[24] Statistics for 1867 were based upon the *Agriculture Report*, 1867, pp. 105-106. Those for 1870 were computed upon the figures of the *Eighth Census*, vol. III, p. vii, and *Ninth Census*, vol. III, p. 81. Both here and throughout the study detailed statistics of losses by individual states have been compiled which it has not been found practicable to include in the paper as printed.

[25] *Ibid.*

[26] *Ibid.*

[27] The decline in the cultivated area for the various states was as follows: Alabama, 20%; Arkansas, 6%; Georgia, 19%; Louisiana, 30%; Mississippi, 16%; North Carolina, 20%; South Carolina, 34%; and Virginia, 28%. In Tennessee there was a gain of 1%; in Texas a gain of 11%; and in Florida a gain of 12%. Data from *Eighth Census*, vol. III, p. vii, and *Ninth Census*, vol. III, p. 81.

[28] See note 27.

[29] *Agriculture Report*, 1867, pp. 95-106.

[30] *Ninth Census*, vol. III, pp. 75-83.

[31] *Ibid*, pp. 75, 82, 87.

[32] *Agriculture Report*, 1871, p. 51. In Arkansas the number of horses (per 100 of population) was reduced from 32 to 18; in Florida, from 9 to 5; in Georgia, from 12 to 6. For milch cows, the reductions in the three states were: Arkansas, 39 to 26; Florida, 66 to 32; Georgia, 28 to 19. For sheep, the reductions were: Arkansas, 46 to 33; Florida, 21 to 14; Georgia, 48 to 35. For swine, the reductions were: Arkansas, 269 to 173; Florida, 193 to 84; Georgia, 192 to 83.

[33] *Ninth Census*, vol. III, p. 75; *Tenth Census*, vol. III, p. 141.

[34] *Eleventh Census*, vol. X, pp. 85, 93, 101; *Twelfth Census*, vol. X, p. cii.

[35] *Ibid;* also *Thirteenth Census,* vol. V, p. 330.

[36] The War had used up the better quality of livestock. The poorer farmers were compelled to use their milch cows as work animals. They were thus over-worked and would not reproduce at a normal rate. *Monthly Report, Department of Agriculture,* 1867, p. 194.

[37] The States of Connecticut, Massachusetts, New York, Pennsylvania, Ohio, Indiana, and Illinois were chosen as a representative group of the older agricultural states of the North. It is not intended to get states in the two sections which are similar, for this is manifestly impossible. These seven northern states are roughly comparable, in state of development, to the eight older states of the Confederacy. In statistical comparisons to discover economic effects of the War, it is desirable to eliminate the expansion upon the frontier. For this reason the three newer states of the Confederacy were excluded. For a similar reason state statistics, rather than totals, have been stressed.

[38] The number of horses is indicative of the livestock development of these northern states. The total (in round numbers) for the seven states in 1860 was 2,728,000; in 1870, 3,589,000. Practically all of the total increase shown in 1870, and more than half of that shown in 1880, however, occured in the state of Illinois. Data from *Ninth Census,* vol III, p. 75, and *Tenth Census,* vol. III, p. 141.

[39] *Eleventh Census,* vol. X, pp. 85, 93, 101; *Twelfth Census,* vol. V, p. cii.

[40] *Eighth Census,* vol. III, p. x; *Ninth Census,* vol. III, p. 81.

[41] *Eighth Census,* vol. III, p. x; *Ninth Census,* vol. III, p. 81; *Agriculture Report,* 1871, p. 49.

[42] *Eleventh Census,* vol. X, pp. 85, 93, 101; *Twelfth Census,* vol. V, p. cii.

[43] *Ninth Census,* vol. III, pp. 81, 86, 90; *Eleventh Census,* vol. X, pp. 84, 92, 100; *Twelfth Census,* vol. V, p. cii.

[44] *Ibid.*

[45] *Statistical Abstract of the United States,* 1907, p. 20; 1920, pp. 139-140.

[46] According to the Superintendent of the Census, F. A. Walker, the evaluations of 1870 were increased by at least 30% through the effects of currency inflation since 1860. *Ninth Census,* vol. III, p. 8.

[47] *Twelfth Census,* vol. VII, p. clxxi.

[48] *Thirteenth Census,* vol. VIII, pp. 57, 60.

[49] Somers, p. 197.

[50] *New York Times,* Sept. 13, 1865, p. 4.

[51] *Senate Report.* No. 41, 42d Cong., 2d Sess., p. 235.

[52] Somers, pp. 79, 210; *Review of Economic Statistics,* July, 1920, p. 16.

[53] Whitelaw Reid, *A Southern Tour* (New York, 1866), pp. 206-207.

[54] Seventy-three wholesale merchants of Charleston issued a notice to their patrons explaining why they could not grant credit and lauding the merits of the cash system. *Charleston Daily News,* April 2, 1866.

[55] Somers, pp. 151, 211; M. B. Hammond, *The Cotton Industry* (New York, 1897), p. 146.

[56] Reid, *A Southern Tour,* pp. 558-573; Somers, p. 268.

[57] For a discussion of this point see "Civil War Finance" by the present writer, in *American Historical Review,* vol. XXX, p. 296.

[58] *Twelfth Census,* vol. VII, p. clxxix.

[59] The author has examined county statistics for Georgia and South Carolina, but a detailed knowledge of local conditions is necessary before any conclusions can be reached.

[60] Trowbridge, *The South,* p. 475.

[61] E. A. Freeman, *William the Conqueror* (London, 1922), p. 119.

[62] *Am. Hist. Rev.,* vol. XXX, p. 296, notes 63, 64.

By calculating and tracing the behavior of gross farm income in the South, Professor Lerner makes an important contribution to the estimated physical and income costs of the War on the southern economy. He stresses especially that southern manufacturing was not affected as seriously as agricultural capacity by the War experience and that this fact conditioned the character of postwar economic development.

SOUTHERN OUTPUT AND AGRICULTURAL INCOME, 1860-1880

By Eugene M. Lerner

WHEREVER WAR touched the South — whether in its "peculiar institution," in its farms, factories or homes, the aftermath was disorganization, ruin, and suffering. For more than two centuries southerners had lived with the institution of slavery. Now that institution crumbled. As federal armies successfully overran the southern states, many freed men tested their new-found liberty by wandering aimlessly into the cities and towns, or by trailing after the advancing Union armies. Some went to other states, while many others drifted back to their old plantation homes where they eventually had to learn the responsibilities of free men. Of those who wandered, uncounted thousands died by the wayside of typhoid or other epidemic diseases;[1] many, unable or unwilling to find work were driven by hunger to petty theft. It was alleged that no chicken roost was safe. Confederate soldiers returned to their farms to find their livestock decimated, their acres gone to weeds, their tools in need of repair. General Pemberton, chief of the Confederate forces at Vicksburg and a wealthy man in prewar days, was reduced to pulling his own plow in order to plant his first postwar crop. His horses had been killed or stolen. Factories were razed to the ground, machinery was worn out and wrecked, houses and barns were burned. In Louisiana a plantation was sold for $6,000 in 1865; the same plantation was valued at $100,000 before the War.

Although there are no inventories of the South's agricultural capacity or physical capital at the close of the War, the several series presented in Table I[2] give some idea of how great was the physical and dollar cost of the Civil War.[3] These series compare the South of 1870, after five full years of recovery, with the South of 1860. Even though they therefore understate the War's destruction, the series still present a startling picture: the number of horses in the 11 states of the Confederacy fell by 29 per cent from 1860 to 1870; the number of cows fell by 32 per cent; the number of swine was reduced by 35 per cent; the value of farm implements declined by 46 per cent; and the value of the farms themselves fell almost by half.

During the decade 1870-1880, the physical capital destroyed by War was replaced, and by 1880, 15 years after the end of the War, most of the series reached or exceeded their 1860 levels. The number of cattle (other than cows) and acres of farms in the South were almost as great in 1880 as they were in 1860; the number of horses, mules, cows, and improved acres in the South ranged from 4 to 27 per cent higher. However, in spite of this growth of resources, the value series, though generally higher in 1880 than in 1870, were still below their 1860 levels. In 1880 the value of farms was 33 per cent below its 1860 level, the value of farm implements was 31 per cent lower and the value of livestock was down 24 per cent. This disparity between the degree of recovery of the physical series on the one hand and the value series on the other requires further analysis.

During the decade of the 1860's, though agricultural capacity fell drastically in the South, it expanded in the rest of the country. For example, in 1860 there were 6.5 million horses in the United States and of these, 1.7 million were in the South. In 1870 there were 7.3 million horses in the United States but only 1.2 million in the South.

During the decade of the 1870's however, many agricultural resources expanded more rapidly in the South than in the country as a whole. In spite of the rapid western expansion of the country during this decade, the South in 1880 held a larger percentage than it did in 1870 of all, except three, of the series examined. The exceptions were: acres in farms, the number of improved acres and the number of swine.

Southern manufacturing[4] during the 15 years after the Civil War followed a much different course. Table II presents several series derived from the United States Census of Manufactures. In every case, the manufacturing series in 1870 are above the corresponding 1860 figures. The number of firms increased by almost 80 per cent between 1860 and 1870; the amount of capital increased by 3 per cent, and the number of laborers by 30 per cent. Some of the manufacturing series presented in Table II measure changes in output or cost of output rather than changes in capacity and so are not directly comparable to the agricultural series.[5] Viewed as a group, however, they suggest a very clear picture: while the resources and output of

TABLE I

INDICATORS OF SOUTHERN[a] AGRICULTURAL CAPITAL AND
CAPACITY AT SELECTED DATES 1850 TO 1880
(*in thousands*)

	No. in South	No. in South as a % of No. in U.S.	Index: 1860=100	No. in South	No. in South as a % of No. in U.S.	Index: 1860=100
	Horses			Mules		
1850	1,421.0	32.7	81.5	405.3	72.4	49.3
1860	1,743.8	27.1	100.0	822.7	71.5	100.0
1870	1,246.2	17.4	71.5	613.5	54.5	74.6
1880	2,083.0	20.1	119.4	1,044.8	57.6	127.0
	Milch Cows			Working Oxen		
1850	2,248.5	35.2	83.1	603.6	35.4	70.7
1860	2,705.7	31.5	100.0	853.6	37.8	100.0
1870	1,852.3	20.7	68.4	507.6	38.4	59.5
1880	2,817.9	22.6	104.1	517.6	52.0	60.6
	Swine			Other Cattle		
1850	15,804.1	52.0	101.6	4,491.4	46.3	59.4
1860	15,562.7	46.4	100.0	7,554.0	57.1	100.0
1870	10,122.6	40.2	65.0	3,623.8	26.7	48.0
1880	13,509.9	28.3	86.8	7,264.4	32.3	96.2
	Acres of Farms			Improved Acres		
1850	....	....	....	43,224.9	38.2	76.0
1860	200,476.3	49.2	100.0	56,832.1	34.8	100.0
1870	156,791.1	38.5	78.2	46,987.1	24.8	82.7
1880	197,002.4	36.7	98.3	67,350.6	23.6	118.5
	Values of Farms			Value of Farm Implements		
1850	793,344.1	24.2	42.9	53,221.3	35.1	64.1
1860	1,850,708.5	27.8	100.0	82,971.4	33.7	100.0
1870	977,142.3	10.5	52.8	45,145.3	13.4	54.4
1880	1,234,958.4	12.1	66.7	57,637.4	14.1	69.5
	Value of Livestock					
1850	196,327.8	36.0	54.2			
1860	362,163.1	33.2	100.0			
1870	279,685.0	18.3	77.2			
1880	276,708.1	18.6	76.4			

a The South is defined as the 11 states that seceded from the Union.
Source: "Tenth Census of the United States," vol. 3.

agriculture fell during the decade 1860-1870, the resources and output of manufacturing increased.

During the decade 1870-1880, the manufacturing series generally show a slight drop in the ratio of the South to the country as a whole. Unfortunately, the many errors in collecting and processing these early census returns make small percentage changes untrustworthy. However, the census figure must be accurate enough to warrant the conclusion that while many resources used in agriculture expanded more rapidly in the South than in the United States as a whole between 1870 and 1880, many in manufacturing did not.

Why did southern manufacturing recover so rapidly from the War in the late 1860's and southern agriculture so slowly? Why did it take until 1880 for the agricultural series to equal their 1860 level when the manufacturing had already surpassed their prewar level in 1870? Why, during the 1870's, did the rate of growth of southern agricultural capital rise relative to that of the nation as a whole, while the rate of growth of manufacturing did not? To answer these

TABLE II

INDICATORS OF SOUTHERN MANUFACTURING
1850 TO 1880

	1850	1860	1870	1880
No. of Establishments				
Establishments in South	123,025	140,433	252,148	253,852
Per Cent of U.S.	13.7	14.7	12.3	11.5
Index, 1860 = 100	87.6	100.0	179.5	180.8
Capital a				
Capital in South (in millions)	55.3	96.0	98.7	133.3
Per Cent of U.S.	10.4	9.5	4.6	4.8
Index, 1860 = 100	57.6	100.0	102.8	138.8
No. of Laborers a				
No. of Laborers	88,390	110,721	144,252	171,674
Per Cent of U.S.	9.2	8.4	7.0	6.3
Index, 1860 = 100	79.8	100.0	130.3	155.0
Cost of Labor				
Wages (in millions)	17.5	28.7	31.0	37.1
Per Cent of U.S.	7.4	7.6	4.0	3.9
Index, 1860 = 100	61.0	100.0	108.0	129.3
Cost of Raw Materials				
Cost of Raw Materials (in millions)	40.8	86.5	116.2	151.8
Per Cent of U.S.	7.4	8.4	4.7	4.5
Index, 1860 = 100	47.2	100.0	134.3	175.5
Value of Products				
Value of Products (in millions)	79.2	155.5	199.0	240.5
Per Cent of U.S.	7.8	8.2	4.7	4.5
Index, 1860 = 100	50.9	100.0	127.9	154.6

a Both series exclude slaves.
Source: "United States Census," various years.

questions, the economy of the South during the Civil War, as well as during the postwar period, must be examined.

During the War, northern ships blockaded the Confederate ports and neither exports, such as cotton and tobacco, nor imports, like manufactured goods, could move easily in or out of the South. In consequence, the price of exports tended to be depressed and the price of imports to be raised.[6] In an effort to bolster their income, planters sent petitions to the Confederate Secretary of the Treasury urging that the Confederate government buy the cotton crop outright or advance a loan on the growing crop. These proposals were rejected for a number of reasons, one of which was that the South needed grain and provisions and the subsidizing of cotton would eliminate the incentive to change crop outputs.[7]

The inaccessibility of foreign markets caused by the northern blockade and the refusal of the Confederate government to extend aid on the cotton crop were powerful incentives for planters to reduce their output of cotton. However, it is less certain that the output of other crops expanded. Indeed, it is more likely that their output also fell.

The War exacted a heavy drain on both agricultural manpower and horses. The old men, women, and children left at home could not manage their farms and slaves as well as the men called to the army. To help correct this decrease in efficiency, legislation was introduced to exempt men from the army if they owned 20 or more slaves. However, this bill quickly gave rise to the complaint "a rich man's war and a poor man's fight," and the measure was dropped. Agricultural inefficiency remained.

What alternatives faced the women left on the farms when their husbands were called to war? One was to try and get along as well as possible, and many of course did just that. Many other women, however, left their plantations and found jobs in industry.

As the blockade restricted the import of many manufactured products, southern manufacturers tried to expand their output of these commodities. New iron works were opened up in Alabama and Virginia and new textile mills were started in the Carolinas. Commodity prices rose faster than wage rates, and this lag undoubtedly increased profits, stimulating the output of all manufactured goods as well as the increase in new plant and equipment. The Confederate government opened quartermaster supply depots in the larger towns and operated salt works, nitrate mines, and ordnance factories. New and expanded enterprises needed laborers. The Confederate army sent troops back from the front to work in war plants. Thousands of women and girls took jobs for the first time in their lives in clothing shops. Manufacturing establishments also began to advertise for slave labor. The Macon Armory advertised for 100 hands;

the Tredegar Iron Works wanted 1,000; the Naval Gun Foundry and Ordnance Works at Selma wanted 200; the salt works in Clark County, Alabama, advertised for 500; and the railroads wanted Negroes by the thousands. Almost every industry was competing for Negro labor. Plantation owners, attracted by relatively high returns, rented more and more of their slaves to mills, factories, and railroads.

The blockade, the price-wage lag, and the increased military demand for manufactured products discouraged the production of exports and stimulated the output of manufactured goods previously imported. The War drained the agricultural management class and encouraged the people left at home to shift their resources out of agriculture and into manufacturing. Combined, these forces tended to reduce agricultural output and expand manufacturing capital and output during the War. Consequently, while there were offsets in manufacturing to the destruction of war, there were no comparable incentives working to encourage agriculture.

After the War, the South's farm labor force, predominantly Negro, became seriously disorganized, thus retarding the recovery of agriculture. The manufacturing labor force, on the other hand, was predominantly white and quickly reorganized.

A pressing farm problem at the end of the War was to get the Negroes to work effectively in the fields. The problems of William Minor, a Louisiana plantation owner, were typical. He wrote in his diary on January 3, 1863:

> Find the negroes are completely demoralised — They are practically free — Going, coming & working when they please & as they please. They destroy everything on the plantation. In one night they killed 30 hogs. They have stolen a number of my best Sd. [Southdown] sheep & sold them in Houma at $1 each. They will not shut a gate or put up a fence; they ride the mules off at night & at all times. The most of them think, or pretend to think, that the plantation & every thing on it belongs to them. . . .[8]

Later in the year Minor described conditions near New Orleans. Some fields appeared to be in good order, but many "were only partially cultivated & some were totally abandoned." He wrote: "The negroes everywhere [are] greatly demoralized, being insolent & idle — working not more than half a day, yet demanding full rations of *every thing*." Conditions had so deteriorated that the planters patrolled the river parishes to watch over their property and guard against the wandering Negroes.[9]

Minor found that wages were not sufficient inducement to keep his Negroes at work so long as they had assurance of rations. He therefore "instructed his overseer to deduct one day's rations for every day a laborer failed to work. As for the married women, who seemed more averse to working than any of the others, their husbands were to be charged for their rations." Minor also explicitly instructed his overseers to use the greatest forbearance and prudence in supervising the Negroes. "They must be got back to the old way of doing business by degrees. Everything must be done to encourage & make them work before resorting to corporeal punishment — If they will not work without it, it must be resorted to & inflicted in a proper manner — To do this you must not punish when you, or the negro to be punished, is *in a passion.*" On the other hand, when the Negroes behaved well, they were given occasional leave to town.[10]

The host of problems associated with the transition of Negroes from slavery to freedom could only be solved with the passing of time. To link laborers' income immediately with their continued output over a crop year, share-cropping and tenant farming developed. Other Negroes were paid only part of their salary at the end of each month and the remainder at the end of the season, if they worked throughout it. In North Carolina, at least, some plantation owners hired Negroes for a season at a stipulated sum. If the Negroes worked extra days, they were paid at the rate of 20 cents per day; if they failed to work on a day that they should have, they were fined from 40 to 50 cents a day. All of these various practices were attempts to develop a dependable agricultural labor force that would work under freedom with some degree of efficiency.

In addition to a disorganized labor force, the destruction of capital itself was a powerful force retarding agricultural expansion. Livestock could only be replaced with the passing of time, and even had the labor force been efficient, fields could not give abundant yields with a shortage of mules, plows, and horses. Moreover, capital markets must have been highly imperfect right after the War. Planters and farmers probably could not borrow to replace their depleted stock, and the principal source of funds available to farmers undoubtedly came from internal sources. Since output was low, savings were low, and recovery retarded. The curse of the poor is their poverty!

Conditions in manufacturing after the War were more favorable for an expansion in output. The predominantly white labor force was not utterly chaotic. The War's destruction created a strong replacement demand for almost all products. New homes and barns, new tools and wagons, new shoes and clothes were urgently needed. Moreover, anticipating some conclusions to be presented later, in spite of the drop in farm capacity, gross farm income experienced a sizable rise between 1866 and 1870. This rise in income allowed the needs of the people to be translated into effective demand and contributed to the rapid recovery in manufacturing.

The reports of manufacturing all testify to rapid rebuilding and expansion programs. The cities of Atlanta and Charleston had minor building booms. Victor S. Clark reported that during the session of 1865-66, the legislature of Georgia incorporated 17 manufacturing companies, "an evidence of a public interest in such enterprises that doubtless outran the possibilities of performance."[11]

Within less than two years of the conclusion of hostilities, the mills at Columbus, Georgia, which had been burned during Wilson's raid, were under reconstruction. The mills at Saluda were rebuilt, and several mills were running in the Greenville district. A number of factories were established in central Alabama, Mississippi, and Texas. As early as 1868, the cotton mills of Augusta received special mention in the report of the Commissioners of the Paris Expositions as illustrating conditions favoring cotton manufacturing in the South.[12]

Southern railroads also recovered rapidly. In spite of Sherman's legendary destructiveness, the attrition through normal wear and tear, and the loss caused by the Confederate government pulling up railroad tracks to lay them elsewhere, one estimate indicates that the total railroad mileage in the South from 1860 to 1865 fell by only 32 miles.[13] During the War, the northern government operated captured southern lines to move federal troops and supplies. In the process the government rebuilt and relaid miles of tracks. After the War, the federal government sold to southern lines rolling stock on credit at less than the market price. During the 1870's, when the southern railroads had difficulty in meeting their payments, Congress relieved them of their obligations. Promoters of both manufacturing establishments and railroads came north to borrow capital, and northern financiers invested heavily, hastening the reconstruction of southern railroad lines, mills, and factories.

James De Bow, the most prominent southern economist of his day, traveled widely through the South during this period and gave, according to the historian, John Stover, a good account of the process of railroad restoration.

In 1866, he found the trains seldom running, accommodations terrible, and the rates twice as high as prewar. By 1867, the railroads were in as good a condition as before the War, with comparable schedules and rates only a quarter higher. He also noted that some companies were paying dividends and that many were meeting interest payments on time. . . . By 1870 the physical restoration and rehabilitation of southern railroads was practically complete.[14]

In summary, the War was a terribly destructive event for the South. It destroyed a large percentage of the South's capacity to produce agricultural products by decimating horses, cattle, and mules. But the War hit agriculture harder than it did manufacturing. In the immediate postwar period, the labor force in manufacturing was not disorganized; the labor force in agriculture was disorganized. The postwar demand for manufactured products was great, and the rise in gross farm income enabled manufacturers to serve an expanding farm market. Therefore, conditions both during and immediately after the War were conducive to manufacturing capacity in the South expanding faster than agricultural capacity. As the data in Tables I and II reveal, manufacturing expanded from 1860 to 1870 while agriculture failed to recover its earlier position.[15]

What happened to agricultural output and farm income as a result of destruction of capacity and the disorganization of the labor force? Table III presents data on crop outputs derived from the estimates of the United States Department of Agriculture's Marketing Service and the United States Census. In every case the average output of crops in the South during the first five postwar years, 1866-70, was considerably below the corresponding 1859 figure. Cotton was almost 50 per cent below its ante-bellum level of output, corn was 44 per cent lower, hay was down 64 per cent. In the rest of the country, output increased. Corn increased in the non-South by 22 per cent, wheat by 52 per cent and hay by 24 per cent. These output figures conform to the resource figures presented earlier. In both instances the southern series in the immediate postwar period fell below the corresponding 1860 levels; in both cases the non-South figures rise above the corresponding prewar figures.

Fifteen years after the War, the output of the South's major crops had expanded rapidly. The average cotton output during the five crop years, 1876-80, was almost twice as high as the average output during the years 1866-70. The average corn output was 56 per cent higher, wheat output was 54 per cent higher, and hay output was 111 per cent higher. In the rest of the country, agricultural output also expanded during these 15 years. In some cases, like hay, potatoes, and oats, the South grew at a faster rate than the non-South; in other cases, like barley, corn, and wheat, the South grew at a slower rate.

The data in Table III also show a growth of output over that in 1860. By 1880 the output of the two most important southern crops, corn and cotton, and the output of two minor crops, potatoes and oats, exceeded their prewar level. Other crops, like wheat and sweet potatoes, closely approximated their prewar level, while still others lagged behind. All of the non-South series in 1880, however, were substantially above their prewar level. These results also roughly conform to the resource figures presented earlier in the chapter.

Considering only the two most important crops of the South, cotton and corn, agricultural production recovered to its prewar level in a little less than 15 years. By 1880 the South's output of these crops was slightly higher than in 1860. However, the agricultural

TABLE III

AVERAGE OUTPUT OF SELECTED CROPS IN THE SOUTH[a] AND NON-SOUTH
IN 1859, 1866-1870 AND 1876-1880

	Cotton (000,000 lbs.)		Barley (000 bushels)	
	South	Non-South	South	Non-South
Output during 1859 [b]	2,373	....	22	15,605
Average output during the five years 1866-1870	1,213	....	121	24,574
Average output during the five years 1876-1880	2,395	....	166	40,827
Average output in ratio:				
1866-70 to 1859	51.1	....	55.1	157.5
1876-80 to 1866-70	197.5	....	136.6	166.1
1876-80 to 1859	100.9	....	75.4	261.6

	Tame Hay (000 tons)		Potatoes (000 bushels)	
	South	Non-South	South	Non-South
Output during 1859 [b]	1,045	18,038	6,600	104,500
Average output during the five years 1866-1870	386	22,489	4,969	111,840
Average output during the five years 1876-1880	817	30,316	7,158	147,696
Average output in ratio:				
1866-70 to 1859	36.9	124.7	75.3	107.0
1876-80 to 1866-70	211.9	134.8	144.1	132.1
1876-80 to 1859	78.2	168.1	108.4	133.6

	Corn (000,000 bushels)		Oats (000,000 bushels)	
	South	Non-South	South	Non-South
Output during 1859 [b]	283	556	20	152
Average output during the five years 1866-1870	188	682	19	228
Average output during the five years 1876-1880	293	1,310	40	367
Average output in ratio:				
1866-70 to 1859	66.4	122.7	93.1	149.9
1876-80 to 1866-70	156.1	192.1	214.6	160.8
1876-80 to 1859	103.7	235.6	199.8	241.1

	Wheat (000,000 bushels)		Sweet Potatoes (000,000 bushels)	
	South	Non-South	South	Non-South
Output during 1859 [b]	31	142	38	4
Average output during the five years 1866-1870	18	216	24	3

TABLE III — (Continued)

	South	Non-South	South	Non-South
Average output during the five years 1876-1880	28	395	32	5
Average output in ratio:				
1866-70 to 1859	58.3	152.3	63.2	81.6
1876-80 to 1866-70	154.3	182.9	132.8	157.8
1876-80 to 1859	90.0	278.6	84.7	128.8

	Rye		Buckwheat	
	(000 bushels)		(000 bushels)	
Output during 1859 [b]	2,201	18,900	572	17,000
Average output during the five years 1866-1870	1,199	16,398	209	10,442
Average output during the five years 1876-1880	983	19,421	219	11,024
Average output in ratio:				
1866-70 to 1859	54.5	86.8	36.5	61.4
1876-80 to 1866-70	82.0	118.4	105.2	105.6
1876-80 to 1859	44.7	102.8	38.4	64.8

	Tobacco		Rice	
	(000,000 lbs.)		(000,000 bushels)	
Output during 1859 [b]	204	231	7	....
Average output during the five years 1866-1870	89	205	2	....
Average output during the five years 1876-1880	133	364	3	....
Average output in ratio:				
1866-70 to 1859	43.8	89.0	34.3	....
1876-80 to 1866-70	149.0	177.4	144.8	....
1876-80 to 1859	65.2	157.8	49.7	....

	Sugar Cane	
	(000 short tons)	
Output during 1859 [b]	116	....
Average output during the five years 1866-1870	42	....
Average output during the five years 1876-1880	107	....
Average output in ratio:		
1866-70 to 1859	36.6	....
1876-80 to 1866-70	253.3	....
1876-80 to 1859	42.6	....

a South defined as the 11 states that seceded from the Union.

b "United States Census."

Sources:

The output figures for each of the crops were derived from the following:

"Cotton and Cottonseed," USDA, Agricultural Marketing Service (June, 1955), Statistical Bulletin No. 164.

"Revised Estimates of Barley Acreage, Yield, and Production, 1866-1929," USDA, Bureau of Agricultural Economics (Feb., 1955), [mimeographed].

"Revised Estimates of Tame Hay Acreage, Yield, and Production, 1866-1929," USDA, Bureau of Agricultural Economics (Dec., 1934), [mimeographed].

"Potatoes, 1866-1950," USDA, Bureau of Agricultural Economics (March, 1953), Statistical Bulletin No. 122.

"Corn by States, 1866-1943," USDA, Agricultural Marketing Service (June, 1954).

"Oats by States, 1866-1943," USDA, Agricultural Marketing Service (June, 1954).

"Wheat, Acreage, Yield, Production, by States, 1866-1943," USDA, Agricultural Marketing Section (Feb., 1955), Statistical Bulletin No. 158.

"Revised Estimates of Sweet Potatoes, Acreage, Yield per Acre, and Production, 1868-1923," USDA, Bureau of Agricultural Economics (Feb., 1937), [mimeographed].

"Revised Estimates of Rye Acreage, Yield per Acre, and Production, 1866-1929," USDA, Bureau of Agricultural Economics (Oct., 1935), [mimeographed].

"Revised Estimates of Buckwheat Acreage, Yield per Acre, and Production, 1866-1929," USDA, Bureau of Agricultural Economics (Aug., 1936), [mimeographed].

"Tobaccos of the United States," USDA, Bureau of Agricultural Economics (July, 1948).

"Gross Farm Income and Indices of Farm Production and Prices in the U.S., 1869-1937," by Frederick Strauss and Louis H. Bean, USDA (Dec., 1940), Technical Bulletin No. 703; and the "New Orleans Price Current, Commercial Intelligences, and Merchants' Transcript" (Aug. 31., 1870); annual report.

output of the non-South continuously expanded throughout this 20-year period. Consequently, the South fell relative to the rest of the country.

Since farm prices fluctuated, the gross farm income of southerners — the product of output times unit prices — behaved differently from southern farm output alone. If the prices and output series move at different rates of speed or in opposite directions, the income and output series will also move by different amounts or even in opposite directions. Farm output, for example, fell drastically immediately after the War, but farm prices were considerably above their prewar level. Consequently, gross southern farm income from crops in current dollars reported in Table IV did not fall after the War by as much as output. In 1866 crop outputs were from 30 to 50 per cent below their prewar level; gross farm income, however, was only 15 per cent below its prewar level.

Between 1866 and 1870 gross farm income from crops rose and in 1870 exceeded its 1859 level. The following year, 1871, was marked by a severe drop in cotton output. The price of cotton, low during the first five months of 1871, rose by almost 50 per cent during the second half of the year. Even this sharp price rise, however, was not enough to compensate for the drop in output, and gross farm income fell. Several of the New Orleans factoring houses that made loans to planters on standing crops found that they had advanced more to planters than the value of their crops. Many of these factors were driven to the wall,[16] and planters as well as businessmen found them-

TABLE IV

GROSS SOUTHERN FARM INCOME FROM SELECTED CROPS[a]

(in millions of dollars)

	Cotton	Tobacco [b]	Sweet Potatoes [c]	Wheat [d]	Potatoes	Corn [e]	Oats [e]	Hay [e]	Rye	Sugar Cane	Rice	Total	1859 =100
1859[f]	277.6	21.4	36.0	33.0	2.8	166.7	7.8	7.5	1.6	18.9	2.2	575.5	100.0
1866	337.1	11.2	(20)[g]	22.4	2.3	79.5	7.9	2.1	.9	5.3	(1)[g]	489.7	85.1
1867	245.0	9.8	(20)[g]	35.4	2.4	164.2	10.0	4.3	1.7	5.8	(1)[g]	499.6	86.8
1868	236.0	12.0	44.2	32.2	3.9	183.7	11.6	4.1	1.7	11.6	(2)[g]	543.0	94.4
1869	310.6	8.3	21.3	25.6	2.4	125.2	12.0	5.5	1.4	11.9	2.8	527.0	91.6
1870	338.8	11.9	25.5	20.8	3.4	162.1	10.4	5.5	1.1	20.5	2.4	602.4	104.7
1871	231.8	9.2	20.6	19.6	4.1	115.0	8.9	7.0	.8	16.9	1.7	435.6	75.7
1872	352.8	12.1	19.2	31.5	3.4	107.6	8.7	7.5	.9	13.8	2.2	559.7	97.3
1873	320.8	11.0	24.4	24.9	4.4	98.1	11.1	7.8	.7	10.3	2.5	516.0	89.7
1874	254.9	8.2	20.4	29.7	4.1	151.7	12.6	7.2	.9	13.0	2.9	505.6	87.9
1875	279.6	14.9	22.4	31.8	3.8	192.2	16.3	7.4	.9	15.7	3.3	588.3	102.2
1876	225.4	7.3	20.4	28.2	3.2	195.6	12.8	7.5	.8	18.6	3.2	473.0	82.2
1877	240.6	10.0	17.8	42.4	4.8	143.4	13.5	6.7	.9	15.0	2.8	497.9	86.5
1878	219.4	7.4	19.7	24.1	3.6	132.0	12.0	7.0	.5	20.6	2.7	449.0	78.0
1879	278.6	8.3	16.6	25.7	4.0	115.3	13.6	5.9	.5	13.2	3.3	485.0	84.3
1880	351.4	9.5	18.2	24.8	3.2	150.0	13.0	9.5	.7	23.5	4.4	608.2	105.7

a Gross farm income is the product of farm output times unit prices. Gross farm output in the South was taken from the sources of Table III. The farm prices per unit of output from 1869 through 1880, were taken from Frederick Strauss and Louis H. Bean, "Gross Farm Income and Indices of Farm Production and Prices in the United States, 1869-1937," USDA, Technical Bulletin, No. 703, Washington, Government Printing Office, 1940. Before 1869 farm prices per unit were computed as follows: an annual index of each crop's price was constructed from Anne Bezanson's "Wholesale Prices in Philadelphia, 1857-1896" (Philadelphia, 1954). In these series, 1869 was used as the base. This base figure was then adjusted to fit Strauss and Bean's figure of the farm price per unit in 1869, and the annual prices during each of the preceding years accordingly.

b The price of tobacco prior to 1869 was taken as equal to the New Orleans price of tobacco leaf, quality, good to fair. For the year 1859, I reduced the 1860 price of tobacco by 55 per cent, since Bezanson reports this was the behavior of Kentucky tobacco.

c The price of sweet potatoes was assumed to behave like the price of white potatoes. The data on the movements of white potato prices were taken from the "Aldrich Report," Part 2, p. 119.

d The price of wheat refers to Bezanson's red wheat price, "Wholesale Prices," p. 504.

e No deductions were allowed in the output of corn, oats, and hay for feed. By using the entire value of these crops, we approximate the cost of production of feeding cattle and livestock and the gross income received from cattle. Consequently, figures presented of gross farm income from crops includes some of the gross farm income received from cattle. These series then overstate the return from crops alone, but understate the return from both crops and livestock. These deficiencies would be serious if an analysis were to be made of the level of farm income. They are less serious, however, for indicating the direction of change in farm income, and the greater part of the discussion in the text is along this line.

f "United States Census."

g These figures are arbitrary. They are based upon an interpretation of contemporary newspaper stories.

selves hard pressed to meet their obligations. In the South, gross farm income during 1871 was lower than during any other postwar year investigated. Not until 1878, the trough year of the longest depression in American history, did gross farm income approach the low figure reached in 1871.

Over the 15 years following the Civil War, gross farm income averaged only 90 per cent of its 1859 level. In only three postwar years, 1870, 1875, and 1880, did gross income exceed its prewar level. In spite of the rise in output over this period, the predominantly downward movement of prices prevented a pronounced upward trend in income.

*This paper was prepared while Mr. Lerner was a Research Assistant at the National Bureau of Economic Research. He wants to thank George Stigler, Clarence Long, and Solomon Fabricant for reading and criticizing earlier drafts of this paper.

[1] U. B. Phillips, "Plantations with Slave Labor and Free," *Agricultural History*, vol. 12 (January, 1938), p. 90.

[2] The census data, the source of this table, are notorious for underreporting items in the rural South, especially in 1870. It is difficult to correct for this defect, and as a result, the data must not be "pressed" too hard. The data are more illustrative of a general condition than assertions of positive values.

[3] None of the series presented is a strict capacity measure. Rather, they show changes in the stock of some of the resources used to produce agricultural output.

[4] The United States Census at this time included, under manufacturing, the output of artisans, such as blacksmiths, carpenters, and the like, some extractive industries, such as lumbering as well as that of mills and factories. The term manufacturing as used in this paper refers to this broad census definition.

[5] Later in this article agricultural output will be investigated directly. Anticipating the conclusions, there is a close conformity between the agricultural output series and the capacity series.

[6] For a more complete statement of the behavior of southern prices during the Civil War, see Eugene M. Lerner, "Money, Prices and Wages in the Confederacy, 1861-65," *The Journal of Political Economy*, vol. 63 (Feb., 1955), p. 28.

[7] Eugene M. Lerner, "The Monetary and Fiscal Programs of the Confederate Government, 1861-65," *The Journal of Political Economy*, vol. 62 (Dec., 1954), p. 514.

[8] J. Carlyle Sitterson, "Transition from Slave to Free Economy on the William J. Minor Plantation," *Agricultural History*, vol. 17 (Oct., 1943), pp. 218-219.

[9] *Ibid.*, p. 220.

[10] *Ibid.*, pp. 219-220.

[11] Victor S. Clark, *History of Manufactures in the United States*, 1607-1929 (3 vols.; New York, 1929) vol. 2, p. 148.

[12] *Ibid.*

[13] John F. Stover, *The Railroads of the South* (Chapel Hill, North Carolina, 1955). In 1860 the total railroad mileage in the South was 9,167 (table, page 5). In 1865 the total railroad mileage in the South was 9,135 (table, page 61).

[14] *Ibid.*, p. 58.

[15] It is interesting to note that manufacturing output recovered more quickly than agricultural output after both world wars of the twentieth century in most of the countries in Europe in which fighting took place.

[16] *The New Orleans Price Current, Commercial Intelligencer and Merchants Transcript*, Aug. 31, 1872.

PART THREE

NATIONAL ECONOMIC POLICY, BUSINESS INTERESTS, AND POLITICAL POWER — THE TARIFF ISSUE

In the postwar years, the social issues in Reconstruction magnified the underlying shifts in political power allegedly created by the War. The brilliant historian, Howard K. Beale, in an article written some 30 years ago, dissected the political alliances and economic pressures generated by the tariff issue. It is a classic article in the historiographic tradition of Charles Beard and Louis Hacker in which the Civil War commands a pivotal position in changing the direction of national economic policy.

The tariff issues were no less important than those which cut across other dimensions of the American economy — banking, domestic aid to income groups, public finance, immigration, land policy, and the like. Nonetheless, discussions of the level and direction of American tariff measures dramatized, for Beale at any rate, the fundamental political re-alignments generated by the War on all matters of public economic policy. The Beale thesis is joined head-on by Stanley Coben in his recent study. The reader may judge for himself the veracity of each author's claim to having isolated the sources of business and political interests on economic policy.

FOR FURTHER READING

The literature on postwar economic policies, business interest, and political pressures is voluminous. This is one of the most intensively studied aspects of American economic history. Three studies in particular should be examined:

J. G. Randall and David Donald, *The Civil War and Reconstruction* (New York: D. C. Heath & Company, 1961), especially Chapters 33, 37 and 38. Contains an exhaustive bibliography.

Robert P. Sharkey, *Money, Class, and Party: An Economic Study of Civil War and Reconstruction*. Johns Hopkins University Studies in Historical and Political Science, Series LXXVII, No. 2 (1959), especially Chapter 4 and Appendix III.

Lance E. Davis, Jonathan R. T. Hughes, and Duncan M. McDougall, *American Economic History: The Development of a National Economy* (Homewood: Richard D. Irwin, Inc., 1961), especially Chapter 18. The discussion of the effect of tariff levels on post-Civil War economic development is the best available in any general textbook.

*In this famous article, Professor Beale argues persuasively that
the elevation of tariff levels in the post-Civil War period was
the special political interest of sectional business interests. In
his judgment the tariff was the fundamental issue of postwar
national economic policy and was central to the politics of
Reconstruction. The ultimate victory of northern business
interests in this controversy established, in Beale's judgment, the
essential guideline of post-Civil War economic development.*

THE TARIFF AND RECONSTRUCTION

By Howard K. Beale

U NDUE EMPHASIS has always been placed upon the purely political
phase of Reconstruction. Rhodes and Dunning, the great
authorities of the period, saw only constitutional principles and a
dispute over the wisdom of rival plans for restoring the Union. Over-
emphasis of the southern problem and the Negro question blinded
them to the social and economic aspects of the struggle.

In reality, the Reconstruction controversy had two phases: one
which concerned the South and its postwar problems, and one which
involved social and economic disputes old as the nation itself, in
which the Civil War was but an interlude. Many were radicals because of honest conviction concerning the South; others, because
they realized that a return of the South to Congress meant a union
of South and West which would deprive the growing business interests of the country of the favors that radical rule would insure to
them. These radicals felt that if such economic questions were at
issue, western radicals would be driven to support Johnson and the
conservatives whose economic policies were more to the western taste.
The difficulty was met by a campaign of vituperation and "waving
of the bloody shirt" which pushed the economic questions into the
background as irrelevant. After November, 1866, the radicals were
supreme. When the South did once more secure a voice in government, the new economic order of New England radicals had been
established beyond danger from agrarian attack.

Among these economic questions that influenced Reconstruction
was the tariff. Eastern manufacturers had lived for many years before
the Civil War under a revenue tariff in which a united South and

West refused to grant "protection" to industry. The withdrawal of southerners in 1861 made possible the passage of a protective measure. During the War, temporary high duties were imposed on imports to offset the heavy war taxes that domestic industry was paying. Moreover, as wartime extravagance was the rule, added protection was easily secured. Besides, while some duties were *ad valorem*, others were specific, and falling prices after the close of the War further increased the protection provided by specific duties. When the War ended, protectionists realized full well that not only the compensatory war rates but the newly acquired protection would be ended, unless the southerners could be kept out of Congress. The southerners were kept out for several years and their states made Republican for several years more by means of Negro suffrage and northern military force. The war taxes were repealed but the compensatory war duties were retained, granting to manufacturers a protection of which they had never dreamed.

The end of the Civil War witnessed the opening of a new economic era, whose industry has been based upon highly protective duties. Protection did not cause the economic development, but it molded its course. Finally, after the new industrial order had depended for years upon a war tariff never repealed, that tariff ceased to be a war tariff and became an integral part of the economic order. Had the conservatives been successful in the election of 1866, the industrial development of the country would have been different, equally great — but different.

During the War, profiteers had been active; legitimate business had made enormous profits. The government had spent money lavishly. Scarcity, created in part by the augmented demands of war and in part by the tariff, had made high prices easily attainable. Not efficiency nor quality, but quantity had counted. As a result manufacturers had adopted extravagant methods, and by the purchase of expensive equipment had expanded their plants beyond all possible peace needs. They had become accustomed to large and easy profits even when methods were inefficient. Cutting off the extra protection of the war period would have forced manufacturers back to efficient methods and normal production; it would have ruined some; it would have brought temporary depression for all during a period of readjustment. There probably would have been little opposition to a retention of the extra protection acquired during the War, but manufacturers actually retained the compensatory duties of wartime after the taxes which they offset were repealed, and they even tried to raise rates.

It was almost universally assumed that if southerners were readmitted to full standing in the Union they would vote solidly for tariff reduction. The question arises whether this would have been the case. Twenty years earlier a strong group of southern Whigs had favored the Clay tariff. Could their support have been won for high postwar protection? The opinion of southerners on the tariff is difficult to determine. They were too vitally concerned with regaining political control of their section, salvaging what was left from the economic wreckage all around them, and warding off threatened Negro suffrage and northern military control, to be thinking much about tariffs. Furthermore, while they were still seeking admission from a northern Congress, only the most foolhardy would have compromised their chances of restoration by opposing the tariff. There would be time for objection after they were safely readmitted. A few like A. H. H. Stuart, representative-elect from Virginia, did urge southerners to accept the tariff because it would bring peace between the sections.[1]

Professor Cole has pointed out that in 1842 leading Whigs of the South favored protection, but that by 1850 "Whig issues were dead."[2] While he found that the old Whig elements were seeking to build up southern industry and were therefore favorable to a tariff, Cole had to depend on city editors for Whig opinion as it was very difficult to get testimony of planters.[3] He concluded, "Sincere protectionist sentiment . . . had doubtless come to be considerably limited in the South [by 1852] and, outside of the border states, it was largely confined to the Whigs of Louisiana."[4] During the prewar decade, 10 commercial conventions met in the South to consider means of increasing prosperity. Encouragement of southern manufacturing was a remedy repeatedly suggested. But no evidence exists of an accompanying interest in a customs wall to develop that hoped-for industry. In fact, an equally popular proposal was the building up of southern shipping companies and direct, southern-controlled connections between cotton fields and European factories.[5] Of course no commercial interest ever favored tariff barriers. Besides, whatever the wishes of southerners before the War, protection after it meant merely added profits for northern manufacturers. In the absence of southern capital, there was no hope of building southern factories except with northern capital and under northern management. The last thing southerners of 1866 desired was to become wage earners for northerners. They would have supported no policy that would have added economic domination to northern military and political control. Toombs, a protectionist Whig of the 1840's, was in Reconstruction days a confirmed opponent of the tariff. In 1880 he wrote Stephens: "The tariff ought to have been the leading subject of Democratic agitation for the last four years. The West is as ready for it as the South, from the enormous amount of her exports of her grain and hog-products, and is, always has been, and always [will] be the most valuable ally of sound principles."[6] By methods akin to those used with the western wool growers, some southern whites might have been induced to support a tariff. But under the conditions of 1866, the number could not have been large. Contemporary opinion in any case seems to have been that the South would use its restored power to oppose the northern tariff.

Northeastern radicals were the leading protectionists. One of the underlying causes of their radicalism was dread of tariff reduction. Among them, danger to protection was an effective argument against Johnson's policy. For example, Brewer of Newport wrote Sumner:

> In a selfish point of view, free suffrage to the Blacks is desirable. Without their support, Southerners will certainly again unite — and there is too much reason to fear successfully, with the "Democrats" of the North, and the long train of evils sure to follow their rule is fearful to contemplate . . . a great reduction of the Tariff doing away with its protective features — perhaps Free Trade to culminate with *Repudiation*, — for neither Southerners nor Northern *Democrats* have any bonds or many greenbacks — and how sweet and complete will be the revenge of the former if they can ruin the North by Free-Trade and repudiation.[7]

New England radicals especially were determined never to allow the South to re-enter the Union as long as New England tariff schemes might thereby be endangered. Wendell Phillips insisted[8] that southerners should not be readmitted until the North had made over "that South in its likeness, till South Carolina gravitates by natural tendency to New England," or as Seymour paraphrased it, "until their ideas of business, industry, money making, spindles and looms were in accord with those of Massachusetts."[9] Radicals even tried to repeal the constitutional prohibition of taxes on exports, in order that they might gain a further advantage over foreign competitors by keeping a cheap cotton supply in the country through a tax on its export.[10] When orators and newspapers spoke of the danger to the Union from a return of southerners to Washington, protectionists understood that among the chief elements of danger was the threat of tariff reduction. But western sensibilities made it impossible for campaign speakers or a sheet like the *Tribune* too openly to avow this motive for radicalism.

Danger of a combination between the South and West was recognized. Ex-Congressman Conway, Kansas anti-slavery leader who went to Richmond after the War to seek his fortune, wrote Sumner that giving the Negro the vote would not help his cause, for the whites would control the Negro. "Nobody can doubt," he added, "that they will cast a Southern vote — a sectional Southern vote;

which through a Northern alliance — say for free trade or anti-protection if you please — will bring them again into power."[11]

In an editorial headed "The Tariff," *The Commercial and Financial Chronicle* of New York declared:

> It cannot certainly be the purpose of the Manufacturing States to provoke such a consolidation [of the South and West] which, should it ever be effected, would rapidly and irresistibly revolutionize our whole commercial system; and it is therefore very important that the manufacturing States themselves, should take timely warning of the perils which they are certain to incur by an over-large desire on the part of their representatives, to push the principle of protection beyond the limits at which it has been fixed for some years past. . . . The utmost judgment is required . . . to avoid pushing a given advantage so far as to unite an overwhelming reaction. . . . A brief retrospect of the part played by the Western States in the late civil war, must satisfy every dispassionate observer that the practical control of our political affairs is destined at no distant date to pass into the hands of the Western people. When the Southern States shall return to their position in the Union as coequal participators . . . the agricultural interests . . . especially when combined with [the] commercial interests, will be entirely irresistible. [This will be the] formidable combination of the future. . . . Manufacturers whose industries . . . yield a present profit . . . are directly concerned. . . . It should be their instant effort to moderate the extreme zeal of those advocates of their interests who threaten to jeopardize protection itself by urging it onward into practical prohibition.[12]

Governor Andrew of Massachusetts said the southern policy was "to impose a greatly reduced duty on European manufacturers . . . with the intent to disintegrate the free States, to break down American manufactures, discourage skilled, intelligent labor, and reduce the laboring classes, by measures alike audacious and insidious, to the dependence held by the slave-power appropriate for the masses of men."[13] The *Tribune* felt that southern support of a tariff would furnish the "plan for the truest, best, and only reconstruction of the South and restoration of the Union." A return of the South without safeguards for the tariff, the *Tribune* feared. "A blended Copperhead and Rebel ascendency," it said, "thinly veneered with office-holding and office-seeking Unionism, could not help assailing the National Debt, disturbing the safeguards of our National Industry, and many other things equally provocative of resistance."[14] Caution was required on the part of a sheet like the *Tribune* that was read in all sections of the North. But even the *Tribune* declared:

In the . . . traitorous section of Northern politics, it is consistent for Americans to advocate and plot with foreigners British Free Trade. The cotton-planters were educated by Calhoun to the policy of keeping the Yankees from manufacturing, and confining them to raising cheap food for their slaves. The failure of their Rebellion has not softened the temper of this education. The reconstructed South would vote solid to destroy the wealth-producing industry of the Loyal States. And their unprincipled slaves in the "copper mines" would lick their shoes while they voted for them.[15]

Tariff fears of the Northeast were recognized in other sections of the country. From Illinois one of the "rising generation" wrote Stevens that he felt justified in the belief "that the representatives from the late insurrectary-states, have an understanding that when they are admitted to seats in Congress; they will raise the standard of 'absolute-free-trade'; bring financial ruin upon the country; and by this means subvert the government and compel the north to permit them to withdraw from the union."[16] George Yeaman, an anti-slavery Unionist ex-Congressman from Kentucky then minister at Copenhagen, wrote McCulloch that in keeping the southerners out from fear that if readmitted they would vote for free trade "the manufacturers and public men of New England are pursuing a hazardous course."[17] In its analysis of the election, the Memphis *Commercial and Argus*[18] explained: "With these appeals to the ignorant and fanatical was the still stronger element of associated wealth in the immense capital invested in manufactures, whose power to extort hundreds of millions of dollars annually from the people . . . through the iniquitous provisions of a protective tariff depends upon the perpetuation of radical ascendancy."

Political opinion was also influenced by changing gold premiums and their important effect upon prices. Beside the fluctuations caused by speculations in gold and by expansion and contraction of the currency, the constant floating of loans abroad during this period caused incessant price movements in international commodities. Contemporaries realized that fluctuating gold premiums had an effect upon the prices of international trade, and hence also upon the profits of men who sold in competition with imported goods. Factory owners usually urged both contraction of the currency and increases in the tariff. The *Tribune*, for instance, speaking for industry, repeatedly urged a resumption of specie payments, which it said would reduce the nominal values and thereby decrease imports.[19]

Recent studies of international prices have shown that an important connection did exist between changing premiums on gold and prices exporters and importers could get for their goods.[20] Graham shows that the constant borrowing in the period from 1862 to 1873 produced several tendencies: a fall in the price of gold measured in paper, a fall in the paper prices of exported commodities, a lowered paper cost of imported commodities, and a relative fall of all three items in comparison with the general price level. The effect of this deflation was that exporting houses suffered, since manufacturers tended to cultivate the more favorable home market instead of sending products abroad. A further effect was a tendency for imports to increase because of the relatively lower paper price of imported goods. This in turn effected a reduction of protection if the customs rates remained constant. The manufacturers were actually affected, therefore, by the movement in gold prices. What they could not see was that borrowing money for further contraction would only increase this tendency, and hence their need for further increases in the tariff and the necessity of keeping the South out until a period of repayment of loans should arrive. In any case, the manufacturer did have a high tariff to protect him.

It was the farmer during this period of falling paper prices of exports who suffered most keenly after the extraordinary war demands ceased, since he was dependent upon world prices, whereas the manufacturer still relied primarily upon the home market and could protect that by tariffs. Neither the farmer nor the manufacturer realized the importance of these factors, but modern theories of international price tendencies substantiate the instinctive feeling of both, and help explain the political importance of the tariff to the manufacturer, and of reduction of the tariff to the farmer who needed to offset in goods he bought the low price he received for goods he sold.

Circumstances, however, played into the hands of the manufacturers. The western wool grower was in a peculiar position. He had overestimated the effect of the reduced cotton supply, and he failed to realize that increased wool production in other parts of the world was more than commensurate with the increased demand. Farmerlike he figured prices in inflated currency values and exaggerated the profitableness of wool growing. Like everyone else he had expanded his business unreasonably during the War. In cold reality, only the tremendous demand of the War had prevented his being ruined in an unfavorable world market. Yet many farmers still believed in 1866 that the future possibilities of wool growing were limitless. These men would support a tariff that included increased profits on their wool. Many, on the other hand, had premonitions of the disaster that we know was staring sheep raisers in the face. In 1867 and 1868 prices of wool fell and many sheep were slaughtered for mutton in spite of the new duty on wool. Only the Wool and Woolens Act prevented a terrific crash.[21] Hayes claimed that the tariff bill of 1866, tabled in the Senate, was passed in the House "mainly through the popularity of the wool and woolens section."[22]

In the sheep states, then, particularly Ohio and Michigan, there was a counterbalancing factor that offset the normal unpopularity of the radical program.

Eastern radicals were shrewd enough to turn this wool interest to their advantage. In September, 1865, the National Association of Wool Manufacturers was organized, under the guiding spirit of John L. Hayes who became the secretary and chief lobbyist. This was the first great business interest to organize, and one of its chief purposes was to secure favorable tariff legislation. Hayes understood the situation. He felt that the South would certainly oppose protection once she returned. He knew the antitariff feeling of the West. He saw that the East alone could never save protection. In his speech at the first meeting of the association, he struck to the very heart of the problem. "There can be no reliance," he warned, "upon a permanent friendly legislation for both interests unless the wool growers are satisfied. Our object is not to reach Congress, but to convince the farmers of the West, who will inevitably control the legislation of this country, of the absolute identity of our interests."[23]

At Hayes's suggestion, a joint meeting of wool manufacturers and wool growers assembled at Syracuse, New York, in December, 1865.[24] There Hayes convinced the sheep raisers, as he had already persuaded the manufacturers, that the future prosperity of both interests depended upon their united demand for a high tariff on both wool and woolens. The convention agreed upon the principle that wool should have high protection, and woolens a duty sufficiently higher to allow the manufacturers to pay the extra price for wool that the tariff would create and still have protection on their woolens. Then in a struggle between the two interests over the apportionment of protection, Hayes and his better organized manufacturers managed to secure a duty on woolens that covered the proposed duty on wool, the old duty on woolens, and new protection all combined. Both interests did finally agree, and then in cooperation pushed their schedule through to final success.

Hayes demonstrated what a well-organized lobby could do. Through it, the wool men wrote their Syracuse schedule into the tariff bill of 1866.[25] The wool manufacturers were glad to work with the other protective interests as long as the general tariff bill seemed likely to pass. But Hayes realized that the western farmer would more willingly support a wool schedule alone than a general tariff. For this reason Bingham introduced the wool and woolens schedule of the Syracuse meeting as a separate bill,[26] and the House passed it.[27] It was allowed to lie on the Senate table, until the general bill failed in 1867, when it was called up by John Sherman[28] to become the Wool and Woolens Act of 1867.[29] Though this wool lobby served both growers and manufacturers, it was the latter who supported it. In fact Hayes commented that since "no agent of the wool growers was present, facts and arguments in favor of increased duties on wool were supplied, even to the wool growing districts of the West."[30]

Johnson's veto was feared, but the same careful management persuaded him to sign the bill. Hayes reported:

Three anxious hours were passed by the friends of the bill, in waiting near the room in the Capitol where the President sat with his Cabinet, signing bills, during the last moments of the session. Hour after hour passed. Such earnest men as Delano and Bingham, from Ohio, were apprised of danger, and hurried from the House to the President's room. These influences, aided by the advice of the Secretary of the Treasury and of the Attorney General, a citizen of the leading wool-growing state, Ohio, prevailed; and, at a moment before the hour of twelve by the President's watch, the bill received the President's signature."[31]

The story of this National Association of Wool Manufacturers is important here not because it is an early example of the successfully organized business lobby, but because it figured significantly in the election of 1866. In that campaign the tariff question would have injured the radicals in the West in spite of the conservative failure to utilize it, had not this clever maneuver won the support of the western wool grower.

Sheep owners still opposed protection in the abstract, but accepted this particular tariff because it promised to aid them personally. H. S. Randall[32] voiced a general sentiment when he declared:

I have never been friendly to the enactment of high tariffs for the purpose of protecting industry. But the exigencies of our government will, in future, demand a high tariff for revenue purposes only; and in adjusting the degree of incidental protection which it must necessarily afford to American industry, we have a right to demand — 1st, That the woolen interest shall be protected equally with other interests of no greater importance; and, 2nd, That the producer of wool shall be protected equally with the manufacturer of wool.[33]

This was a period, too, of rapid expansion of industry into the West. Vast lumber interests, the newly opened iron mines of the Northwest, iron works, steel mills just beginning to use the new Bessemer process, and other types of manufactories were beginning to give growing groups in the West, especially in Michigan and Ohio, an interest in tariffs. The West was still an agricultural region, but it required an imagination no more highly developed than that of the average westerner to picture a great future for manufacturing interests whose seeds had already been planted in scattered localities. Amid

114

the shouting of 1866, nascent industrialism played a quiet, unperceived role.[34] It silenced opposition to the radicals in some regions which their tariff views would otherwise have alienated. Still, even with the wool men, benefit from the tariff schedule only sugar-coated a bitter tariff pill that as farmers and westerners they would gladly have declined to swallow.

In spite of claims of the radicals that the tariff was not an issue in 1866, vigorous protests against their protective policy poured in from the agricultural Northwest.[35] In Indiana a part of the Democratic strength during the War had been based upon opposition to the "Yankee tariff."[36] Leaders like Hendricks had inveighed against New England's selfishness which used the War to get rich at the expense of western farmers. In the spring of 1866 western opposition to protectionism began to organize in agricultural associations and Johnson clubs.[37] Thomas Ewing, a prewar protectionist of Ohio, felt that no industry which had not been able to establish itself under the high protection of the past four years ought to be protected. He was certain that no party could sustain itself on higher rates, since it was "the overburdened community" that must pay.[38] "The high pressure for an extreme and almost prohibitory tariff" was rapidly driving Grimes of Iowa "into free trade."[39] Washburne, who opposed protection, predicted in 1865 that the tariff question would "resume its former importance" and again "divide parties." His friend Burchard, a member of the Illinois legislature, later a Republican congressman, wrote that though he had always been a protectionist, consideration of what was for the interest of Illinois and the western agricultural states had changed his view.[40] Charles Ray, a clever politician formerly editor of the Chicago *Tribune*, congratulated Trumbull on his opposition to the tariff, and added:

We are being consumed by the good of New England and Pennsylvania. If matters are not regulated and on a fairer and juster principle, the West will be badly injured before five years. . . . The Protectionists are very bitter as all men are whose profits are threatened, and very harmful as all men are who have great amounts of money and are willing to use it. . . . The remedy for the evils of which I complain will not be found until the process of robbing by law becomes plain to the farmers whose money is now so profusely poured into the capacious pockets of the manufacturer.[41]

Horace White of the Chicago *Tribune*, though a strong radical, opposed the party's protective tendencies. He wrote Washburne:

[the Internal Revenue Commission] propose to give the American manufacturer a bounty of five cents per pound for exporting, which bounty has to be paid by you and me. [Then] they propose to put a tariff of five cents a pound on all imported cotton goods which tariff you and I and all consumers have to pay. But it does not end here, for this five cents a pound tariff will operate to raise the price of all domestic cotton goods five cents a pound in addition to the five cents tax on raw cotton, and of this extra five cents the government will get nothing, while the people will be paying it all the time. Have we killed King Cotton to set up King Sheeting?[42]

In June the Chicago *Tribune* wrote: "We tell these gentlemen," the manufacturers of the East, "that they are traveling to destruction as fast as they can go. They are cutting open the goose to get all the golden eggs at once. They are legislating the Government funds into their pockets too rapidly for the permanence of the system."[43] Again: "The increased rates of duties (except possibly on wool) are wholly unnecessary and unjustifiable, and if adopted will work injury to revenue and to public interest. The present tariff is high enough. . . . On increase one man would make his thousands, while 50 would lose their hundreds."[44] Two days later: "The new tariff Bill . . . is a financial monstrosity, the like of which is rarely seen in any age or clime. . . . Turn which way we will, a new mountain of taxation arises before us — taxation avowedly *not* to put money into the National treasury but to keep it out."[45] Finally: "Western members . . . are in favor of a tariff that will yield the largest amount of revenue and at the same time afford adequate protection to American manufacturers. . . . The existing tariff does both . . . the West favors it. On the other hand the Eastern members are clamoring for a prohibitory tariff that will cut off all importations and reduce the revenue from imports from forty to seventy millions of dollars per annum. This is the issue."[46]

Even in the East there was some opposition to the tariff. Bennett and the New York *Herald* fought it consistently;[47] Parke Godwin and the *Evening Post* opposed it; Godkin and the *Nation* favored free trade. Laboring men where their votes were not controlled by employers objected to protection. Merchants fought it. Gay of the *Tribune* wrote Sumner[48] that a desire for free trade was affecting the *Post's* attitude toward Reconstruction and the blacks. "The devil has got into it," he said, "and it is now far more mischievous than the most virulent of the Copperhead papers." In 1865 a Free Trade League was organized in New York with George Bancroft, Francis Lieber, William Cullen Bryant, Parke Godwin, Cyrus W. Field, and J. A. Roosevelt among the founders.[49] In July, 1866, the Chamber of Commerce of the State of New York sent Congress this remonstrance[50] against the proposed tariff:

In the first place the title of the bill is misleading, the enhanced duties it proposes being in many cases so high that they must prove prohibitive. Its adoption could not fail to

diminish rather than to increase the revenues from imports
. . . it seems impolitic to do so coincident with the abandonment of many of the existing sources of internal revenue. . . .
But your remonstrants object to the measure on other and
broader grounds. They believe its adoption would prove injurious to commerce by diverting it from its established channels, by lessening our foreign trade and by leaving our large
mercantile marine without adequate or profitable employment. It would mar the prosperity of agriculture by increasing
the cost of its supplies without enhancing the prices of its
products, which are governed, as are those of all exportable
commodities, by the foreign market value. It would injure
mechanics by increasing the cost of living, without enhancing
wages, and finally, through its exorbitant production, it would
endanger the permanent prosperity of the manufacturing interests itself, which it specially intended to protect and foster.
It proposes to increase that production by adding from ten to
fifty per cent to the high rates of thirty at the moment when
the amended internal revenue laws relieve that interest from a
heavy excise tax. The joint effect of the two measures would
be to confer on that interest a rate of protection, ranging from
fifty to one hundred per cent; and this protection will be absolute with the excise taxes annulled, and the premium on exchange and on gold to pay duties, compensating the manufacturers for the adverse effects of a depreciated currency; this
degree of protection being at least twice as large as that interest
has hitherto enjoyed under the revenue laws most favorable
to-day, we may expect to see it engender our home competition, which will ultimately prove fatal to its prosperity. We
may also expect to see the people soon become so restive under
this unwarrantable boon conferred on a favored interest, as to
demand its repeal, and the substitute of a tariff strictly
grounded on the principle of revenue. This, combined with
the perils of home competition, would be liable to involve the
manufacturing interest of our country in general bankruptcy.
Even in New England antitariff men could be found.[51]

In the spring and summer of 1866 Congress was considering a
tariff bill which provided increased rates. Various interests cried for
special favor. Advocates of the old system of tariff for revenue only
attacked each increase. But every interested member acquiesced in
the gains of "the other fellow" provided he was allowed his share,
too. At last the bill, overloaded with augmented duties, passed the
House and reached the Senate. The Senate postponed it until after
the fall elections.

When the Senators turned to further consideration of the bill in the following session, they were confronted by an alternative draft prepared by David A. Wells,[52] and recommended by Secretary McCulloch. The Wells bill[53] approached the problem in a new spirit: it equalized inconsistencies in the existing Act of 1864; it reduced the duties on certain raw materials; it maintained duties on manufactured goods at about the old rate; all this provided not reduction, but reform much needed after five years of scrambling for special favor. The protected interests wanted the House bill, but were willing to accept Wells's offer since even this provided high protection.[54] After a long discussion the Wells bill somewhat modified was adopted in the Senate. Protectionists in the House were not satisfied, but as the end of the session was near, under the lead of Morrill and Stevens, they rallied to its support. But western Republicans would not support high protection even under party pressure. Garfield appealed to party loyalty and asked members of the Union party not to "aid our enemies in tying the hands of the House."[55] Western distaste for protection was, however, stronger than party loyalty. In order to pass the bill before March 4, Morrill moved a suspension of the rules. On the test vote,[56] though they secured a majority of 106 to 64, the protectionists failed to secure the necessary two thirds. Two amendments were made adding duties on wool and foodstuffs as a bail for western support. Then Stevens again moved suspension of the rules. But even the powerful whip of Stevens failed; the vote was less favorable than before.[57]

. The distribution of votes was significant. Had there been no wool clause the count would have been more striking, but in spite of the wool duty, the vote indicates low tariff sentiment in the Northwest and eastern border states, and high protectionism in the Northeast. The House gave the radical tariff bill 95 ayes and 52 nays.[58] Of the ayes, 4 were in the Far West,[59] 63 in the Northeast,[60] and only 28 in the Northwest;[61] of these 28, 19 were from the sheep states of Ohio and Michigan. New England, New York, and Pennsylvania voted 58 to 5 for the bill, the other four northeastern states,[62] 5 to 8 against it. The Northwest stood 28 to 39 against it; the Northwest, aside from the two great sheep-growing and manufacturing states of Ohio and Michigan, 9 to 36 against it. Not one vote was cast against the bill in all New England; not one vote for it in Delaware, Indiana, or Illinois. Had the full southern representation been admitted enhanced by the abolition of the three-fifths rule, the total vote[63] instead of 95 to 52 for it, might have been 95 to 125 against the tariff, or under the old three-fifths rule for counting Negroes, 95 to 110. More significant still, with only the representation provided under the Fourteenth Amendment in case the Negro did not vote, the South could still have turned a 95 to 50 tariff victory into a tie.

A similar situation obtained when Stevens tried to force a sus-

pension of the rules to pass the milder tariff of February, 1867.[64]
In this case the vote was 102 to 69. Of the ayes, 5 were in the Far
West, 64 in the Northeast, and 31 in the Northwest; of those 31,
19 were again in Ohio and Michigan. In New England, New York,
and Pennsylvania taken together, the vote was this time 58 to 15,
with two negative votes from Massachusetts and ten from New York;
in the other states of the Northeast[65] it was 6 to 7 against the bill.
The Northwest voted 31 to 41 against it, or excepting Ohio and
Michigan, 12 to 37. Had full southern representation been present
with the southerners untrammeled and in control of their own local
governments, the measure might have been defeated, 102 to 142, and
under the three-fifths rule, 102 to 127. Even the provisions of the
Fourteenth Amendment might have turned a 102 to 69 majority into
a 102 to 112 defeat. In the Senate the vote was 27 to 10 for the
tariff of 1867.[66] Of the ayes, four were in the Far West, sixteen in
the Northeast, and only seven in the Northwest; of this seven, four
were from Ohio and Michigan, one from Illinois, one from Wisconsin, and one from Minnesota. Not a single negative vote was
cast by the whole Northeast. Not an affirmative vote was cast by
Indiana, Kentucky, Missouri, Iowa, or Kansas. Had the South been
back in Congress instead of winning a 27 to 10 victory, the radical
tariff bill might have suffered a 27 to 30 defeat.

On the wool and woolens bill which passed 31 to 12, the Senate
vote was strikingly different.[67] This time instead of 16 to 0, the vote
of the Northeast was 12 to 7, with both Massachusetts senators,
Sprague of Rhode Island, and Buckalew of Pennsylvania opposed to
the measure. Instead of opposing it 7 to 8, the Northwest supported
the wool and woolens bill by a 14 to 3 vote, Kentucky, Missouri, and
Indiana casting the only three votes against it. In these votes are
found the key to the factor that enabled the radicals to suppress the
tariff issue, ample evidence of the potential force of the tariff as a
campaign issue had the conservatives used it, and clear explanation
of the radical determination not to let southerners return to Congress.

During the War the country had acquiesced in the tariff as
necessary to secure victory. S. S. Cox, the one man in Congress with
the temerity to oppose it, had won the stigma of Copperheadism.[68]
After the War, people were thoroughly imbued with the idea that a
high tariff was essential to the payment of the war debt. For this
reason many who in principle opposed protection and in practice
suffered from it, resigned themselves to it as inevitable, merely
attempting to secure some of its benefits. T. C. Jones, for instance,
told Ohio farmers that the need of revenue would make a tariff
necessary for years, and urged them to present a "consistent and solid
front" in demanding as much protection for the farm as for the
factory.[69] The radicals were glad to offer protection on foodstuffs,

since the amount imported was negligible. Neither manufacturer nor farmer was much affected, but the farmer could feel that he was somehow benefiting. About this time, too, a chance factor aided the protectionist. The western farmer felt that the only serious competitor he faced was the wheat grower of Canada. For 11 years Canadian grain had been free from duty under a Canadian reciprocity treaty.[70] As the end of the War approached, the farmer who no longer had armies to feed, and who still paid war taxes and inflated prices for all that he brought, began to regard this treaty as a menace. Notice of abrogation was therefore given, and the treaty expired in February, 1866. Henceforth the northwestern wheat farmer felt he had something to gain from a duty on wheat. He opposed protection in principle, but the new customs barrier between him and Canada blunted the edge of his opposition.[71]

But western opposition to protection was only dulled. Since most westerners were still antiprotectionist from interest and inborn prejudices, the tariff was a potential force in the impending political battle. Had Johnson brought the tariff forward in the early phases of the campaign, and staunchly opposed protection as his political training would have inclined him to do, and as advisers like McCulloch urged, he might have won the election. Had the Philadelphia Convention drawn up a platform with a tariff reduction plank in it, had it pointed out that safeguarding a high tariff was a large factor in radical opposition to restoration, it could have thrown a bomb into the radical camp, for the eastern wing of the party could not have defended protection without alienating western followers. Yet not to have defended it, would have been to relinquish, before the fight, the choicest fruit of victory. The opportunity to create this dilemma was neglected.

Johnson's shrewdest supporters tried to emphasize the tariff factor. Ex-Governor Seymour, for instance, in a speech at Cooper Institute said:

[The House bill] will fall heavily upon the commercial and farming interests of our country. It will harm this great city. It will lengthen the hours of labor, and will scant the food and clothing of the poor; but who hears of this amid the howlings of sectional rage? . . . This question of tariffs and taxation, and not the negro question keeps our country divided. . . . The men of New York [are] called upon to keep out the Southern members, because if they [were] admitted they would vote to uphold your commercial greatness and the interests of Western agricultural States.[72]

But other counsel prevailed. In fact, conservative determination not to do anything until the South was readmitted, actually helped the radicals push the tariff into the background.

Northwestern radicals realized both the importance of the tariff issue and the strong opposition to protection among some of their constituents. They handled the situation admirably. In the West, they dodged the tariff as irrelevant to the campaign. When they awoke to its dangerous potentialities in the election, the pending tariff bill was quickly tabled. The *Herald* said it "died of party apprehension"[73] because in the Northwest "even the Radicals" began to understand that "that which is clear profit in the way of tariff protection to the New England and Pennsylvania manufacturers and importers with heavy stocks on hand, is dead loss to the great West."[74]

Fear of the political consequences of the bill was general. Horace White of the Chicago *Tribune* wrote to Senator Trumbull:

Would not it be well to get that fatal tariff bill postponed, smothered, or in some way out of sight when it comes to the Senate? There is absolutely no difference of opinion about it here — Protectionists and Free Traders both agreeing in considering it a bill of abominations. The only class who favor it are those who have stocks of goods on hand — a very small class numerically. Mr. Medill, the oracle of the Protectionists in the West, has written the most pressing letters to his fellow Protectionists in the House telling them that the bill must be killed, or both Protectionism and Republicanism will be killed in Indiana, Illinois, and Iowa. I have written as strongly as possible on this subject to Senators Fessenden and Wilson.[75]

John L. Hayes, woolens lobbyist, said: "The postponement of the bill . . . by votes of Senators known to be generally favorable to a protective policy, was undoubtedly due to national considerations believed to be more important than any industrial necessities."[76] Some of the strongest protectionists urged postponement of a bill that gave the highest protection the country had ever seen.[77] It might have failed. What radical leaders feared was its passage just before the election. On this issue, a veto could not have been sustained, and the bill would have furnished the conservatives a weapon ready made.

The radical strength lay in being able to use the tariff in the East where it was patently a stake in the struggle, and to avoid it in the West where, despite the new interests, protection was generally unpopular. A clear-cut tariff issue with public and constant iteration in the West that a desire to maintain the protective system was an important cause of radical opposition to Johnson's southern policy, would have split the radical party and won back many western radicals to conservatism. Through a skillfully handled campaign of claptrap and vituperation, the radicals escaped from this danger, and kept the South subjected to military rule while they insured the permanence of a protective system, which since the election of 1866 has been seriously threatened only twice and never overthrown.

[1] Speech quoted in New York *Tribune* (Semi-Weekly), April 20, 1866.

[2] Arthur C. Cole, *The Whig Party in the South*, pp. 101-102, 221.

[3] *Ibid*, pp. 206-211.

[4] *Ibid.*, p. 221.

[5] Evidence gathered by E. H. Roseboom and H. Easterby on the southern Commercial Conventions for a Harvard Seminar in 1922.

[6] R. Toombs to A. H. Stephens, March 25, 1880, American Historical Association, *Annual Report*, 1911, vol. II, p. 740.

[7] July 7, 1865, Sumner MSS. (in the Widener Library of Harvard University), vol. LXXIV. The Stevens MSS. (in Library of Congress) and Sumner MSS. give ample evidence that in many radical minds the danger to the government from unrepentant rebels who sought to overthrow it was the certainty of tariff reduction.

[8] Speech at Cooper Institute, New York *Tribune*, Oct. 26, 1866.

[9] Speech at Cooper Institute, New York *Herald*, Oct. 31, 1866.

[10] Blaine proposed an amendment of this kind in 1864 and Stevens in 1865, but neither was successful. *Congressional Globe*, 38th Cong., 1st Sess., p. 1261; and 39th Cong., 1st Sess., p. 10.

[11] Jan. 16, 1866, Sumner MSS., vol. LXXVI.

[12] *The Commercial and Financial Chronicle*, vol. III (July 7, 1866), p. 3.

[13] Gov. John A. Andrew, *Address of His Excellency to the Two Branches of the Legislature of Massachusetts, Jan. 6, 1865*, p. 95.

[14] New York *Tribune* (Semi-Weekly), Feb. 23, April 20, Oct. 5, 1866.

[15] New York *Tribune* (Semi-Weekly), April 3, 1866.

[16] April 18, 1866, Stevens MSS., vol. VII.

[17] Dec. 27, 1866, McCulloch MSS. (in Library of Congress), vol. III.

[18] Nov. 8, 1866, quoted in the New York *Herald*, Nov. 13, 1866.

[19] New York *Tribune* (Semi-Weekly), May 22, June 5, June 22, 1866.

[20] F. W. Taussig, "International Trade under Depreciated Paper," *Quarterly Journal of Economics*, vol. XXXI (1917), p. 380 ff.; F. D. Graham, "International Trade under Depreciated Paper: the United States, 1862-1879," *ibid.*, XXXVI (1922), p. 220 ff.; J. W. Angell, *The Theory of International Prices*, pp. 160-167.

[21] For full discussion see H. K. Beale, "The Decision of Reconstruction" (MS. doctoral dissertation in Widener Library), pp. 351-364.

[22] U. S. Department of Agriculture, "Special Report on the History and Present Condition of the Sheep Industry of the United States," *House Miscellaneous Documents*, 52d Sess., 2d Sess., No. 105, pp. 551-561.

[23] Hayes, *Speech before the First Annual Meeting of National Association of Wool Growers*, Sept. 6, 1865, p. 63.

[24] See *Report of the Proceedings of the Convention of Delegates from the National Association of Wool Manufacturers and from the Several Organizations of the Wool Growers of the United States, at Syracuse, New York, Dec. 13, 1865*.

[25] *Joint Report of the Executive Committee of the National Association of Wool Manufacturers, and the Executive Committee of the National Wool-Growers' Association, Addressed to the United States Revenue Commission, Feb. 9, 1866*.

[26] *Congressional Globe*, 39th Cong., 1st Sess., p. 4046.

[27] *Ibid.*, p. 4253. The bill itself is printed here.

[28] March 1, 1867, *ibid.*, 39th Cong., 2d Sess., p. 1924.

[29] It passed the Senate March 2, 1867, 31 to 12; *ibid.*, p. 1958.

[30] Hayes, *Report of Second Annual Meeting of National Association of Wool*

Manufacturers, Oct. 3, 1866.

[31] *Third Annual Report of the National Association of Wool Manufacturers*, Oct. 2, 1867, p. 13.

[32] It was to Randall as president of the New York wool growers that Hayes addressed his call for the Syracuse conference of wool growers and manufacturers.

[33] "Address to Ohio Wool Growers," *Ohio State Board of Agriculture, Eighteenth Annual Report*, 1863, p. 356.

[34] See H. K. Beale, "The Decision of Reconstruction," pp. 365-371.

[35] See Clarence L. Miller, "Attitude of the Northwest toward the Tariff, 1864-1883" (unpublished M.A. thesis at the University of Chicago). Miller ascribes this opposition to the fact that it took money from westerners' pockets to make the East richer, the fact that the shutting out of foreign goods removed the only means Europe had of paying for western agricultural products, and the fact that the duty on iron, by doubling the cost of building, decreased the number of railroads, and increased freight rates, to the detriment of the western farmer.

[36] J. A. Woodburn, "Party Politics in Indiana during the Civil War," *American Historical Association, Annual Report*, 1902, p. 238.

[37] E.g., the Johnson Club of Nevada City, Mo., which sent Johnson a resolution that the tariff was unjust — oppressive to the West, and South, and to the poor man, June 7, 1866, Johnson MSS. (in Library of Congress), vol. XCV.

[38] T. Ewing to E. J. Williams, Sept. 6, 1865, Ewing MSS. (in Library of Congress), "Letter-book."

[39] Welles MS. Diary (in Library of Congress), June 27, 1866; vol. II, p. 542 in printed version.

[40] "Upon every pound of iron used," he wrote, "the farmer must pay a bonus to the owner of the mines and manufactories of other states. He must sell, or pay the price of, one bushel of oats, *to pay the extra cost imposed by the tariff*, when he has a horse shod 'all around.' . . . . Illinois must be an agricultural state . . . 50,000,000 bushels of wheat are shipped as grain or flour from Chicago annually . . . let us get in exchange for it as cheaply as we can the products of other regions and if the English Importer will sell us in New York more iron or other commodities for it, than the manufacturers of the Eastern States, let us buy of him." (Italics are Burchard's.) Nov. 16, 1865, Washburne MSS. (in Library of Congress), vol. XCIII.

[41] Feb. 2, 1866, Trumbull MSS. (in Library of Congress), vol. LXIII.

[42] Jan. 30, 1866, Washburne MSS. (in Library of Congress), vol. LIII.

[43] *Chicago Tribune*, June 22, 1866.

[44] *Ibid.*, June 26, 1866.

[45] *Ibid.*, June 28, 1866.

[46] *Ibid.*, July 3, 1866.

[47] To its thousands of subscribers it sent out such editorials as this: "The manufacturers will get a higher price for their goods, almost anything they choose to ask. . . . But who pays for all this? The farmers of the West and North, the planters, the mechanics, laborers, and all the industrial classes. They pay for it in enormous high prices, and all to enrich a bloated monopoly. The masses are taxed for the benefit of a few . . . not to support the government . . . but to increase the profits of a few manufacturers and iron and coal capitalists in New England and Pennsylvania. It is the most invidious, partial and infamous legislation ever known in the history of this country." July 3 and 12, 1866.

[48] March 1, 1866, Sumner MSS., vol. LXXVII.

[49] "Printed Invitation," Feb. 11, 1865, Sumner MSS., vol. LXXIII.

[50] "Action of the New York Chamber of Commerce against the Proposed Tariff" (printed), John Sherman MSS. (in Library of Congress), vol. CVI., July 5, 1866.

[51] E.g., Pratt, a Republican leader of Connecticut who later deserted Johnson,

thought the Tariff Bill "perfectly damnable." J. Pratt to G. Welles, July 19, 1866, Welles MSS., vol. LXI.

[52] Special Commissioner of the Revenue.

[53] *Senate Executive Documents*, 39th Cong., 2d Sess., No. 2. See Taussig's discussion, *Tariff History of the United States*, 7th ed., pp. 175-178.

[54] Wells later opposed high protection, but either at this time had not been converted, or else as a practical man felt the futility of seeking reduction until the South returned.

[55] *Congressional Globe*, 39th Cong., 2d Sess., p. 1657.

[56] *Ibid.*, p. 1658.

[57] It was 102 to 69. *Ibid.*, p. 1659.

[58] July 10, 1866, *ibid.*, 39th Cong., 1st Sess., p. 3725.

[59] The "Far West" embraced Oregon with many New England settlers, California, and the radical 'war baby,' Nevada, admitted to give two senatorial votes to the radicals.

[60] "Northeast" is here used to include New England, New York, New Jersey, Pennsylvania, West Virginia, Maryland, and Delaware.

[61] "Northwest" is used to include the Old Northwest, Minnesota, Iowa, and the western border states of Kentucky, Missouri, and Kansas.

[62] New Jersey, Delaware, Maryland, West Virginia.

[63] The conjectural votes are compiled from the *Census of 1870*, and the *Congressional Directory*.

[64] Feb. 28, 1867, *Congressional Globe*, 39th Cong., 2d Sess., p. 1659.

[65] New Jersey, Delaware, Maryland, West Virginia.

[66] Jan. 31, 1867, *ibid.*, p. 931.

[67] March 2, 1867, *ibid.*, p. 1958. In the House the vote was not recorded.

[68] E.g., *Congressional Globe*, 38th Cong., 1st Sess., p. 2675.

[69] Ohio State Board of Agriculture, *Twenty-first Annual Report*, 1866, p. 77.

[70] Chalfant Robinson, *History of Two Reciprocity Treaties*.

[71] Economists might question whether this new barrier actually helped the farmer, but he felt it did, and consequently the psychological effect was the same whether he benefited or not.

[72] New York *Herald*, Oct. 31, 1866.

[73] *Ibid.*, July 14, 1866.

[74] *Ibid.*, July 15, 1866.

[75] July 5, 1866, Trumbull MSS., vol. LXVIII.

[76] John L. Hayes, *Second Annual Report of the National Association of Wool Manufacturers*, p. 14.

[77] The New York *Tribune*, July 13, 1866, said Sumner and four others who should have supported it killed the tariff because they were tired of hearing New England denounced as selfishly seeking protection.

*Stanley Coben attacks the Beale thesis. Coben argues that the
political allegiance of northeastern business interests to the
tariff issue and national economic policy was less precise and
exceedingly more complicated than Beale concluded.*

NORTHEASTERN BUSINESS AND RADICAL RECONSTRUCTION: A RE-EXAMINATION

By Stanley Coben

HISTORIANS have generally accepted the view that Radical Reconstruction "was a successful attempt by northeastern business, acting through the Republican party, to control the national government for its own economic ends: notably, the protective tariff, the national banks [and] a 'sound' currency."[1] The Radical program is also said to have been "the method by which the 'Masters of Capital' . . . expected to exploit the resources of the southern states" behind federal protection.[2] Western hostility to these eastern business designs was avoided by large appropriations for rivers, harbors, railroads, free land, and pensions, and by use of the ever-potent "bloody shirt." Thus is supposed to have been prevented by a union of western and southern agrarian opposition to the industrial and financial masters of the East.[3]

This thesis has met with little serious challenge and has been subjected to only occasional qualification. It continues to influence studies of the political and economic history of the post-Civil War era.[4] Yet a closer examination of the important economic legislation and congressional battles of the period, and of the attitudes of businessmen and influential business groups, reveals serious divisions on economic issues among Radical legislators and northeastern businessmen alike. Certainly neither business leaders nor Radicals were united in support of any specific set of economic aims. Considerable evidence also suggests that the divisions among businessmen often cut across sectional as well as industrial lines. Furthermore, evidence indicates that few northeastern business groups were interested in southern investments in the early postwar years, and that these few were hostile to Radical Reconstruction.

The evident need for new interpretations of the motivation of northern Radicals and of the economic history of the entire period is demonstrated by a re-examination of the most important of the "economic ends" usually agreed upon as motives for Radical Reconstruction: the tariff and the currency issues, and the charge that northern business interests sought federal protection for the exploitation of the South.

The tariff split northeastern businessmen more than any other issue.[5] So fierce was business competition in this era, and so eager were the antagonists to use every possible means of winning an advantage, that almost all important tariff schedules became battlegrounds between industries, as well as between firms within the same industry. The copper, iron, linseed, and woolen textile industries, for example, were bitterly divided on crucial tariff schedules. The most significant split, however, was between certain high protectionist Pennsylvania interests on one side and influential low-tariff groups in New England and New York on the other. Pennsylvania coal mine operators feared the competition of rich Nova Scotia deposits, mined by low-wage labor, close to major American markets. Iron and steel manufacturers, the largest highly protected interest, were faced with the competition of long-established, technologically advanced English producers, whose wage scale was only a fraction of that of the Americans. Pennsylvania carpet, glass, and wool industries demanded protection for similar reasons. The Keystone State was the largest extractor of iron and steel, of carpets, glass, and chemicals. On the other hand, powerful opposition to the tariff objectives of the Pennsylvanians came from the cotton and many of the woolen textile manufacturers of New England, and from the interwined importing, financial, and railroad interests of New York.

New Englanders had become strong advocates of lower tariffs in the 1850's. The sharp tariff reductions of 1857 were accomplished chiefly by southern and New England votes.[6] New England manufacturers, especially textile producers, desired cheap imported raw materials in order to lower the price of their finished goods on the international market. Furthermore, they agreed to reduced rates on manufactured goods to discourage the growth of domestic competition.[7] Among American manufacturers, New England producers as a group were farthest from domestic sources of raw materials, closest to sources of cheap foreign commodities. Cheap supplies of coal, lumber, flaxseed, building stone, fine wool, and other commodities were available in nearby Canada and Nova Scotia. Scottish and British iron, Indian linseed, and Russian and Philippine hemp were imported into Boston in large quantities for the benefit of manufacturers.[8] Hardly any wool for the finer grades of cloth was produced in America, either before or after the War; nor were the rough, lowest grades, used in carpets and blankets, available at home.[9] By the end of the War, northeastern cotton manufacturers were importing the cheap Indian Surat cotton already widely used in England.[10]

English textile manufacturers, rivals of the New Englanders both in world markets and in America, obtained their raw materials free of duty.[11] There were good reasons for northeastern producers to believe that only the American system of imposts kept them from equaling the British in world trade. By the 1850's, many American mills had been in operation for three generations. They had experienced managers and weavers, cheap and abundant credit, modern machinery and production methods. In cotton cloth manufacturing, for which machinery could be used most extensively, New England labor was the most productive in the world. By 1860, the average number of looms per weaver was four in America, two in Great Britain. French and German manufacturers lagged even farther behind in methods and machinery.[12]

In addition to high productivity which made their goods competitive in the world markets, and the need to import cheap raw materials, many New England manufacturers preferred low tariffs from a fear that high textile duties would foster the growth of new competitors at home. New producers might bring cutthroat competition and periodic chaos to the industry by their poor judgment of market conditions. A special committee of the Boston Board of Trade acknowledged in 1858 that New England textile manufacturers had potentially dangerous rivals, especially in Pennsylvania; but the committee concluded that the tariff reduction of 1857 removed any immediate threat. "Under the impulse of a high protective tariff they accomplished so little, that now, under a change of policy, there seems no present cause of alarm."[13] When the higher Morrill duties came before the House in 1860, Representative Alexander H. Rice of Massachusetts, speaking for the manufacturers of his state, declared that "excessive protection" would stimulate "ruinous and irresponsible competition at home." In the Senate, textile manufacturer Henry Wilson proclaimed: "A high protective policy . . . is calculated to raise up rivals at home, and is more injurious to us than foreign competition."[14]

After the War, fear of the growth of protected competition continued to influence New England tariff sentiment. Edward Atkinson, president of the Cotton Spinners of New England, and a director of the Boston Board of Trade, wrote to Henry Wilson in 1866: "The strongest men in the trade are more afraid of the unskillful competition built up at home by high duties than they are of foreign competition."[15] Enoch R. Mudge, one of the most influential New England textile men, told the organizing meeting of the National Association of Cotton Manufacturers and Planters in 1868: "When we speak of protection, I think it should be given only at the point where the cotton manufacturer requires it."[16] For well-established, efficient New England producers, of course, there were comparatively few points at which protection was necessary. They had seen evidence of the success of their low tariff theories in the few years the 1857 schedules were in force. "The operation of the tariff of 1857 has contributed largely to the prosperity of our woolen manufactures," one of Boston's largest wool dealers reported in 1859.[17] Exports of cotton cloth had risen steadily, from an average of $7,000,000 in the years 1851 through 1856, to almost $11,000,000 in 1860.[18]

The government's need for revenue allowed protectionists an almost unchallenged ascendancy during the Civil War,[19] but the battle between northeastern business groups over tariff schedules was resumed after Appomattox. For example, when a resolution for lower tariffs was placed before the National Board of Trade convention in 1869, delegates from the Boston Board of Trade and Boston Corn Exchange voted 6 to 1 for the resolution; Philadelphia delegates voted 7 to 0 against it.[20] The Boston Board of Trade also worked unsuccessfully to prevent abrogation of the reciprocity treaty with Canada; Philadelphia's Board joined western agricultural interests in demanding an end to reciprocity.[21]

These divisions within the business community were likewise reflected in the congressional debates and voting on important tariff schedules. Cotton manufacturers resumed their prewar demands for lower schedules, even for cotton textiles. Senator William Sprague, whose sprawling Rhode Island mills were relatively inefficient, protested against the 25 per cent cut in cotton textile duties proposed in 1867. He was answered by Senator William P. Fessenden of Maine, sponsor of the measure: "I am informed by the commissioner [Revenue Commissioner David A. Wells] that these duties were fixed at a rate perfectly satisfactory to those engaged in the manufacture of cottons, who appeared before him. . . . The cotton interest of this country has got so that it can stand of itself pretty much."[22]

Schedules on coal similarly came under attack. As power looms replaced hand looms, and steam power replaced water power, New England manufacturers became increasingly interested in lower coal duties.[23] Under reciprocity and the low tariff of 1857, imports of coal into Boston rose steadily from 88,531 tons in 1858, to 209,225 tons in 1865, most of this being cheap Nova Scotia fuel.[24] Representative George S. Boutwell and Senator Charles Sumner of Massachusetts tried in vain to prevent higher coal schedules from being placed in the proposed tariffs of 1866 and 1867. Sumner acknowledged that there was a lot of coal in Pennsylvania, West Virginia, and the West. "But why," he asked, "should New England, which has a natural resource comparatively near at home, be compelled at a great sacrifice to drag her coal from these distant supplies?" Sumner's amendment was defeated 11 to 25, with eight New Englanders, both New Yorkers, and one senator from Oregon comprising those favoring lower duties on coal.[25]

Many other schedules in the proposed bills of 1866 and 1867 were fought out by competing or conflicting business interests. Manufacturers, especially New Englanders, dependent upon cheap imported raw materials, were continually in opposition to the combined efforts of raw material producers and competing manufacturers closer to these native sources of supply. When Senator Benjamin F. Wade of Ohio moved to raise the duty on linseed, largely grown in the West, Fessenden of Maine accused him of asking the higher rate "for this simple selfish reason: that the trade of crushing seed and manufacturing oil on the sea-coast may be utterly destroyed for the benefit of crushers of seed and manufacturers of oil in the West."[26]

Rolling mills, chiefly eastern, which controlled the American Iron and Steel Association,[27] almost forced through an extremely low duty on scrap iron. Such a duty would allow the mills to import huge quantities of cheap European used rails, and to re-roll them in lieu of using domestic pig iron for new rails. Senator Zachariah Chandler, from the iron producing state of Michigan, demanded that the proposed duty on wrought scrap iron be quadrupled, and the duty on cast iron be almost tripled. Lower schedules, he declared, would close the iron mines, put out every blast furnace, and mean "total ruin to the iron interests of the United States. . . . It is a bill gotten up to suit the railroad rolling-mills, and to sacrifice every other iron interest in the United States." The rolling mills won one Senate vote, but Chandler forced another, which was won by those sympathetic with the mine operators and pig iron producers. Almost all the western senators and both Pennsylvanians voted for higher duties on scrap metal. All but one senator from New England and New York voted for the low schedule.[28]

The only tariff adjustment besides the wool and woolens bill to become law in the early postwar years was a measure passed in 1869, greatly increasing the duties on copper. Eastern smelters, who used a combination of eastern and cheap South American ores, were forced out of business by this bill, passed for the benefit of Lake Superior mine operators, whose domestic ores did not require smelting. The Lake Superior mine owners, some of whom were eastern financiers, were thus given a monopoly of the American market. They were thereby enabled to charge much higher than world prices at home and to dump their surplus abroad at much lower prices.[29] Similar conflicts among business interests developed on tariff schedules for salt (used for scouring wool), zinc, lead, nickel, and building stones.[30]

The wool and woolens bill of 1867, which considerably raised most schedules, has been cited as a prime example of the cooperation of business interests, because it was devised in a conference between a committee of wool growers and representatives of the National Association of Wool Manufacturers. What has generally been overlooked is the fact that the manufacturers' association, like the American Iron and Steel Association, was dominated by a well-organized segment of the industry, in this case by worsted and carpet manufacturers, whose interests conflicted with those of other important groups within the woolen industry.

Most influential of the men who negotiated the agreement for the manufacturers were Erastus B. Bigelow, president and founder of the Association, and America's leading carpet manufacturer; John L. Hayes, permanent secretary of the Association; and J. Wiley Edmonds, treasurer of the giant Pacific Mills, a leading worsted producer. Hayes reported to the membership that "for six months Mr. Bigelow gave himself unremittingly to the great work . . . [and to him they] must attribute the happy results of the conference." Before this "happy" conclusion, Hayes conceded, most woolen manufacturers "were becoming more and more disposed to look abroad for the chief supply of raw material . . . and were inclined to advocate the British policy of free trade in raw materials, including wool."[31] Certainly the results of the conference were not so happy for manufacturers of woolen cloth, the largest item of domestic woolen output. These producers would be forced to pay much higher rates for imported raw wool than the worsted manufacturers with whom they competed. Carpet and blanket manufacturers would pay by far the lowest rates.[32]

The largest manufacturer of wool cloth taking part in the negotiations with the growers was Edward Harris of the Harris Manufacturing Company, Woonsocket, Rhode Island. Harris later declared that he had no part in deciding the schedules, and that his name had been appended to the agreement without his knowledge or consent.[33] Senator Henry Wilson of Massachusetts, a manufacturer of fine woolen cloth, told the Senate Finance Committee that if the new schedules were put into effect, he would have to close his factory. He subsequently declared in the Senate: "Some of the very ablest men in Massachusetts and in New England earnestly believe that this bill, so far as it concerns two thirds of the woolen manufacturers of the country, is not so good as the present tariff. [Only] the carpet manufacturers are abundantly satisfied." Wilson's statement was reinforced by other New England senators. William Sprague of Rhode Island, William P. Fessenden of Maine, and Lot M. Morrill of Maine reported similar opinions of the wool and woolens bill among the cloth manufacturers in their constituencies.[34] Nevertheless, there was no organized opposition in Washington to the energetic Hayes or to the large number of western congressmen who were anxious to honor an agreement which gave protection to wool growers. The wool and woolens bill passed easily despite adverse votes from men like Wilson, Sumner, and Sprague who had close associations with the New England woolen industry.[35]

Northeastern opposition to the cloth schedules continued after the passage of the bill, and in the winter of 1869-1870, Edward Harris and 43 other New England woolen manufacturers petitioned Congress to reduce the duties on wool for cloth as low as carpet wool duties, which were one fifth as high. On reaching Washington with this petition, Harris was informed that the wool growers and John Hayes, who said he represented 300 companies and individuals associated with the woolen industry, had first claim on congressmen's votes.[36] In 1889, the woolen cloth manufacturers obtained 530 signatures from wool manufacturers and dealers asking for lower duties — and again failed. Finally, in 1909, the cloth manufacturers formed a separate organization to do permanent battle in Washington with the worsted and carpet interests.[37]

For somewhat different reasons a low-tariff sentiment similar to that in New England was also strong in New York City, by far the largest importing and financial center in the country. New York merchants, shippers, and those who financed their activities opposed tariffs which might restrict imports, while the railroad financiers protested that under the proposed tariff of 1866 the Erie and the New York Central systems alone would have to pay out annually about two million dollars by way of protection."[38] The New York Chamber of Commerce had opposed the Morrill bill of 1861 as "a radical change in the tariff policy of the country," but had patriotically refrained from strenuous protests as tariff rates steadily rose during the War.[39] In listing the organization's postwar objectives, however, Secretary John Austin Stevens declared: "The principles of free, unshackled trade, which it has ever upheld, must be reaffirmed."[40] A few months after the War's end, the *Commercial and Financial Chronicle* observed: "Signs are not wanting that the subject of Free Trade will be made the text of the next political agitation in this country." The *Journal of Commerce* also began agitating for lower tariffs soon after the War; and the introduction of the first postwar tariff bill, providing for generally increased rates, naturally brought a strong protest from the New York Chamber of Commerce.[41]

Clearly, then, New England cotton manufacturers and many wool and other manufacturers preferred and worked for lower tariff schedules — as did most of New York's financial and mercantile community. This fact was obvious to contemporary protectionists, especially the fervent Pennsylvanians. They recognized the role New

Yorkers and New Englanders played in reducing many schedules, and in defeating, by obstructionist tactics, bills of which they disapproved. A delegate from Philadelphia's Board of Trade complained to the National Board of Trade in 1869 that New England's industries had been built up behind tariff walls. "Now they are marked disciples of free trade. . . . They overlook the interests yet in their infancy. . . . Is this right? Is this just?"[42] Henry C. Carey, leading spokesman for Pennsylvania iron, coal, and other protected interests, charged in 1867 that for 20 years, on tariff questions, "It has pleased the representatives of Massachusetts to array themselves on the side of cotton planters, slave owners, railroad monopolists."[43]

Northeastern businessmen were thus far from united in support of high tariffs after the Civil War. Leading business interests of New England and New York believed that they lost more than they gained from high postwar tariffs. Had reconstruction politics allowed them a choice, it seems likely that these important groups would have preferred a return to the coalition which had produced the low tariff of 1857 — a coalition which included the South. Certainly they would not have opposed the return of southern representatives in order to retain high imposts.

The business interests of the Northeast were divided into fiercely competing groups not only by the tariff issue, but by currency questions as well. These conflicts were brought into the open shortly after the Civil War by attempts to contract the swollen wartime currency. Secretary of the Treasury Hugh McCulloch's proposals for contraction, designed for quick resumption of specie payments, won a cordial response from many importers and financiers, who would gain materially from the elimination of the premium on gold and a consequent rise in the market value of government bonds.[44] Many businessmen longed for the currency stability they believed resumption would bring. But McCulloch met with warnings and protests from other important northeastern business groups. The Philadelphia Board of Trade immediately warned against hasty action, "lest by injudicious measures and rapid contraction," the people's interests should be sacrificed. A few weeks later, the Commercial and Financial Chronicle, a firm advocate of hard money, was forced to admit: "There is little doubt that the depression in public confidence, of which a proof will be found in our account of the week's fluctuation in the Stock Market, is closely connected with the anticipated effects of the contraction movement of the Secretary of the Treasury."[45]

Although only a moderate amount of currency was taken out of circulation, businessmen continued to fear that goods bought at high prices with inflated Greenbacks might have to be sold at much lower prices if McCulloch were allowed to proceed with contraction. Wholesale prices fell sharply after January, 1866, confirming their fears.[46] As general price depreciation continued through 1866 and 1867, businessmen's objections to contraction became increasingly loud and widespread. The Commercial Exchange of Philadelphia adopted a resolution in January, 1867, "That premature resumption will prove a curse and not a blessing." A vice president of the New York Chamber of Commerce, who approved contraction, recalled "living in the midst of the clamor against that process, where almost every man I met was denouncing the Secretary and predicting ruin upon all the interests of the country unless the policy was discontinued."[47]

Opposition to McCulloch's policy spread to Congress, where Representative William D. Kelley of Pennsylvania called it the "road to bankruptcy."[48] Finally, in January, 1868, Senator John Sherman of Ohio introduced legislation to end contraction. "We hear the complaint from all parts of the country," he said, "from all branches of industry . . . that industry for some reason is paralyzed and that trade and enterprise are not so well rewarded as they were. Many, perhaps erroneously, attribute all this to the contraction of the currency."[49]

Passage of Sherman's measure, however, did not end the conflict among northeastern businessmen over currency. Most seem to have favored a stable money supply, and to have opposed currency expansion and quick resumption alike. Many of the more conservative bankers, importers, and merchants, however, continued to support an early return to specie payments. There was also an influential and vocal group of businessmen which persistently called for currency inflation. This last group found adherents among those manufacturers and merchants who sought to take advantage of great postwar demand for their products, but who had difficulty obtaining capital for plant and inventory expansion, even at extremely high interest rates. Many of those who borrowed large sums for investments in factories, mines, and railroads, were apt to favor currency expansion, which they believed would lower interest rates, raise prices, and make debts easier to pay. Radical Senator Sprague, for example, in control of a Rhode Island empire of factories, real estate, utilities, and banks, complained to the Senate that "The interest paid by the borrower today is just double what it was at the close of the War." He placed the blame on "the power centralized in New York."[50]

It is significant that Jay Cooke, once an ardent hard money man, became something of an inflationist after he borrowed millions to build the Northern Pacific, and saw his corporation become a huge land speculator through government grants. In a letter to his brother and partner, written in 1868, Cooke called for moderate currency expansion which would keep pace "with the new habits and enlarged area of Country." "Why," he asked, "should this Grand and Glorious Country be stunted and dwarfed — its activities chilled and its very life blood curdled by these miserable 'hard coin' theories — the musty theories of a by gone age?"[51]

Pennsylvania iron and steel men, through their representatives and periodicals, led eastern demands for an increased supply of currency. Their industry was expanding rapidly behind high tariff walls, stimulated by the postwar spurt in railroad building. Iron manufacturer Thaddeus Stevens was a leader in congressional schemes to inflate the currency. Both Stevens and Kelley of Pennsylvania supported textile manufacturer Benjamin F. Butler's resolution to pay the wartime bonds in paper rather than gold.[52] Representative Daniel J. Morrell, a bank president as well as former general manager of the giant Cambria Iron Works in Pennsylvania, called for more circulation, and contended that under a program of inflation "Capital would be less valuable, and a larger share of the increase in wealth would go to the enterprise and labor which created it."[53] Pennsylvania iron and steel periodicals took up the fight against the bankers. "In the seaboard cities," said *Iron Age* in 1867, "the money power seeks to attain a position of irresistible control, and to subdue and subordinate to itself all the interests of industry."[54] The lines of battle were perhaps drawn most succinctly and cogently in a speech by Representative Kelley in January, 1867. "The contest," he said, "is between the creditor and the debtor class — the men of investments and the men of enterprise."[55]

The issue, however, was not as simple as Kelley put it. Most foreign goods were paid for with gold, not Greenbacks. Customs duties were also payable in gold. As long as specie payments could be postponed, the premium on gold would remain. In the early postwar years, the premium fluctuated between 30 and 40 per cent. The effect was to raise the cost of foreign goods about one third above what their cost would be if specie resumption should occur.[56] Monetary inflation would tend to raise the premium and consequently the price of imports even higher. This fact was not lost on the Pennsylvanians. As early as 1863, the Philadelphia Board of Trade noted that the "premium on foreign exchange adds greatly to tariff and transportation costs."[57] In 1864, Samuel J. Reeves, iron manufacturer and chairman of the executive committee of the American Iron and Steel Association, wrote the Commissioner of Internal Revenue: "The constant advance in the price of gold has acted as so much protection to the home manufacturer above the duty. . . . The iron manufacture now finds its safety only in the high cost of gold; what is to become of it when there will be no premium on gold?"[58] The answer, so far as many iron manufacturers were concerned, was to retain the premium on gold.

The significance of the Pennsylvanians' currency policies was obvious to importers, financiers, and many manufacturers in New York and New England. Most of these favored hard money and low tariffs. The Boston Board of Trade's "Wool Report" for 1863 noted the effect of the gold premium on the price of wool.[59] New York merchants protested that the high price of gold seriously discouraged imports, and the city's Chamber of Commerce adopted a resolution charging that "Powerful interests are striving to perpetuate the existing depreciation of the currency."[60]

When contraction was abruptly ended and tariff reform failed, in 1867-1868, some businessmen in New York and New England felt that the government's policies were falling under the control of high tariff and paper money men. On the other hand, Henry C. Carey, spokesman for Pennsylvania protectionists, charged that New England, aided by New Yorkers, was attempting to create a monopoly in money and manufacturing. One instrument of the monopolists, said Carey, was a low tariff, which New England manufacturers could afford because of their low interest charges and modern machinery, and which they used to ruin domestic competition and to obtain cheap foreign raw materials to aid New England producers. A second instrument, he continued, was the banking system — "a great money monopoly for the especial benefit of the Trading States." Even with this monopoly, Carey complained, the traders wished to contract the currency, further reducing the pittance allowed Pennsylvania and further raising interest charges manufacturers would have to pay. Either the New Englanders would change their ways, he warned, or they would be compelled to do so by a combination of southern, western, and middle states, in which Pennsylvania would take the lead.[61] In reply, cotton manufacturer Edward Atkinson "rejoiced" at this analysis of New England's advantage, and assured Carey that henceforth the New England representatives would support the low tariff and hard money policies even more strongly. Instead of fearing the threatened combination of sections under Pennsylvania's leadership against those policies, he prophesied that New England would join with the South and the West in promoting them.[62]

Both Carey and Atkinson overstated the unity of New England manufacturers, oversimplified the varied and conflicting interests in the West, and conjectured about the probable political and economic alignments of the postwar South. Nevertheless, both were more realistic than historians who have explained northeastern leadership of Radical Reconstruction in terms of a unified northeastern business interest anxious to keep the South out of the Union in order to protect high tariffs and hard money.

Nor can the direction and support which northeastern representatives gave to Radical Reconstruction be accurately explained as an attempt to "make easy the road for northern economic penetration and exploitation of the South."[63] Few important northeastern capitalists had any desire to place their money in a war-torn, unsettled region. Eventually, northerners invested huge sums in southern factories, mines, railroads, and real estate; but it is significant that only a small number did so as long as Radicals controlled southern state legislatures.

Many southern leaders and periodicals recognized the need for northern capital after the Civil War, and numerous cordial invitations were extended.[64] That such invitations were futile was obvious to businessmen, North and South. "We want capital attracted to the South," said the *Commercial and Financial Chronicle* of New York City, "and this cannot be, so long as the States are under semi-military rule." And from the South *De Bow's Review* echoed, "It is idle to ask capital to venture until order is restored." South Carolina exempted manufacturers from all state and local taxation, but failed to attract northern capital partly because of the uncertainties of Reconstruction.[65] Thomas W. Conway, a former Freedmen's Bureau official, who toured the North in 1866 trying to induce businessmen to make southern investments, reported to the New York Chamber of Commerce, which had encouraged his mission: "The substantial men met by me in all parts of the country are sick of the delay in regard to the settlement of our national political difficulties." Until such settlement occurred, he predicted, there would be continued uncertainty and violence in the South, and poor prospects for northern investment.[66]

Even Pennsylvania's Representative William D. Kelley, who was both a Radical leader and an enthusiastic advocate of northern investments in the postwar South, soon found that Radical Reconstruction interfered with southern industrial growth. In March, 1868, Kelley demanded immediate readmission of Alabama — a potential economic paradise, he said, whose wealth was "paralyzed" while Reconstruction ran its violent course. Thaddeus Stevens, less interested in southern industrial development than was Kelley, fought against his colleague's haste, insisting that Alabama must first guarantee the suffrage rights of Negroes.[67]

New England cotton manufacturers, dealers, and shippers feared that northerners' refusal to send their capital south would result in an insufficient cotton crop. Edward S. Tobey, Boston cotton merchant and manufacturer, recommended that the Freedmen's Bureau be authorized to take over the role of private capital in organizing Negro labor for cotton cultivation. The South's deficiency of capital, Tobey told the Boston Board of Trade in a famous speech in November, 1865, was proved by "frequent applications from Southern men to Northern capitalists to invest in cotton lands at low prices." It would be ideal if private investors could supply this want; but capital,

136

Tobey observed, "is seldom placed by its possessors where society is disorganized and life and property comparatively unprotected by a stable and efficient government." The Board approved Tobey's suggestion.[68]

A few months after Tobey's speech, however, the New Englanders' plans were changed by a sudden shift in the cotton market. The southern cotton crop was larger than expected. Furthermore, the English, with new machinery and methods for manufacturing with cheap Indian Surat cotton, had become increasingly less dependent upon American producers. New England manufacturers and dealers were caught with large supplies of cotton as the price dropped almost 40 per cent in the first four months of 1866.[69] The momentary interest New England businessmen had shown in reconstruction legislation dropped with the price of cotton. The Boston Board of Trade's "Review of the Boston Market for the Year 1867," declared: "Business men, generally, are loud in their complaints against the course of legislation for two years past. Important interests have been neglected by Congress, and too much time has been wasted on questions which only led to discord and bad feeling in the different branches of the Government."[70]

Most large northern investors, instead of being concerned over the difficulties of investing in the South, turned their attention to the many lucrative opportunities elsewhere — in Minnesota timberlands, Michigan iron and copper mines, Pennsylvania coal and oil, and railroads in almost every state. Significantly, the Pennsylvania Railroad, with abundant capital and great influence in Congress, did not attempt to create its "Southern empire" until Radical Reconstruction was nearing its conclusion. Until 1871, the Pennsylvania preferred to take advantage of investment opportunities in the Northwest. When Thomas A. Scott, who guided the railroad's expansion, decided to move south, he dealt with Conservative governors and legislators in the South as successfully as he had with Democrats and Republicans in the North and West.[71]

Only one important northeastern business group was strongly attracted by investment opportunities in the South immediately after the War: New York financiers, the true "masters of capital," who had long-standing commercial ties with the South, and had sufficient funds to risk large amounts in a turbulent area. New York merchants, shippers, and financiers were as interested as Bostonians in large postwar cotton crops, but they emphatically disagreed with the Boston proposal to use the Freedmen's Bureau to grow cotton. When Tobey's plan was put before the executive committee of the New York Chamber of Commerce, the committee reported: "Our best reliance for attaining the desired end is to present to capitalists this most inviting field."[72]

Insofar as northern capital was invested in southern railroads, both before and immediately after the War, most of it was provided by New Yorkers. A recent study shows, for example, that of some 280 directors of 25 major southern lines in 1867-1868 only 11 were northerners, and 10 of these were from New York.[73] Two important New York investors in southern railroads were elected to Congress and were thus in a position to speak publicly about reconstruction legislation. One of the two was William E. Dodge, metal importer, iron manufacturer, land speculator, railroad investor, and president of the New York Chamber of Commerce; the other was William W. Phelps, director of four large banks and eight railroads.[74] The evidence suggests that the opinions these men expressed of Radical Reconstruction were typical of those held by New York's financial leaders.

When Thaddeus Stevens's bill for dividing the South into military districts reached the floor of the House in January, 1867, Dodge voted against it; and in explaining his vote he told his Republican colleagues: "I claim to be as loyal as any other man . . . [but] if these southern states are still to be kept year after year in this state of disquietude we at the North, sympathizing with them in our social and business relations, must to a certain extent suffer with them." Furthermore, said Dodge, businessmen believed that this bill would result in continued high taxation to support an army of occupation in 10 states.[75] And in the debate on Butler's civil rights bill in 1875, Phelps — one of three Republicans to vote against it in the House — expressed sentiments long held in the New York financial community. "You are trying to do," he said, "what it seems to me this House everlastingly tries in one form or another to do — to legislate against human nature. You are trying to legislate against human prejudice, and you cannot do it. . . . Let us end this cruel policy."[76]

Many New York financiers made public their support of President Andrew Johnson in his battle against the Radicals. When Johnson vetoed the bill for the continuation of the Freedmen's Bureau, in February, 1866, a mass meeting to celebrate the veto was arranged by the city's business leaders, and a committee was sent to Washington to offer the President New York's aid. Among those on the committee were Moses Taylor, dean of New York bankers, and William B. Astor, known as the "landlord of New York."[77] Six months later, when Johnson visited New York as part of his "swing around the circle," a grand dinner was given for him at Delmonico's. Chairman of arrangements was Alexander T. Stewart, the "dry goods king"; treasurer for the dinner was Henry Clews, probably second only to Jay Cooke as a dealer in government bonds, and second to none as a dealer in southern railroad securities. A large number of New York's leading businessmen attended the dinner.[78] This was followed on September 17, 1866, by a giant National Union celebration to demonstrate the city's support of the President at the height of his crucial campaign against the Radicals. The reception committee for this impressive meeting included Stewart, Taylor, Clews, Edwards Pierrepont, and August Belmont. Among those who gave public notice of their approval of Johnson's policies by allowing their names to be listed as vice presidents of the meeting were such well-known financiers as William H. Aspinwall, Cornelius Vanderbilt, John J. Cisco, and Henry Grinnell, as well as numerous important merchants and manufacturers.[79]

Similar indications of support or approval of the presidential reconstruction program rather than that of Congress also came from the New York Chamber of Commerce and from the financial press. In 1866 the Chamber of Commerce adopted a resolution, introduced by the banker brother of Radical leader Roscoe Conkling, which expressed the hope that Reconstruction "may be everywhere signalized by magnanimity and clemency and that it may nowhere be stained by a single act which will be condemned as needlessly harsh or revengeful." A copy of this resolution was sent to Washington as encouragement to the President.[80] As early as July, 1865, *Hunt's Merchants' Magazine* and the *Commercial and Financial Chronicle* — two of the leading business journals of the period — had applauded Johnson's program for the speedy restoration of the seceded states. As the Radicals gathered their forces in the fall of 1865, the *American Railroad Journal* announced that Reconstruction "is going on as well as could be hoped. The President . . . sets the example of kindness and benignity and a large majority of both parties . . . are evidently disposed to support his policy." And in January, 1866, the *Journal of Commerce* proclaimed its support of Johnson.[81]

From evidence such as this, the reconstruction program of the Radicals cannot be explained as an organized attempt by the business interests of the Northeast either to preserve and promote their own economic advantages or to obtain protection for economic exploitation of the South. Actually, northeastern businessmen had no unified economic program to promote. Important business groups within the region opposed each other on almost every significant economic question, and this lack of a common interest was likewise reflected in the economic views of Radical congressmen. Thaddeus Stevens, for example, dominant Radical leader in the House, was a fervent protectionist and a proponent of paper money inflation; Charles Sumner, Senate Radical leader, spoke and voted for lower tariff schedules and for resumption of specie payments. With both the businessmen and the legislators thus divided on economic issues, and with the New York merchants and financiers — who were in a position to gain most from economic exploitation of the South —

definitely critical of the Radicals' program, it seems clear that factors other than the economic interests of the Northeast must be used to explain the motivation and aims of Radical Reconstruction.

[1] This is the conclusion of the most recent survey of historians' attitudes toward Radical Reconstruction. T. Harry Williams, "An Analysis of Some Reconstruction Attitudes," *Journal of Southern History*, vol. XII (Nov., 1936), p. 470. Williams calls this the "Beale thesis," because it has been most completely developed by Howard K. Beale in his *The Critical Year: A Study of Andrew Johnson and Reconstruction* (New York, 1930), and his "On Rewriting Reconstruction History," *American Historical Review*, vol. XLV (July, 1940), pp. 807-827.

[2] William B. Hesseltine, "Economic Factors in the Abandonment of Reconstruction," *Mississippi Valley Historical Review*, vol. XXII (Sept., 1935), p. 191.

[3] Helen J. and T. Harry Williams, "Wisconsin Republicans and Reconstruction, 1865-1870," *Wisconsin Magazine of History*, vol. XXIII (Sept., 1939), pp. 17-39.

[4] For recent expressions of the "Beale thesis," see C. Vann Woodward, *Origins of the New South, 1877-1913* (Baton Rouge, 1951), pp. 23-24; George R. Bentley, *A History of the Freedmen's Bureau* (Philadelphia, 1955), pp. 34-36; William B. Hesseltine, *Confederate Leaders in the New South* (Baton Rouge, 1950), p. 136; Arthur S. Link, *American Epoch: A History of the United States since the 1890's* (New York, 1955), pp. 4-5; George R. Woolfolk, *The Cotton Regency: The Northern Merchants and Reconstruction, 1865-1880* (New York, 1958).

Earlier statements of the thesis may be found in Charles A. and Mary R. Beard, *The Rise of American Civilization* (2 vols.; New York, 1927), vol. II, Chap. XX; Louis M. Hacker, *The Triumph of American Capitalism* (New York, 1940), Chap. 25; Richard N. Current, *Old Thad Stevens: A Story of Ambition* (Madison, 1942), Introduction, Chap. IV, and pp. 226, 249, 260; Matthew Josephson, *The Politicos, 1865-1896* (New York, 1938), Chap. I. James S. Allen, *Reconstruction: The Battle for Democracy, 1865-1867* (New York, 1937), is a Marxist version of the thesis.

[5] For a very different point of view, see Howard K. Beale, "The Tariff and Reconstruction," *American Historical Review*, vol. XXXV (Jan., 1930), pp. 276-294.

[6] Davis R. Dewey, *Financial History of the United States* (New York, 1903), p. 263. Dewey calculated the House vote for the 1857 tariff by section: New England 18 to 9 in favor; South 60 to 2 in favor; West 14 to 33 opposed; Middle States 24 to 28 opposed. There was no roll call on the final vote in the Senate, but see speeches by Senator Henry Wilson of Massachusetts, *Cong. Globe*, 34th Cong., 3d Sess., Appendix, pp. 333-334 (Feb. 26, 1857), and Senator Daniel Clark of New Hampshire, *ibid.*, 36th Cong., 2d Sess., p. 1023 (Feb. 19, 1861). See also Richard Hofstadter, "The Tariff Issue on the Eve of the Civil War," *American Historical Review*, vol. XLIV (Oct., 1938), pp. 50-55.

[7] George W. Bond and George Livermore, *Report of the Boston Board of Trade on Wool for 1859* (Boston, 1860), p. 2; Frank W. Taussig, *The Tariff History of the United States* (8th ed.; New York, 1931), p. 142; Melvin T. Copeland, *The Cotton Manufacturing Industry of the United States* (Cambridge, 1912), p. 14.

[8] See, for example, "Review of the Boston Market for the Year 1865," *Twelfth Annual Report of the Boston Board of Trade* (Boston, 1866), pp. 72-95.

[9] Arthur H. Cole, *The American Wool Manufacture* (2 vols.; Cambridge, 1926), vol. II, pp. 310, 319, 330; John L. Hayes, *Statement of Fact Relative to Canada Wools and the Manufacture of Worsted* (Boston, 1866), pp. 10, 19.

[10] "It may soon become imperatively necessary to us to be able to obtain foreign cotton on even terms with English manufacturers if we expect to compete with them in other markets." *Boston Board of Trade: Report of a Committee upon the Cotton Tax* (Boston, 1867); *Ninth Annual Report of the Boston Board of Trade* (Boston, 1863), Appendix, p. 99.

[11] Shepard B. Clough and Charles W. Cole, *Economic History of Europe* (3d ed.; Boston, 1952), pp. 472-476, 605-607.

[12] Copeland, *Cotton Manufacturing Industry*, p. 10. "What this country wants," Massachusetts cotton manufacturer Edward Atkinson wrote Senator Henry Wilson in 1866, "is cheap iron. Our cotton mills now cost to build $30 per spindle complete with looms, etc., etc., against $10 to $12 in England." Atkinson to Wilson, July 7, 1866, Harold F. Williamson, *Edward Atkinson: The Biography of an American Liberal* (Boston, 1934), p. 67.

[13] *Fifth Annual Report of the Boston Board of Trade* (Boston, 1859), pp. 96-97.

[14] *Cong. Globe,* 36th Cong., 1st Sess., p. 1867 (April 26, 1860); *ibid.,* 36th Cong., 2d Sess., p. 1026 (Feb. 19, 1861). Rice later became president of the Boston Board of Trade, then governor of Massachusetts.

[15] Atkinson to Wilson, July 7, 1866; Williamson, *Atkinson,* pp. 67-68.

[16] *Proceedings of a Convention for the Purpose of Organizing the National Association of Cotton Manufacturers and Planters* (Boston, 1868), p. 13.

[17] Bond and Livermore, *Report on Wool,* p. 2.

[18] Copeland, *Cotton Manufacturing Industry,* p. 14; Taussig, *Tariff History,* p. 142.

[19] Dewey, *Financial History,* pp. 265-267, 272, 301-304; Taussig, *Tariff History,* pp. 150, 159-162; Edward Stanwood, *American Tariff Controversies in the Nineteenth Century* (2 vols.; Boston, 1903), vol. II, p. 130.

[20] *Proceedings of the Second Annual Meeting of the National Board of Trade* (Boston, 1870), p. 321.

[21] *Eleventh Annual Report of the Boston Board of Trade* (Boston, 1865), p. 42; *Thirteenth Annual Report of the Boston Board of Trade* (Boston, 1867), pp. 2-3; *Thirty-first Annual Report of the Philadelphia Board of Trade* (Philadelphia, 1864), p. 17.

[22] *Cong. Globe,* 39th Cong., 2d Sess., pp. 709, 744 (Jan. 24, 25, 1867)

[23] Copeland, *Cotton Manufacturing Industry,* p. 29; J. Herbert Burgy, *The New England Cotton Textile Industry: A Study in Industrial Geography* (Baltimore, 1932), pp. 24, 30, 34, 100.

[24] *Twelfth Annual Report of the Boston Board of Trade* (Boston, 1866), p. 75.

[25] *Cong. Globe,* 39th Cong., 1st Sess., pp. 3569 (July 3, 1866); 39th Cong., 2d Sess., pp. 830, 857 (Jan. 29, 30, 1867).

[26] *Ibid.,* 39th Cong., 2d Sess., p. 705 (Jan. 24, 1867). Linseed oil was important in the manufacture of paints, dyes, and varnishes.

[27] Pig iron producers, still the dominant segment of the iron and steel industry in the early 1870's, withdrew from the American Iron and Steel Association in 1871 and formed their own association, which by 1873 numbered 200 firms. For the sharp division which this Association saw between itself and the American Iron and Steel Association, see *The American Pig Iron Manufacturing Association, Meeting Held in New York City, February 19, 1873* (Philadelphia, 1873), pp. 32, 64.

[28] *Cong. Globe.,* 39th Cong., 2d Sess., pp. 799-801 (Jan. 28, 1867) pp. 860-862 (Jan. 30, 1867).

[29] Taussig, *Tariff History,* pp. 219-221; *Letter of Henry Martin, Esq., President of the Baltimore Copper Company, to the Senate of the United States in Opposition to the Bill Increasing the Duty on Imported Copper Ores* (Baltimore,

1869); Bliss Perry, *Life and Letters of Henry Lee Higginson* (Boston, 1921), pp. 263-264; William B. Gates, *Michigan Copper and Boston Dollars* (Cambridge, 1951), pp. 33-35, 45-47.

[30] *Cong. Globe*, 39th Cong., 2d Sess., pp. 680, 765, 793, 798, 821 (Jan. 23, 26, 28, 29, 1867).

[31] *Transactions of the National Association of Wool Manufacturers, Second Annual Report* (Boston, 1866), pp. 12, 20. For interesting evidence of Edmonds' part in this agreement, see speech by Senator Jonathan P. Dolliver, *Cong. Record*, 61st Cong., 1st Sess., p. 1717 (May 4, 1909). For the protectionist ideas of Bigelow and Hayes, see Erastus B. Bigelow, *Objects and Plan of the National Association of Wool Manufacturers* (Boston, 1865), pp. 3-4; John L. Hayes, *The Fleece and the Loom: An Address before the National Association of Wool Manufacturers at the First Annual Meeting in Philadelphia, September 6, 1865* (Boston, 1866), p. 60.

[32] For more detailed discussion of the schedules, see Chester W. Wright, *Wool Growing and the Tariff* (Cambridge, 1910), pp. 213-215; Haldor R. Mohat, *The Tariff on Wool* (Madison, 1935), pp. 23-25; Taussig, *Tariff History*, pp. 195-218.

[33] Edward Harris, *Memorial of Manufacturers of Woolen Goods to the Committee on Ways and Means* (Washington, 1872), p. 22.

[34] *Cong. Globe*, 39th Cong., 2d Sess., pp. 909-911 (Jan. 31, 1867).

[35] *Ibid.*, p. 1958 (March 2, 1867). A relatively small but well-informed and organized group within the woolen industry was able to write schedules to suit itself because they had to be phrased in complicated, technical language. See Senator Dolliver's comments on this subject, *Cong. Rcord*, 61st Cong., 1st Sess., p. 1715 (May 4, 1909). The major reason for passage, however, was the fact that the schedules pleased leading wool growers.

[36] Edward Harris, *The Tariff and How It Effects the Woolen Cloth Manufacture and Wool Growers* (Woonsocket, 1871), pp. 14-15; *Carded Wool Bulletin* (Boston), vol. I (May, 1910), p 6; Edward Atkinson, *Reply to the Argument by Mr. John L. Hayes* (Woonsocket, 1872).

[37] Mohat, *Tariff on Wool*, p. 19; Taussig, *Tariff History*, pp. 316-317.

[38] Statement of Representative Henry J. Raymond of New York, *Cong. Globe*, 39th Cong., 1st Sess., p. 3516 (June 30, 1866).

[39] *Fourth Annual Report of the Chamber of Commerce of the State of New York* (New York, 1862), pp. 2-3; *Fifth Annual Report of the Chamber of Commerce of the State of New York* (New York, 1863), pp. 4-5. Senator Edwin D. Morgan, a member of the Chamber, voted for tariff increases during the War, then reverted to fighting high schedules in 1866. James A. Rawley, *Edwin D. Morgan, 1811-1883: Merchant in Politics* (New York, 1955), pp. 207-209.

[40] *Centennial Celebration of the Chamber of Commerce of the State of New York . . . . Report of Proceedings* (New York, 1868), p. 21; also, *Ninth Annual Report of the Chamber of Commerce of the State of New York* (New York, 1867), Part I, p. 5.

[41] *Commercial and Financial Chronicle* (New York), vol. I (July 8, 1865), p. 38; *New York Journal of Commerce*, May 23, 1865; *Ninth Annual Report of the Chamber of Commerce of the State of New York*, Part I, pp. 29, 30, 60, 61. The Chamber's protest could not be ignored. The organization's membership included many of the largest campaign contributors to both parties, including, in 1866, such merchants and importers as Moses Grinnell, Alexander T. Stewart, William E. Dodge, Horace Claflin, and Senator Edwin D. Morgan; and such financiers as Henry Clews, Levi P. Morton, John Austin Stevens, Moses Taylor, John J. Cisco, and J. Pierpont Morgan.

[42] *Proceedings of the Second Annual Meeting of the Naional Board of Trade* (Boston, 1870), p. 312. For a justification of their low tariff policies, see the

comments by New England textile men in *First Annual Meeting of the National Board of Trade* (Boston, 1869), pp. 127-134.

[43] Henry C. Carey, *Reconstruction: Industrial, Financial and Political, Letters to the Hon. Henry Wilson, Senator from Massachusetts* (Philadelphia, 1867), p. 34. As Carey observed, votes on the complex tariff bills of 1866 and 1867 were not an accurate indication of tariff sentiment. Some additional insight into these bills is provided by Herbert R. Ferleger, *David A. Wells and the American Revenue System, 1865-1870* (New York, 1942), pp. 22-168; Williamson, *Atkinson*, pp. 64-71; Taussig, *Tariff History*, pp. 175-177. Carey was especially hurt by what he considered the apostasy of his friend, Revenue Commissioner Wells, who went over to the camp of the low-tariff New Englanders in 1866-1867.

[44] It should be noted that while immediate resumption would have raised the market value of federal bonds, it would also have reduced the value of interest payments, which were made in gold. Important dealers in government bonds, like Henry Clews and Jay Cooke, opposed contraction. Cooke wrote his brother in 1867, "As to getting back to specie payments, the least said about that the better, as it is the premium on gold that enables us to sell the 5-20's." Jay Cooke to Henry D. Cooke, Sept. 20, 1867, Henrietta M. Larson, *Jay Cooke: Private Banker* (Cambrdige, 1936), pp. 204, 209-110.

[45] *Thirty-third Annual Report of the Philadelphia Board of Trade* (Philadelphia, 1866), p. 1. *Commercial and Financial Chronicle*, vol. II (Jan. 13, 1866), p. 31; *Iron Age* (New York), vol. V (Nov. 7, 1867), pp. 2, 4.

[46] Wesley C. Mitchell, *Gold, Prices, and Wages under the Greenback Standard* (Berkeley, 1909), p. 26; "Review of the Boston Market for the Year 1866," *Thirteenth Annual Report of the Boston Board of Trade* (Boston, 1867), p. 43. Wholesale prices fell fastest, affecting manufacturers and the larger merchants and importers more than retailers. Both wholesale and retail prices fell faster than wages and farm prices.

[47] *Proceedings of the First Annual Meeting of the National Board of Trade* (Boston, 1869), pp. 114, 173.

[48] "Contraction, the Road to Bankruptcy," reprinted in William D. Kelley, *Speeches, Addresses, and Letters on Industrial and Financial Questions* (Philadelphia, 1872), p. 210.

[49] *Cong. Globe*, 40th Cong., 2d Sess., pp. 407, 537, 674 (Jan. 9, 15, 22, 1868).

[50] *Ibid.*, 40th Cong., 1st Sess., pp. 65, 361 (March 15, 30, 1867). Sprague's overextended empire went into bankruptcy in 1873 when his loans were called in. Zechariah Chafee, Jr., "Weathering the Panic of '73," *Dorr Pamphlets* (Providence), No 4 (1942).

[51] Jay Cooke to Henry D. Cooke, Nov. 23, 1869, Larson, *Jay Cooke*, p. 205.

[52] *Cong. Globe*, 40th Cong., 2d Sess., pp. 212-213 (Dec. 16, 1867).

[53] *Ibid.*, 41st Cong., 2d Sess., Appendix, p. 142 (March 10, 1870).

[54] *Iron Age*, vol. V (Oct. 24, 1867), p. 4; *ibid.* (Nov. 7, 1867), p. 4; *Industrial Bulletin* (Philadelphia), vol. VIII (Nov., 1871), p. 4.

[55] Kelley, *Speeches, Addresses, and Letters*, p. 226.

[56] See statement of costs of English rails in *Bulletin of the American Iron and Steel Association* (Philadelphia), No. 2, Supplement (Feb. 6, 1867), p. 186. The Association's figures show the premium to have been a greater share of total cost than was the tariff duty.

[57] *Thirtieth Annual Report of the Philadelphia Board of Trade* (Philadelphia, 1863), p. 40.

[58] "Extracts from a letter to the Hon. Joseph J. Lewis . . . from Samuel J. Reeves," *Thirty-second Annual Report of the Philadelphia Board of Trade* (Philadelphia, 1865), p. 76.

[59] Bond and Livermore, *Report on Wool*, p. 3.

[60] *Eighth Annual Report of the Chamber of Commerce of the State of New York* (New York, 1866), Part II, p. 90; *Memorial to the Honorable the Senate and House of Representatives* (New York, 1869), signed by A. A. Low and Samuel Babcock for the New York City Chamber of Commerce; remarks by A. A. Low in *Eighth Annual Report of the New York Chamber of Commerce* (New York, 1866), Part I, p. 28; and *Ninth Annual Report of the New York Chamber of Commerce* (New York, 1867), Part I, pp. 74, 76.

[61] Carey, *Reconstruction*, pp. 4, 8, 21, 24-26, 50, 53-58, 67-68.

[62] Atkinson to Carey, Nov. 11, 1867, Williamson, *Atkinson* pp. 79-80. For further details of this controversy see Henry Wilson to Carey, Sept. 21, 1867; Carey to Wilson, Sept. 25, 1867; George L. Ward to Carey, Oct. 16, 1867; Carey to Ward, Oct. 18, 1867; David A. Wells to Carey, Nov. 1, 6, 1867; Carey to Atkinson, Nov. 18, 1867; Henry C. Carey Papers, Edward Carey Gardiner Collection (Historical Society of Pennsylvania, Philadelphia).

[63] Hesseltine, *Confederate Leaders in the New South*, p. 136.

[64] For example, see Petersburg (Va.) *News*, quoted in New York *Journal of Commerce*, May 20, 1865. A number of similar appeals for northern capital are cited in John F. Stover, *The Railroads of the South 1865-1900: A Study in Finance and Control* (Chapel Hill, 1955), pp. 54-55. See also Broadus Mitchell, *The Rise of Cotton Mills in the South* (Baltimore, 1921), p. 237.

[65] *Commercial and Financial Chronicle*, vol. II (Feb. 17, 1866), p. 198; *De Bow's Review* (Nashville), After the War Series, vol. IV (Nov., 1867), p. 451; Francis B. Simkins and Robert H. Woody, *South Carolina during Reconstruction* (Chapel Hill, 1932), pp. 290-291.

[66] Thomas W. Conway, "Introduction of Capital and Men into the Southern States of the Union," *Ninth Annual Report of the Chamber of Commerce of the State of New York* (New York, 1867), Part II, pp. 8-13.

[67] *Cong. Globe*, 40th Cong., 2d Sess., pp. 2139-2141 (March 26, 1868). For another significant conflict between Kelley and Stevens see *ibid.*, 39th Cong., 1st Sess., pp. 3687-3688 (July 9, 1866).

[68] Edward S. Tobey, *The Industry of the South . . . : A Speech Delivered before the Boston Board of Trade, November 27, 1865* (Boston, 1878). See also *Twelfth Annual Report of the Boston Board of Trade* (Boston, 1866), p. 57.

[69] *Thirteenth Annual Report of the Boston Board of Trade* (Boston, 1867), p. 47.

[70] *Fourteenth Annual Report of the Boston Board of Trade* (Boston, 1868), p. 122. For further evidence of the New Englander's rapid change of heart, see Williamson, *Atkinson*, pp. 59-61, and Boston Board of Trade, *Report of a Committee upon the Cotton Tax* (Boston, 1867).

[71] Stover, *Railroads of the South*, pp. 99-121. According to Stover, "While many southerners in the postwar years had eagerly sought northern capital for their stricken railways, their entreaties up to 1870 had rarely resulted in more than visits of railroad carpetbaggers." John F. Stover, "The Pennsylvania Railroad's Southern Rail Empire," *Pennsylvania Magazine of History and Biography* (Philadelphia), vol. LXXXI (Jan., 1957), p. 28.

[72] *Eighth Annual Report of the Chamber of Commerce of the State of New York* (New York, 1866), Part I, p. 70. One of the few influential New Englanders interested in "exploiting" the South was former abolitionist Governor John A. Andrew of Massachusetts. His small American Land Company and Agency was forced out of business in 1866. Andrew was not sympathetic to the Radicals' program, and favored turning southern state governments over to the old leaders of southern society — businessmen, politicians, former Confederate officers. Henry G. Pearson, *The Life of John A. Andrew* (2 vols.; Boston, 1904), vol. II, pp. 267, 270, 273.

[73] Stover, *Railroads of the South*, p. 38.

[74] For one example of southern railroad investments by Dodge and Phelps see Hugh M. Herrick (comp.), *William Walter Phelps: His Life and Public Service* (New York, 1904), pp. 31-32 The other two men who took part in this investment were Moses Taylor, president of the National City Bank, and John J. Cisco, investment banker and treasurer of Credit Mobilier. Both Taylor and Cisco also opposed Radical Reconstruction.

[75] *Cong. Globe*, 39th Cong., 2d Sess., pp. 627-629 (Jan. 21, 1867).

[76] *Ibid.*, 43d Cong., 2d Sess., p. 1002 (Feb. 4, 1875). For similar earlier statements see *Commercial and Financial Chronicle*, vol. I (Aug. 26, 1865), p. 260; New York *Journal of Commerce*, May 25, 1865.

[77] New York *Morning Herald*, Feb. 23, 1866. Among the organizers of the meeting were Dodge; banker and brokerage house president George Opdyke; Dodge's predecessor as Chamber of Commerce president, A. A. Low; and financier and merchant Moses Grinnell. See also George Fort Milton, *The Age of Hate: Andrew Johnson and the Radicals* (New York, 1930), pp. 289-296.

[78] *Dinner to the President of the United States in Honor of His Visit to the City of New York, August 29, 1866*, printed program in Samuel J. Tilden Papers (New York Public Library); also Henry Clews to Samuel J. Tilden, Sept. 6, 1866, Tilden Papers. In Philadelphia, banker Anthony J. Drexel met with other leading businessmen in the Merchants' Exchange and planned Johnson's welcome to the city. Philadelphia *Age*, Aug. 28, 1866. For evidence of Jay Cooke's disgust with Radical Reconstruction, see Ellis P. Oberholtzer, *Jay Cooke: Financier of the Civil War* (2 vols.; Philadelphia, 1907), vol. II, p. 22.

[79] *National Union Celebration at Union Square, September 17, 1866* (New York, 1866). After the 1866 election, when it was apparent that Johnson could not be re-elected in 1868, these men began to switch their support to Grant, who was known to be safe and sound on the currency, and who seemed most likely to bring peace to the South. Many northern businessmen were antagonized by Johnson's undignified campaign. New York *Tribune*, Dec. 5, 1867.

[80] *Eighth Annual Report of the Chamber of Commerce of the State of New York* (New York, 1866), Part I, p. 4.

[81] *Hunt's Merchants' Magazine and Commercial Review* (New York), vol. LIII (July, 1865), pp. 28-30, 43; *Commercial and Financial Chronicle*, vol. I (July 1, 1865), pp. 3, 5; (July 29, 1865); p. 133; *American Railroad Journal* (New York), vol. XXXIII (Oct. 7, 1865), p. 949; New York *Journal of Commerce*, January 9, 1866.

Although lack of space necessitated the omission from this article of discussions of government bonds and national banks, the antagonism to Radical Reconstruction of the great financiers, their organizations and periodicals, is perhaps the best evidence of the remote relationship between these financial issues and congressional reconstruction policies. For the negative attitude of the New York bankers toward the national banking system, both during and after the Civil War, see Fritz Redlich, *The Molding of American Banking: Men and Ideas* (2 vols.; New York, 1951), vol. II, pp. 105, 106, 108, 121, 140-146; Larson, *Jay Cooke*, pp. 140-142.

PART FOUR

The War and National Economic Growth

The following two selections discuss the most fundamental issue involved in the appraisal of the economic impact of the Civil War: did it have any long-term effect on the pace of American economic development? Professor Cochran argues in the negative. Dr. Salsbury draws the issue into the mainstream of economic historiography: he challenges the Cochran thesis on empirical grounds and relates the problem to the broader issues of political economic development pioneered by Charles Beard.

In a very real sense, all the preceding selections have a direct bearing on the issues discussed in the Cochran and Salsbury papers. The article of Victor Clark, for example, arrives at a conclusion fundamentally not at issue with that of Cochran. Similarly, Lerner's regional postwar study of southern agriculture offers additional support for the Cochran findings. Finally, the Beale and Coben articles are a primary factor in the historiographic and methodological issues examined and criticized by Dr. Salsbury.

The reader may make his own judgment about the logic and rationale of the respective arguments presented in these and previous selections. To assist in this task, a summary of useful and convenient statistical materials is provided in the next section. Tables VI 1-4 and VII 1-5 in Part Five are especially relevant to the Cochran-Salsbury papers.

FOR FURTHER READING

In addition to the sources cited in the footnotes of the Cochran and Salsbury papers, a classic article by Chester Wright should also be consulted:

Chester Wright, "The More Enduring Consequences of America's Wars," *Journal of Economic History*, Supplement (Dec., 1943), pp. 9-26.

There is also a penetrating article by Curtis Nettles covering somewhat different ground:

Curtis Nettles, "Economic Consequences of War: Costs of Production," *Journal of Economic History*, Supplement (Dec., 1943), pp. 1-9.

One of the most provocative discussions of the impact of war as regards secular, economic, and cultural matters is a fascinating book by John U. Neff:

John U. Neff, *War and Human Progress* (Cambridge: Harvard University Press, 1950).

Finally, perhaps the best balanced treatment of war and eocnmic development in a general textbook is to be found in:

Herman Krooss, *American Economic Development* (New York: Prentice-Hall, Inc., 1955), Chapter 14.

Professor Cochran's article is fast becoming a classic. Utilizing the most recent quantitative research he attempts to answer the question posed in the article's title. Professor Cochran also argues that the impact of the War as stressed by American historians has tended to obscure the very real achievements of the American economy in the two prewar decades.

DID THE CIVIL WAR RETARD INDUSTRIALIZATION?

By Thomas C. Cochran

IN MOST TEXTBOOKS and interpretative histories of the United States the Civil War has been assigned a major role in bringing about the American Industrial Revolution.[1] Colorful business developments in the North — adoption of new machines, the quick spread of war contracting, the boost given to profits by inflation, and the creation of a group of war millionaires — make the war years seem not only a period of rapid economic change but also one that created important forces for future growth. The superficial qualitative evidence is so persuasive that apparently few writers have examined the available long-run statistical series before adding their endorsement to the conventional interpretation. The following quotations taken from the books of two generations of leading scholars illustrate the popular view.[2]

"The so-called Civil War," wrote Charles A. and Mary R. Beard in 1927, " . . . was a social war . . . making *vast changes* in the arrangement of classes, in the accumulation and distribution of wealth, *in the course of industrial development.*"[3] Midway between 1927 and the present, Arthur M. Schlesinger, Sr., wrote: "On these tender industrial growths the Civil War *had the effect of a hothouse.* For reasons already clear . . . nearly every branch of industry grew lustily."[4] Harold U. Faulkner, whose textbook sales have ranked near or at the top, said in 1954: "In the economic history of the United States the Civil War was extremely important. . . . In the North *it speeded the Industrial Revolution* and the development of capitalism by the prosperity which it brought to industry."[5] The leading new text of 1957, by Richard Hofstadter, William Miller, and Daniel Aaron, showed no weakening of this interpretation: "The growing demand for farm machinery as well as for the 'sinews of war' led to American industrial expansion. . . . Of necessity, *iron, coal, and copper production boomed during the war years*."[6] A sophisticated but still essentially misleading view is presented by Gilbert C. Fite and Jim E. Reese in a text of 1959: "The Civil War proved to be a boon to Northern economic development. . . . Industry, for example, was not created by the war, but wartime demands *greatly stimulated and encouraged industrial development* which already had a good start."[7] In a reappraisal of the Civil War, in *Harper's Magazine* for April, 1960, Denis W. Brogan, a specialist in American institutions, wrote: "It may have been only a catalyst but the War *precipitated the entry* of the United States *into the modern industrial world*, made 'the take-off' (to use Professor W. W. Rostow's brilliant metaphor) come sooner."[8]

In all of these reiterations of the effect of the Civil War on industrialism, statistical series seem to have been largely neglected. None of the authors cited reinforce their interpretations by setting the war period in the context of important long-run indexes of industrial growth. Since 1949, series for the period 1840 to 1890 that would cast doubt on the conventional generalizations have been available in *Historical Statistics of the United States, 1789-1945.*[9] In 1960 a new edition of *Historical Statistics* and the report of the Conference on Research in Income and Wealth on *Trends in the American Economy in the Nineteenth Century* have provided additional material to support the argument that the Civil War retarded American industrial development.[10] These volumes give data for many growth curves for the two decades before and after the war decade — in other words, the long-run trends before and after the event in question. The pattern of these trends is a mixed one which shows no uniform type of change during the Civil War decade, but on balance for the more important series the trend is toward retardation in *rates* of growth rather than toward acceleration. This fact is evident in many series which economists would regard as basic to economic growth, but in order to keep the discussion within reasonable limits only a few can be considered here.

Robert E. Gallman has compiled new and more accurate series for both "total commodity output," including agriculture, and "value added by manufacture," for two most general measures of economic growth available for this period. He writes: "Between 1839 and 1899 total commodity output increased elevenfold, or at an average decade rate of slightly less than 50 per cent. . . . Actual rates varied fairly widely, high rates appearing during the decades ending with 1854 and 1884, and a very low rate during the decade ending with 1869."[11] From the over-all standpoint this statement indicates the immediately retarding effect of the Civil War on American economic growth, but since most of the misleading statements are made in regard to industrial growth, or particular elements in industrial growth, it is necessary to look in more detail at "value added by manufacture" and some special series. Gallman's series for value added in constant dollars of the purchasing power of 1879 shows a rise of 157 per cent from 1839 to 1849; 76 per cent from 1849 to 1859; and only 25 per cent from 1859 to 1869.[12] By the 1870's the more favorable prewar rates were resumed, with an increase of 82 per cent for 1869-1879, and 112 per cent for 1879-1889. Thus two decades of very rapid advance, the 1840's and the 1880's, are separated by thirty years of slower growth which falls to the lowest level in the decade that embraces the Civil War.

Pig-iron production in tons, perhaps the most significant commodity index of nineteenth-century American industrial growth, is available year-by-year from 1854 on. Taking total production for five-year periods, output increased 9 per cent between the block of years from 1856 to 1860 and the block from 1861 to 1865. That even this slight increase might not have been registered except for the fact that 1857 to 1860 were years of intermittent depression is indicated by an 81 per cent increase over the war years in the block of years from 1866 to 1870.[13] If annual production is taken at five-year intervals, starting in 1850, the increase is 24 per cent from 1850 to 1855; 17 per cent from 1855 to 1860; 1 per cent from 1860 to 1865; and 100 per cent from 1865 to 870. While there is no figure available for 1845, the period from 1840 to 1850 shows 97 per cent increase in shipments, while for the period 1870 to 1880 the increase was 130 per cent. To sum up, depression and war appear to have retarded a curve of production that was tending to rise at a high rate.

Bituminous coal production may be regarded as the next most essential commodity series. After a gain of 199 per cent from 1840 to 1850 this series shows a rather steady pattern of increase at rates varying from 119 to 148 per cent each decade from 1850 to 1890. The war does not appear to have markedly affected the rate of growth.[14]

In the mid-nineteenth century copper production was not a basic series for recording American growth, but since three distinguished authors have singled it out as one of the indexes of the effect of the war on industry it is best to cite the statistics. Before 1845 production of domestic copper was negligible. By 1850 the "annual recoverable content" of copper from United States mines was 728 tons, by 1860 it was 8,064 tons, by 1865 it was 9,520 tons, and by 1870 it was 14,112 tons. In this series of very small quantities, therefore, the increase from 1850 to 1860 was just over 1,000 per cent, from 1860 to 1865 it was 18 per cent, and from 1865 to 1870 it was 48 per cent.[15]

Railroad track, particularly in the United States, was an essential for industrialization. Here both the depression and the war retarded the rate of growth. From 1851 through 1855 a total of 11,627 miles of new track was laid, from 1856 through 1860, only 8,721 miles, and from 1861 through 1865, only 4,076 miles. After the war the rate of growth of the early 1850's was resumed, with 16,174 miles constructed from 1866 through 1870. Looked at by decades, a rate of over 200 per cent increase per decade in the twenty years before the war was slowed to 70 per cent for the period from 1860 to 1870, with only a 15 per cent increase during the war years. In the next two decades the rate averaged about 75 per cent.[16]

Next to food, cotton textiles may be taken as the most representative consumer-goods industry in the nineteenth century. Interference with the flow of southern cotton had a depressing effect. The number of bales of cotton consumed in United States manufacturing rose 143 per cent from 1840 to 1850 and 47 per cent from 1850 to 1860, but fell by 6 per cent from 1860 to 1870. From then on consumption increased at a little higher rate than in the 1850's.[17]

While woolen textile production is not an important series in the over-all picture of industrial growth, it should be noted that, helped by protection and military needs, consumption of wool for manufacturing more than doubled during the war, and then fell somewhat from 1865 to 1870. But Arthur H. Cole, the historian of the woolen industry, characterizes the years from 1830 to 1870 as a period of growth "not so striking as in the decades before or afterwards."[18]

Immigration to a nation essentially short of labor was unquestionably a stimulant to economic growth. Another country had paid for the immigrant's unproductive youthful years, and he came to the United States ready to contribute his labor at a low cost. The pattern of the curve for annual immigration shows the retarding effect of both depression and war. In the first five years of the 1850's an average of 349,685 immigrants a year came to the United States. From 1856 through 1860 the annual average fell to 169,958, and for the war years of 1861 to 1865 it fell further to 160,345. In the first five postwar years the average rose to 302,620, but not until the first half of the 1870's did the rate equal that of the early 1850's. Had there been a return to prosperity instead of war in 1861, it seems reasonable to suppose that several hundred thousand additional immigrants would have arrived before 1865.[19]

In the case of farm mechanization the same type of error occurs as in the annual series on copper production. "Random" statistics such as the manufacture of 90,000 reapers in 1864 are frequently cited without putting them in the proper perspective of the total number in use and the continuing trends. Reaper and mower sales started upward in the early 1850's and were large from 1856 on, in spite of the depression. William T. Hutchinson estimates that most of the 125,000 reapers and mowers in use in 1861 had been sold during the previous five years.[20] While the business, without regard to the accidental coming of the war, was obviously in a stage of very rapid growth, the war years presented many difficulties and may actually have retarded the rate of increase.[21] Total sales of reapers for the period 1861-1865 are estimated at 250,000 — a quite ordinary increase for a young industry — but the 90,000 figure for 1864, if it is correct, reinforces the evidence from the McCormick correspondence that this was the one particularly good year of the period. During these years William S. McCormick was often of the opinion that the "uncertainties of the times" made advisable a suspension of manufacturing until the close of the war.[22]

For a broader view of agricultural mechanization the series "value of farm implements and machinery" has special interest. Here the census gives a picture which, if correct, is explicable only on the basis of wartime destruction. Based on constant dollars the average value of machinery per farm *fell* nearly 25 per cent in the decade of the war and showed nearly a 90 per cent gain in the 1870's.[23] Differing from these census figures is a series prepared by Marvin W. Towne and Wayne D. Rasmussen based on the production of farm machinery. While this obviously does not take account of destruction of existing equipment or the rapid increase in the number of farms, the record of new production is hard to reconcile with the census figures. The production of implements and machinery reckoned in constant dollars is a sharply rising curve from 1850 on, with increases of 110 per cent from 1850 to 1860; 140 per cent from 1860 to 1870; and 95 per cent from 1870 to 1880.[24] Meanwhile the number of farms increased by about one third in each of the decades of the 1850's and 1860's and by one half in the 1870's.[25] Whatever interpretation is given to these figures, it does not appear that the war greatly increased the trend of agricultural mechanization. The series for gross farm product in constant dollars shows wide variations in increase from decade to decade, with the 1860's in the low group. The gains were 23 per cent, 1840 to 1850; 42 per cent, 1850 to 1860; 21 per cent, 1860 to 1870; 52 per cent, 1870 to 1880; and 20 per cent, 1880 to 1890.[26]

Much American business expansion was financed by short-term bank loans continuously renewed. Thus major increases in business activity should be mirrored in increases in bank loans, both for financing short-term transactions and for additions to plant and working capital that would, in fact, be paid off gradually. If there was a really great Civil War boom in business activity it should be indicated in the series "total loans" of all banks. But it is not. In constant dollars, bank loans fell slightly between 1840 and 1850, and rose nearly 50 per cent by 1860. It should be noted that none of these three decadal years were periods of high prosperity. During the war Confederate banking statistics were not reported by the comptroller of the currency, but by 1866 there is a comparable figure for the nation as a whole, and in constant dollars it is some 35 per cent below that of 1860. Even by 1870 the constant dollar value of all loans was more than 15 per cent lower than just before the war. If instead of examining loans one looks at total assets of all banks the decline in constant dollars from 1860 to 1870 is reduced to 10 per cent, the difference arising from a larger cash position and more investment in government bonds.[27]

Net capital formation would be a more proper index of economic growth than bank loans or assets. Unfortunately, neither the teams of the National Bureau of Economic Research nor those of the Census Bureau have been able to carry any reliable series back of 1868. From colonial times to 1960, however, the chief single form of American capital formation has undoubtedly been building construction. Farm houses, city homes, public buildings, stores, warehouses, and factories have year by year constituted, in monetary value, the leading type of capital growth. Gallman has drawn up series for such construction based on estimating the flow of construction materials and adding what appear to be appropriate markups.[28] Admittedly the process is inexact, but because of the importance of construction in reflecting general trends in capital formation it is interesting to see the results. The rate of change for the ten-year period ending in 1854 is about 140 per cent; for the one ending in 1859 it is 90 per cent; for 1869 it is 40 per cent; and for 1879 it is 46 per cent. Taking a long view, from 1839 to 1859 the average decennial rate of increase was about 70 per cent, and from 1869 to 1899 it was about 40 per cent.[29] The rate of advance in construction was declining and the war decade added a further dip to the decline.

Since the decline in rate is for the decade, the exact effect of the war years can only be estimated, but the logic of the situation, reinforced by the record of sharp cut-backs in railroad building, seems inescapable: the Civil War, like all modern wars, checked civilian construction. The first year of war was a period of depression and tight credit in the Middle West, which checked residential and farm construction in the area that grew most rapidly before and after the war. In both the East and the West the last two years of the war were a period of rapid inflation which was regarded by businessmen as a temporary wartime phenomenon. The logical result would be to postpone construction for long-term use until after the anticipated deflation. The decline in private railroad construction to a small fraction of the normal rate exemplifies the situation.

Lavish expenditure and speculation by a small group of war contractors and market operators gambling on the inflation seem to have created a legend of high prosperity during the war years. But the general series on fluctuations in the volume of business do not bear this out. Leonard P. Ayres's estimates of business activity place the average for 1861 through 1865 below normal, and Norman J. Silberling's business index is below its normal line for all years of the war.[30] Silberling also has an intermediate trend line for business, which smooths out annual fluctuations. This line falls steadily from 1860 to 1869.[31] Much of Silberling's discussion in his chapter "Business Activity, Prices, and Wars" is in answer to his question: "Why does it seem to be true that despite a temporary stimulating effect of war upon some industries, wars are generally associated with a long-term retarding of business growth . . . ?"[32] He puts the Civil War in this general category.

Collectively these statistical estimates support a conclusion that the Civil War retarded American industrial growth. Presentation of this view has been the chief purpose of this article. To try to judge the nonmeasurable or indirect effects of the war is extremely difficult. But since further discussion of the conventional qualitative factors may help to explain the prevailing evaluation in American texts, it seems appropriate to add some conjectural obiter dicta.

Experience with the apparently stimulating effects of twentieth century wars on production makes the conclusion that victorious war may retard the growth of an industrial state seem paradoxical, and no doubt accounts in part for the use of detached bits of quantitative data to emphasize the Civil War's industrial importance.[33] The resolution of the paradox may be found in contemporary conditions in the United States and in the nature of the wartime demand. The essential wastefulness of war from the standpoint of economic growth was obscured by the accident that both of the great European wars of the twentieth century began when the United States had a high level of unemployment. The immediate effect of each, therefore, was to put men to work, to increase the national product, and to create an aura of prosperity. Presumably, the United States of the mid-nineteenth century tended to operate close enough to full employment in average years that any wasteful labor-consuming activities were a burden rather than a stimulant.

By modern standards the Civil War was still unmechanized. It was fought with rifles, bayonets, and sabers by men on foot or horseback. Artillery was more used than in previous wars, but was still a relatively minor consumer of iron and steel. The railroad was also brought into use, but the building of military lines offset only a small percentage of the overall drop from the prewar level of civilian railroad construction. Had all of these things not been true, the

Confederacy with its small industrial development could never have fought through four years of increasingly effective blockade.

In spite of the failure of direct quantitative evidence to show accelerating effects of the war on rates of economic growth, there could be long-run effects of a qualitative type that would gradually foster a more rapid rate of economic growth. The most obvious place to look for such indirect effects would be in the results of freeing the slaves. Marxists contended that elimination of slavery was a necessary precursor of the bourgeois industrialism which would lead to the socialist revolution. The creation of a free Negro labor force was, of course, of great long-run importance. In the twentieth century it has led to readjustment of Negro population between the deep South and the northern industrial areas, and to changes in the use of southern land.

But economically the effects of war and emancipation over the period 1840 to 1880 were negative. Richard A. Easterlin writes: "In every southern state, the 1880 level of per capita income originating in commodity production and distribution was below, or at best only slightly above, that of 1840. . . . [This] attests strikingly to the impact of that war and the subsequent disruption on the southern economy."[34] In general the Negroes became sharecroppers or wage laborers, often cultivating the same land and the same crops as before the war. In qualification of the argument that free Negro labor led to more rapid industrialization it should be noted that the South did not keep up with the national pace in the growth of nonagricultural wealth until after 1900.[35]

Two indirect effects of the war aided industrial growth to degrees that cannot accurately be measured. These were, first, a more satisfactory money market, and, secondly, more security for entrepreneurial activity than in the prewar period. The sharp wartime inflation had the usual effect of transferring income from wage, salary, and interest receivers to those making profits. This meant concentration of savings in the hands of entrepreneurs who would invest in new activities; and this no doubt helps to explain the speculative booms of the last half of the 1860's and first two years of the 1870's which have been treated as the prosperity resulting from the war. Inflation also eased the burdens of those railroads which had excessive mortgage debts. But a great deal of new research would be needed to establish causal connections between the inflationary reallocation of wealth, 1863 to 1865, and the high rate of industrial progress in the late 1870's and the 1880's.

The National Banking Act, providing a more reliable currency for interstate operations, has been hailed as a great aid to business expansion although it would be hard to demonstrate, aside from a few weeks during panics, that plentiful but occasionally unsound currency had seriously interfered with earlier industrial growth.[36] The existence of two and a half billion dollars in federal bonds also provided a basis for credit that was larger than before the war. This led to broader and more active security markets as well as to easier personal borrowing. But two qualifications must be kept in mind. First, local bank lending to favored borrowers had probably tended to be too liberal before the war and was now put on a somewhat firmer basis. In other words, since 1800 a multiplication of banks had made credit relatively easy to obtain in the United States, and in the North this continued to be the situation. Second, the southern banking system was largely destroyed by the war and had to be rebuilt in the subsequent decades. It should also be remembered that by 1875 some 40 per cent of the banks were outside the national banking system.[37]

Because of a few colorful speculators like Jay Gould, Daniel Drew, and Jim Fisk, and the immortality conferred on them, initially by the literary ability of the Adams brothers, the New York stock exchange in the postwar decade appears to have mirrored a new era of predatory wealth. But one has only to study the scandals of the London and New York stock exchanges in 1854 to see that there was little growth in the sophistication or boldness of stock operators during these fifteen years.[38] In any case, the exploits of market operators were seldom related in a positive way to economic growth. Even a record of new issues of securities, which is lacking for this period, would chiefly reflect the flow of capital into railroads, banks, and public utilities rather than into manufacturing. Very few "industrial" shares were publicly marketed before the decade of the 1880's; such enterprises grew chiefly from the reinvestment of earnings.

There was strong government encouragement to entrepreneurial activity during the Civil War, but to ascribe to it unusual importance for economic growth requires both analysis of the results and comparison with other periods. Government in the United States has almost always encouraged entrepreneurs. The federal and state administrations preceding the Civil War could certainly be regarded as friendly to business. They subsidized railroads by land grants, subscribed to corporate bond issues, and remitted taxes on new enterprise.[39] Tariffs were low, but railroad men and many bankers were happy with the situation. Whether or not American industrialism was significantly accelerated by the high protection that commenced with the war is a question that economists will probably never settle.

The building of a subsidized transcontinental railroad, held back by sectional controversies in the 1850's, was authorized along a northern route with the help of federal loans and land grants when the southerners excluded themselves from Congress. Putting more than a hundred million dollars into this project in the latter half of the 1860's, however, may have had an adverse effect on industrial growth. In general, the far western roads were built for speculative and strategic purposes uneconomically ahead of demand. They may for a decade, or even two, have consumed more capital than their transportation services were then worth to the economy.

To sum up this part of the obiter dicta, those who write of the war as creating a national market tied together by railroads underestimate both the achievements of the two decades before the war and the ongoing trends of the economy. The nation's business in 1855 was nearly as intersectional as in 1870. Regional animosities did not interfere with trade, nor did these feelings diminish after the war. By the late 1850's the United States was a rapidly maturing industrial state with its major cities connected by rail, its major industries selling in a national market, and blessed or cursed with financiers, security flotations, stock markets, and all the other appurtenances of industrial capitalism.

But when all specific factors of change attributable to the war have been deflated, there is still the possibility that northern victory had enhanced the capitalist spirit, that as a consequence the atmosphere of government in Washington among members of both parties was more friendly to industrial enterprise and to northern-based national business operations than had formerly been the rule. It can be argued that in spite of Greenbackers and discontented farmers legislation presumably favorable to industry could be more readily enacted. The Fourteenth Amendment, for example, had as a by-product greater security for interstate business against state regulation, although it was to be almost two decades before the Supreme Court would give force to this protection. By 1876, a year of deep depression, the two major parties were trying to outdo each other in promises of stimulating economic growth. This highly generalized type of argument is difficult to evaluate, but in qualification of any theory of a sharp change in attitude we should remember that industrialism was growing rapidly from general causes and that by the 1870's it was to be expected that major-party politics would be conforming to this change in American life.

Massive changes in physical environment such as those accompanying the rise of trade at the close of the Middle Ages or the gradual growth of industrialism from the seventeenth century on do not lend themselves readily to exact or brief periodization. If factory industry and mechanized transportation be taken as the chief indexes of early industrialism, its spread in the United States was continuous and rapid during the entire nineteenth century, but in general, advance was greater during periods of prosperity than in depressions. The first long period without a major depression, after railroads, canals, and steamboats had opened a national market, was from 1843 to 1857. Many economic historians interested in quantitative calculations would regard these years as marking the appearance of an integrated industrial society. Walter W. Rostow, incidentally, starts his "take-off" period in the 1840's and calls it completed by 1860.[40] Others might prefer to avoid any narrow span of years. Few, however, would see a major stimulation to economic growth in the events of the Civil War.

Finally, one may speculate as to why this exaggerated conception of the role of the Civil War in industrialization gained so firm a place in American historiography. The idea fits, of course, into the Marxian frame of revolutionary changes, but it seems initially to have gained acceptance quite independently of Marxian influences. More concentrated study of the war years than of any other four year span in the nineteenth century called attention to technological and business events usually overlooked. Isolated facts were seized upon without comparing them with similar data for other decades. The desire of teachers for neat periodization was probably a strong factor in quickly placing the interpretation in textbooks; thus, up to 1860 the nation was agricultural, after 1865 it was industrial. Recent study of American cultural themes suggests still another reason. From most standpoints the Civil War was a national disaster, but Americans like to see their history in terms of optimism and progress. Perhaps the war was put in a perspective suited to the culture by seeing it as good because in addition to achieving freedom for the Negro it brought about industrial progress.

[1] This article is based on a paper presented by the author at the annual meeting of the Mississippi Valley Historical Association in Louisville in April, 1960.

[2] These particular authors are cited merely as examples of historical opinion, not because they are more in error than others. The reader needs only to take down other texts from his own shelf to find similar statements.

[3] *The Rise of American Civilization* (2 vols.; New York, 1927), vol. II, p. 53. In this and the following quotations the italics are mine.

[4] Homer C. Hockett and Arthur M. Schlesinger, *Land of the Free: A Short History of the American People* (New York, 1944), p. 355. Schlesinger wrote the section beginning with the Civil War.

[5] *American Economic History* (7th ed.; New York, 1954), p. 345. The same statement appears in a later edition (New York, 1960), p. 345.

[6] *The United States: The History of a Republic* (Englewood Cliffs, N. J., 1957), p. 381.

[7] *An Economic History of the United States* (Boston, 1959), p. 284.

[8] "A Fresh Appraisal of the Civil War," *Harper's Magazine* (New York), vol. CCXX (April, 1960), p. 140.

[9] U. S. Bureau of the Census, *Historical Statistics of the United States, 1789-1945* (Washington, 1949).

[10] U. S. Bureau of the Census, *Historical Statistics of the United States: Colonial Times to 1957* (Washington, 1960); *Trends in the American Economy*

in the Nineteenth Century (Princeton, 1960), published by the National Bureau of Economic Research as Volume XXIV of its Studies in Income and Wealth.

[11] Trends in the American Economy, p. 15.

[12] Historical Statistics (1960 ed.), p. 402. "Constant" or "real" means dollars adjusted to eliminate price changes. It should be remembered that all series expressed in current dollars need to be corrected for rather violent price movements during these fifty years. Precise adjustments would vary with every series, and would involve many problems, but the movement of wholesale prices in general (Warren-Pearson Index) may be roughly summarized as follows: In 1850 prices were 12 per cent lower than in 1840, but by 1860 they were 11 per cent higher than in 1850. From 1860 to 1865 prices rose 99 per cent, but by 1870 the increase for the decade was only 46 per cent. By 1880 the decline for the decade was 26 per cent, and for the decade ending in 1890 it was 18 per cent. Historical Statistics (1960), p. 115. In other words, current dollars are a very unreliable indicator, particularly as applied to wholesale prices.

[13] Ibid., pp. 365-366.

[14] Ibid., p. 357.

[15] Ibid., p. 368.

[16] Ibid., pp. 427-428.

[17] Historical Statistics (1949 ed.), p. 187. This table is not carried back to 1840 in the 1960 edition.

[18] Arthur H. Cole, The American Wool Manufacture (2 vols.; Cambridge, 1926), vol. I, p. 392.

[19] Historical Statistics (1960 ed.), p. 57.

[20] William T. Hutchinson, Cyrus Hall McCormick (2 vols.; New York, 1930-1935), vol. II, p. 67.

[21] Ibid., vol. II, pp. 67-95.

[22] Ibid., vol. II, p. 88.

[23] Historical Statistics (1960 ed.), p. 285. For price index see note 12, above.

[24] Trends in the American Economy, p. 276.

[25] The percentage increases were 41 per cent (1860 over 1850); 30 per cent (1870 over 1860); and 51 per cent (1880 over 1870). Historical Statistics (1960 ed.), p. 278.

[26] Ibid., p. 284.

[27] Ibid., p. 624. The reader is again warned that deflation of current dollar values for this early period is an inexact process.

[28] Trends in the American Economy, pp. 60-64.

[29] Ibid., p. 24. Gallman has two alternate series which I have averaged. For the purposes of this paper either series leads to the same conclusions.

[30] Leonard P. Ayres, Turning Points in Business Cycles (New York, 1939), p. 14; Norman J. Silberling, The Dynamics of Business (New York, 1943), p. 50.

[31] Silberling, Dynamics of Business, p. 61.

[32] Ibid., p. 66.

[33] Ayres, Silberling, and some other students of economic activity such as Herbert Hoover, however, blame the breakdown of the 1930's on the dislocations caused by World War I. Ibid., pp. 65-66. See also The Memoirs of Herbert Hoover: The Great Depression, 1929-1941 (New York, 1952), p. 105.

[34] Trends in the American Economy, p. 85.

[35] Simon Kuznets (ed.), Population Redistribution and Economic Growth: United States, 1870-1950 (2 vols.; Philadelphia, 1957-1960), vol. I (Methodological Considerations and Reference Tables), pp. 729-732; vol. II (Analysis of Economic Change), p. 109.

[36] See Bray Hammond, Banks and Politics in America: From the Revolution to the Civil War (Princeton, 1957), pp. 663-667, 670.

[37] *Historical Statistics* (1960 ed.), pp. 628, 638.

[38] See James K. Medbury, *Men and Mysteries of Wall Street* (Boston, 1870), p. 319 ff.; Margaret G. Myers, *The New York Money Market* (2 vols.; New York, 1931), vol. I, p. 140.

[39] Myers, *New York Money Market*, vol. I, p. 296; National Bureau of Economic Research, *Capital Formation and Economic Growth* (Princeton, 1955), p. 382. See also Carter Goodrich, *Government Promotion of American Canals and Railroads, 1800-1890* (New York, 1960).

[40] W. W. Rostow, *The Stages of Economic Growth* (Cambridge, Eng., 1960), p. 95.

Dr. Salsbury examines critically the issues raised in Professor Cochran's paper. Salsbury wisely cautions against the misuse of statistics in attempting to explain complicated historical events. Dr. Salsbury also analyzes the impact of the War on American economic development within the broader issues of historical interpretation raised by Charles Beard and Louis Hacker.

THE EFFECT OF THE CIVIL WAR ON AMERICAN INDUSTRIAL DEVELOPMENT

By Stephen Salsbury

MUCH HAS BEEN WRITTEN about the Civil War. Until quite recently, however, historians were concerned mainly with its cause and they largely ignored the economic effects of the War. In the nineteenth century most northerners simply blamed the War on slavery. In the same period southerners merely accused politicians of being irresponsible and claimed that fanatical abolitionists ignited the conflict. But to Charles A. Beard, writing in the 1920's, these old statements seemed unconvincing.

Beard viewed America's history as a great movement away from Jefferson's agrarian type of society to the capitalistic, industrial, mechanized, and urban society that we have now. In his view, the forces that moved people were economic ones and not idealistic concerns over states' rights or over the immorality of slavery. Beard's pre-Civil War America consisted of a northern, capitalistic, industrial economy with, opposing it, the southern agricultural system. He saw the economic interest and political power of the South, in the Electoral College, the Senate, House of Representatives, and Supreme Court, as frustrating the economic needs of the rapidly growing industrial north.

Professor Louis Hacker stated the Beard thesis in its most extreme and naked form in his book, *The Triumph of American Capitalism.* "By 1860," he summarized,

a critical situation had arisen in American affairs. Because the southern planter capitalists were in control of the instrumentalities of the national state and, as a result, were thwarting the advance of the (too slowly) growing northern industrial capitalism, their claims to power had to be challenged. This the newly formed Republican party did. The partial success of the Republican party at the polls in 1860 drove the southern leaders — pushed on by extremists in their midst who were under heavy economic pressures — into secession. The Civil War broke out. The Union government, after the departure of the southern legislators, was now wholly possessed by the Republican party.[1]

In Beard's words, the Civil War was the "social cataclysm in which the capitalists, laborers, and farmers of the North and West drove from power in the national government the planting aristocracy of the South. Viewed under the light of universal history, the fighting was a fleeting incident; the social revolution was the essential portentous outcome."[2]

This explanation of the causes of the Civil War lead Beard and Hacker to the conclusion that the conflict spurred economic growth in the United States:

The Second American Revolution (Civil War) while destroying the economic foundation of the slave-owning aristocracy, assured the triumph of business enterprise. As if to add irony to defeat, the very war which the planters precipitated in an effort to avoid their doom augmented the fortunes of the capitalist class from whose jurisdiction they had tried to escape. Through financing the federal government and furnishing supplies to its armies, northern leaders in banking and industry reaped profits far greater than they had ever yet gathered during four years of peace. When the long military struggle came to an end they had accumulated huge masses of capital and were ready to march resolutely forward to the conquest of the continent — to the exploitation of the most marvelous natural endowment ever bestowed by fortune on any nation.[3]

But Beard made no systematic use of statistical evidence in trying to analyze the War's effect.

Prior to 1860 southern planters successfully used their power in the national government to oppose measures such as the tariff, the Homestead Bill, national banking, etc., favored by the northern industrialists and western farmers. Beard, however, made no attempt truly to evaluate the importance of such measures in economic terms and merely assumed that because northern capitalists could not get their way, their plans for expansion and profits were hindered and that economic growth was thus retarded. Starting with this assumption, Beard saw the War as aiding industrialism. He argued that the transference of power from the Democratic to the Republican party (a condition which lasted, with two short exceptions, from the 1860's until 1932) enabled businessmen to shape government policies in ways that were most helpful to their plans for profit and expansion.

Beard cited the policies and legislation which, he claimed, specifically aided economic growth. He considered as most important the direct federal aid to the vast transcontinental railroad projects; it started with the subsidy and land grant to the Union Pacific and Central Pacific railroads in 1862 and included federal land grants in the following years to the Northern Pacific, Kansas Pacific, Santa Fe (Atlantic and Pacific), and Southern Pacific routes. The protective tariff was named as specifically aiding economic growth. He named also the acts designed to make easy the removal of land (whether farmland, timberland, or mineral land) from the public domain to private hands, the Immigration Act of 1864 which gave federal blessing to the importation of workingmen under contracts "analogous to the indentured servitude of colonial times," and the national banking laws and many others.[4]

But more important than any specific legislative act, according to Beard's interpretation, was the ascendancy of the Republican party in Washington; this created a climate that tolerated no interference with the private capitalists. Gone were the Jacksonian ideas that opposed the concentration of economic power in the hands of large corporations. After 1860, Leland Stanford, Collis P. Huntington, John D. Rockefeller, John M. Forbes, Jay Gould, and Mark Hanna had almost unlimited freedom to do as they pleased. And when men such as these ran into trouble with labor, their control of the government assured them that federal power would be used to smash opposition.

Charles Beard's main effort was to explain why the United States in the period between 1860 and 1910 became the world's most productive and powerful industrial nation. In giving his explanation, he made only a random use of statistics. But while he was perfectly content to make almost totally undocumented assertions, such as that which attributed the post-Civil War boom to "huge masses of capital made available by war profits far greater than . . . [capitalists] had ever yet gathered," Louis Hacker attempted to support this argument by statistical evidence. He used, for instance, an analysis of the census data to substantiate the thesis that "industrial capitalism (more particularly, *heavy* industry) benefited from the Civil War and it continued to make great forward strides (despite a severe depression) after the political victory was firmly secured."[5]

Lately, the role of the Civil War in positively contributing to the American Industrial Revolution has been questioned. Among the most recent and able of these questioning re-evaluations is Thomas C. Cochran's *"Did the Civil War Retard Industrialization?"*[6] In "reiterations of the effect of the Civil War on industrialism," he writes, giving examples, "statistical series seem to have been largely neglected."[7] Cochran's conclusion, after an examination of statistics (available mainly in the 1949 and 1960 editions of *Historical Statistics of the United States*[8] and in the report of the Conference of Research on Income and Wealth in *Trends in the American Economy in the Nineteenth Century*), strongly suggests that the Civil War slowed industrial growth.

Cochran observes that generally during the two decades preceding the Civil War (1840-1860) and the two decades (1870-1890) following the ten-year census period in which the war occurred, the rate of growth exceeded that of the "war decade" (1860-1870). In short, he points to rapid expansion between 1840 and 1860, then actual stagnation in some areas, and but slight increases in most others during the war period (1861-1865), which caused a slower growth rate for the decade 1860-1870, and finally a resumption of rapid growth in the decades between 1870 and 1890.

Behind Cochran's conclusion that the Civil War retarded industrial growth lies the very unstatistical and also partly unsubstantiated assumption that by 1840 all the ingredients favorable to fast industrial growth were overwhelmingly present in the American society. This implies that by the end of the Van Buren administration, the ground was laid for an almost continuous and uninterrupted expansion. This expansion, however, did not occur and the assumption is made that disruptive effects of the Civil War removed vital capital building goods and services from the economy between 1861 and 1865, making the growth after 1865 less rapid than it otherwise would have been.

Now, available statistics do indicate certain American economic reverses during the War. Cotton production almost ended, cotton textile manufacturing in the North fell sharply, and so did the construction of new railroad tracks. Yet, despite this, other segments such as bituminous coal, Pennsylvania anthracite, pig iron, and railroad rails continued to expand, although some at a slightly reduced rate. From this point of view, statistics show that the economy grew less rapidly during the five Civil War years than at other times. We might fairly conclude that war disruption was partially, at least, responsible for this.[9]

Yet the conclusions of Beard, Hacker, and the other historians who claim that the Civil War speeded the Industrial Revolution do not stand or fall on an analysis of the short run, immediate effects which the War had upon the economy. Rather, these conclusions, which see the War as assuring the "triumph of capitalism," and as producing a long term surge of industrial production, rest on longer range analyses.

Professor Cochran's arguments may be met by comparing the post-Civil War growth rate with prewar activity. If one does this, some surprising results present themselves. Let us, for example, instead of comparing the three decades 1850-1860, 1860-1870, 1870-1880, as Cochran does, compare the decade preceding the Civil War (1850-1860), with that immediately following it (1865-1875).[10] Pig iron production in tons, which he considers as "the most significant commodity index of nineteenth century American industrial growth."[11] increased about 50 per cent between 1850 and 1860, but more than doubled between 1865 and 1873 before it fell, due to the depression which started in 1873.[12] Bituminous coal, "the second most essential commodity series,"[13] tells a similar story: here production increased slightly less than 100 per cent during the decade of 1850-1860, while during the years 1865-1875 it increased by about 145 per cent. Railroad track construction, which he deems "essential for industrialization," tells an even more striking story: during the period 1850-1860 about 20,000 miles of track were laid down, compared to roughly 40,000 during the decade 1865-1875. Clearly then, in these three areas which Cochran considers the most important indicators of nineteenth century economic growth, the postwar decade evidences a substantial boom with growth rates much above those of the pre-Civil War era.[14]

Although this kind of analysis tends to cast doubt on the argument and could be used to support Hacker's assertion that "industrial capitalism (more particularly, heavy industry) benefited from the Civil War," such a conclusion would have the weakness which plagues any attempt to assess the economic effects of the Civil War by reference to growth rates, and industrial or agricultural output. Such statistics tell us only how much was produced, or how much the growth rate declined or increased, but they do not tell us why. This returns us to the nonstatistical explanation of Beard which conflicts dramatically with Cochran's underlying assumption that all the ingredients for rapid economic growth dominated the American society by the beginning of William Harrison's administration.

Professor Cochran recognizes that what he calls "indirect effects" may have had some influence upon post-Civil War economic development. For purposes of analysis we can put these "indirect effects" into two categories. First, there were the changes in the political and social system which the War produced; and second there were the stimulants, such as inflation and the creation of a substantial federal debt, which resulted directly from the War itself. Relative to the second category, Cochran admits that "sharp wartime inflation had the usual effect of transferring income from wage, salary, and interest receivers to those making profits, . . . (which) meant concentration of savings in the hands of entrepreneurs who would invest in new activities."[15] He also points out that inflation "eased the burdens of those railroads which had excessive mortgage debts."[16] But Cochran seems willing to dismiss these effects of the War with the casual statement that "a great deal of new research would be needed to establish causal connections between the inflationary reallocation of wealth, 1863 to 1865, and the high rate of industrial progress in the late 1870's and 1880's."[17] With this sentiment one can only agree. We add that until such attempts are made one must be careful about characterizing the Civil War as a retarder of industrialization.

Cochran's analysis is similar in his statements about the effect of expanded and superior credit resulting from the establishment of national banks and the increase of the national debt from $64,000,000 in 1860 to over $2,700,000,000 in 1866.[18] He gives no statistics which would indicate the impact of the new banking system and the enormous federal debt, but merely states that "since 1800 a multiplication of banks had made credit relatively easy to obtain in the United States, and in the North this continued to be the situation."[19] Further, he observes that the War destroyed southern banking, and that by 1875 some 40 per cent of the banks were still outside the national banking system. With these statements there can be little disagreement, yet it is difficult to see how they prove or disprove the thesis that the War retarded economic growth. In precise terms, how easy was credit to obtain before 1860? Was there ample credit for large scale ventures? Was there any change in this picture after 1865? If there was, did it result from the War? These questions still remain to be answered. And the fact that some "40 per cent of the banks" in 1875 were outside the national banking system seems almost irrelevant without a great deal of additional analysis which is not supplied.

Finally, Cochran recognizes that he must meet the argument which asserts that the Civil War changed the social structure of the nation. He agrees that there is a "possibility that the northern victory had enhanced the capitalist spirit"; but he maintains that this "highly generalized argument is difficult to evaluate." This is undoubtedly true (and the same statement could be made about most attempts to explain human behavior). But the Beard thesis is not so vague but what it is subject to some trenchant criticism. It is possible to analyze in detail the measures which the Republican Party enacted, and to determine how they affected economic growth. It has already been suggested that it may be feasible to measure the amount of investment capital made available by the creation of the national banking system, and the large national debt. There might also be a thorough quantitative study of government aid to internal improvements. While it is true that "federal and state administrations preceding the Civil War could . . . be regarded as friendly to business," it might be well to compare, as Professor Cochran suggests, federal and state aid during and after the Civil War with that in other periods. This

166

should include an attempt to determine the precise amount in constant dollars made available to transportation enterprises by the various state and local governments and the national Congress. We do have readily available information on federal land granted for such purposes. Some idea of the new Republican attitude can be gained from the fact that, in the single year 1865, the national government granted more land for internal improvements than in all years prior to 1861.[20]

There can be no doubt that the exodus from Washington of southern congressmen speeded by ten years or more the building of our entire transcontinental railroad network. Mr. Cochran suggests that such ventures were "built for speculative purposes uneconomically ahead of demand . . . " and thus concludes without supplying any evidence that they may "for a decade or even two have consumed more capital than their transportation services were then worth to the economy."[21] Although this judgment is not necessarily wrong, it will take much research to prove it one way or the other. Certain it is that the building of our vast transcontinental railway systems, which is partially reflected in 40,000 miles of track laid down between 1865 and 1875, had enormous economic effects both from the point of view of consuming (thus stimulating) the products of heavy industry, and of opening up agricultural land in California, Kansas, Nebraska, Wyoming, Colorado, Utah, Idaho, Montana, Washington, Oregon, Arizona, Nevada, and New Mexico. Here it must be noted that since the first transcontinental road was not finished until May, 1869, the statistical impact of these roads in agriculture would not be seen until the decade 1870-1880.

Professor Cochran's assertion that the Union Pacific, during its first decade, was a drain on the economy has been sharply challenged by Robert Fogel. Fogel not only analyzes the rate of return on the Union Pacific's cash expenditures; he also presents estimates of the line's "social return," that is, the increased national income due to the railroad but not reflected in the company's earnings. In both respects Professor Fogel finds the Union Pacific a success, returning an average of 11.6 per cent on its cash expenditures for the first decade of its operation, and an average social return of 29.9 per cent for the same period.[22] While it must be conceded that the social return statistics as yet mean little since we have few comparable figures for other railroads or other kinds of investments, it is only by this type of investigation that we will finally be able, through the aid of numbers, to shed light upon the question of the economic effect of the Civil War on the railroads.

Finally, however, we must face the inherent limits of statistics. Cochran's argument that the Civil War's contribution to the "spirit of capitalism" is difficult to measure is all too correct. Such actions as those of the Republican-appointed Supreme Court, which interpreted the Fourteenth Amendment to the Constitution to insure the sanctity of corporate property and to protect it from attacks by hostile state legislatures, are not subject to statistical measurement. Yet they vitally affected industrial development, at least the industrialism which characterized nineteenth century America.

In summary, historians must not discard or avoid statistics; they can prove invaluable in drawing a clear picture of what happened. Numbers may even answer questions such as, was the Union Pacific a stimulant to economic growth? and if so how? and in what areas of the economy? Yet the broader question — did the Civil War accelerate industrialism by placing in undisputed power men of business? — is only partially susceptible to statistical analysis. We can gain insight into the impact of some measures (tariffs, aid to railroads, land distributed under the Homestead Act, etc.) through numerical data, yet historians must never fail to integrate such information with interpretations based upon nonstatistical social, political, and psychological analysis.

[1] Louis M. Hacker, *The Triumph of American Capitalism* (New York, 1940), p. 339.

[2] Charles A. Beard and Mary R. Beard, *The Rise of American Civilization* (New York, 1933), vol. II, p. 54.

[3] *Ibid.*, p. 166.

[4] Beard and Beard, *Rise of American Civilization*, vol. II, p. 106.

[5] Hacker, *Triumph of American Capitalism*, p. 438.

[6] Thomas C. Cochran, "Did the Civil War Retard Industrialization?", *Mississippi Valley Historical Review*, vol. XLVIII (Sept., 1961), p. 198.

[7] *Ibid.*, p. 198.

[8] Bureau of the Census, *Historical Statistics of the United States 1789-1945* (1949), and Bureau of the Census, *Historical Statistics of the United States Colonial Times to 1957* (1960).

[9] EDITOR'S NOTE: See especially Tables VI-2 and VI-3 of Part Five.

[10] Note that many of the series used by Professor Cochran, especially those in *Trends in the American Economy in the Nineteenth Century*, are not year-by-year statistics but show changes only every tenth year (usually the census year) and thus it is not possible strictly to compare the decade 1850-1860 with the decade 1865-1875.

[11] Cochran, "Did the Civil War Retard Industrialization?", p. 200.

[12] See Table VI-2, Part Five.

[13] Cochran, "Did the Civil War Retard Industrialization?", p. 200.

[14] See Table VI-2, VI-3, Part Five.

[15] Cochran, "Did the Civil War Retard Industrialization?", p. 207.

[16] *Ibid.*

[17] *Ibid.*

[18] See Table IX-1, Part Five.

[19] Cochran, "Did the Civil War Retard Industrialization?", p. 207.

[20] See Table VII-5, Part Five.

[21] Cochran, "Did the Civil War Retard Industrialization?", p. 209.

[22] Robert W. Fogel, *The Union Pacific Railroad, A Case in Premature Enterprise*, pp. 95-103.

STATISTICAL SUPPLEMENT: SELECTED STATISTICS ON THE DEVELOPMENT OF THE AMERICAN ECONOMY, 1850-80

The purpose of bringing together in one source a wide array of quantitative materials is quite central to the approach of this book: The economic consequences of the Civil War are by no means simple and clear-cut. Nearly all the authors in the preceding selections have used quantitative evidence to support opposing or contradictory conclusions. It is certainly not a simple matter to compile a set of unambiguous statistics. Nevertheless, warned in advance of the inherent shortcomings as well as of the benefits to be gained by use of statistical material in historical research, the student is urged to come to his own conclusions of the issues raised by the various authors.

The data in these tables can be used to inspect the arguments of Clark, Cochran, and Salsbury. Because these are aggregate data for the entire economy, however, they bear directly on the explanation of the War's impact offered by all the writers in the text.

The statistics presented here are by no means exhaustive: one or more groups of tables is related directly to the arguments of the respective articles in the text. To supplement the data in the following tables, students should consult the most valuable collection of historical statistics contained in the U. S. Dept. of Commerce, Bureau of the Census, Historical Statistics of the U. S.: From Colonial Times to the Present (Washington: Government Printing Office, 1959).

I.

One of the major reasons why honest men differ in interpreting the impact of the War on national economic development is the paucity and inadequacy of available statistics. National income and product data, for example, are virtually nonexistent for the years before 1869, when the estimates of Simon Kuznets begin. The veracity of the R. F. Martin data, available since 1939, has been seriously questioned by Kuznets and other scholars working at the National Bureau of Economic Research.[1] Recently Robert Gallman has attempted to push back the Kuznets estimates to the period before the Civil War. Some results of Gallman's efforts, shown as regards commodity output are given in part, in Table I-1. These data, which may be taken as a first approximation to national income and product statistics, compare the rates of growth in commodity production and population. They also show productivity growth in commodity production.

The data in Table I-2 show the value added by broad economic groups in prices prevailing in each year examined and for a base price period of 1879. Broadly speaking, the value added for each group is the difference between the dollar value of raw materials and the dollar value of a finished product.

[1] See Simon Kuznets, *Income and Wealth of the U.S.: Trends and Structure* (Cambridge: Bowes and Bowes, 1950), pp. 221-241.

TABLE I-1

U. S. COMMODITY OUTPUT, POPULATION, AND GAINFUL WORKERS IN COMMODITY PRODUCTION, QUINQUENNIAL, 1839-1859 AND 1869-1899

Year or End of Decade	Output	Population	Output per Capita	Gainful Workers	Output per Worker
ABSOLUTE FIGURES					
	(mill.)	(thous.)		(thous.)	
1839	$ 1,094	17,120	$ 64	4,484	$244
1844	1,374	20,182	68		
1849	1,657	23,261	71	6,190	268
1854	2,317	27,386	85		
1859	2,686	31,513	85	8,140	330
1869	} 3,271	39,905	82	{ 9,695	337
1869				{ 9,635	339
1874	4,297	45,073	95		
1879	5,304	50,262	105	12,850	413
1884	7,300	56,658	129		
1889	8,659	63,056	137	16,570	523
1894	10,258	69,580	147		
1899	11,751	76,094	154	19,512	602
DECENNIAL RATES OF CHANGE					
(per cent)					
1849	52	36	11	38	10
1854	69	36	24		
1859	62	36	20	32	23
1869	23	27	− 4	19	2
1874					
1879	62	26	29	33	22
1884	70	26	35		
1889	63	25	30	29	27
1894	41	23	15		
1899	36	21	13	18	15
Averages:					
1839-99	49	28	16	28	16
1839-59	57	36	16	35	16
1869-99	54	24	24	27	21

SOURCE: Robert E. Gallman, "Commodity Output 1839-1899," Trends in the American Economy in the Nineteenth Century, p. 16.

TABLE I-2

Value Added by Selected Industries in Current and 1879 Prices: 1839 to 1899
[*In billions of dollars*]

Year	Current Prices					1879 Prices					
	Total	Agriculture	Mining	Manufacturing	Construction	Total	Agriculture	Mining	Manufacturing	Construction	Value of output of fixed capital
1839	1.04	.71	0.01	.24	.08	1.09	.79	0.01	.19	.11	.25
1844	1.09	.69	.01	.31	.08	1.37	.94	.01	.29	.13	.....
1849	1.40	.83	.02	.45	.11	1.66	.99	.02	.49	.16	.39
1854	2.39	1.46	.03	.66	.23	2.32	1.32	.03	.68	.30	.....
1859	2.57	1.50	.03	.82	.23	2.69	1.49	.03	.86	.30	.73
1869	4.83	2.54	.13	1.63	.54	3.27	1.72	.07	1.08	.40	1.09
1874	5.40	2.53	.15	2.07	.65	4.30	1.98	.11	1.69	.52	.....
1879	5.30	2.60	.15	1.96	.59	5.30	2.60	.15	1.96	.59	1.64
1884	7.09	2.84	.20	3.05	1.01	7.30	3.00	.23	3.22	.86	.....
1889	7.87	2.77	.28	3.73	1.10	8.66	3.24	.35	4.16	.92	2.72
1894	7.83	2.64	.29	3.60	1.30	10.26	3.27	.39	5.48	1.12	.....
1899	10.20	3.40	.47	5.04	1.29	11.75	3.92	.55	6.26	1.02	3.35

SOURCE: Adapted from Historical Statistics of the U.S., (1960), p. 139.

TABLE I-3

GROSS NATIONAL PRODUCT, TOTAL AND PER CAPITA, 1869-1893
[Kuznets's concept: 5-year periods are annual average.]

Year or Period	Current Prices		1929 Prices	
	Total [in billions of dollars]	Per Capita [in dollars]	Total [in billions of dollars]	Per Capita [in dollars]
1869-1873	$ 6.71	$165	$ 9.11	$223
1872-1876	7.53	171	11.2	254
1877-1881	9.18	186	16.1	327
1882-1886	11.3	204	20.7	374
1887-1891	12.3	199	24.0	388
1889-1893	13.1	204	26.1	405

SOURCE: Adapted from Historical Statistics of the U.S. (1960), p. 139.

II.

The data in Table II-1 are self explanatory: they contain the total debt of the federal government outstanding and its distribution by type of financial instrument, 1851-1880.

The table shows quite clearly the enormous increase in the absolute and per capita volume of the public debt during the war years. The influence of government spending on economic behavior, the subject explored by Mitchell's article in Part One, may be assessed by close examination of this table. Finally, the student may find an interesting statistic by computing the proportion that computed annual interest charges were to gross national product and to the Gallman estimate of commodity production. Were the interest charges excessive in terms of the economy's over-all performance? Were the absolute dollar amounts in interest payments significant enough to redistribute income from the population at large to the relatively smaller group of investors who held the interest-bearing government securities?

TABLE II-1
PUBLIC DEBT OF THE FEDERAL GOVERNMENT: 1851-1880

| Year | Principal of public debt outstanding | | | | | Computed annual interest charge |
| | Total gross debt | | Matured | Non-interest-bearing [a] | Interest-bearing [b] | |
	Amount	Per capita				
	1,000 dollars	Dollars	1,000 dollars	1,000 dollars	1,000 dollars	1,000 dollars
1851	68,305	2.85	....	....	....	....
1852	66,199	2.67	....	....	....	....
1853	59,805	2.32	162	....	59,642	....
1854	42,244	1.59	199	....	42,045	....
1855	35,588	1.30	170	....	35,418	2,314
1856	31,974	1.13	169	....	31,805	1,869
1857	28,701	0.99	198	....	28,503	1,673
1858	44,913	1.50	170	....	44,743	2,447
1859	58,498	1.91	165	....	58,333	3,126
1860	64,844	2.06	161	....	64,683	3,444
1861	90,582	2.80	159	....	90,423	5,093
1862	524,178	15.79	231	158,591	365,356	22,049
1863	1,119,774	32.91	172	411,767	707,834	41,854
1864	1,815,831	52.08	367	455,437	1,360,027	78,853
1865	2,677,929	75.01	2,129	458,090	2,217,709	137,743
1866	2,755,764	75.42	4,436	429,212	2,322,116	146,068
1867	2,650,168	70.91	1,739	409,474	2,238,955	138,892
1868	2,583,446	67.61	1,246	390,874	2,191,326	128,460
1869	2,545,111	65.17	5,112	388,503	2,151,495	125,524
1870	2,436,453	61.06	3,570	397,003	2,035,881	118,785
1871	2,322,052	56.72	1,949	399,406	1,920,697	111,949
1872	2,209,991	52.65	7,927	401,270	1,800,794	103,988
1873	2,151,210	50.02	51,929	402,797	1,696,484	98,050
1874	2,159,933	49.05	3,216	431,786	1,724,931	98,796
1875	2,156,277	47.84	11,426	436,175	1,708,676	96,856
1876	2,130,846	46.22	3,902	430,258	1,696,685	96,104
1877	2,107,760	44.71	16,649	393,223	1,697,889	93,161
1878	2,159,418	44.82	5,594	373,089	1,780,736	94,654
1879	2,298,913	46.72	37,015	374,181	1,887,716	83,774
1880	2,090,909	41.60	7,621	373,295	1,709,993	79,634

SOURCE: Adapted from Historical Statistics of the U.S. (1960), p. 721.

a Includes old demand notes; U.S. notes (gold reserve deducted since 1900); postal currency and fractional currency less the amounts officially estimated to have been destroyed; and also the deposits held by the Treasury for the retirement of Federal Reserve banknotes, and for national banknotes of national banks failed, in liquidation, and reducing circulation, which prior to 1890 were not included in the published debt statements. Does not include gold, silver, or currency certificates, or Treasury notes of 1890 for redemption of which an exact equivalent of the respective kinds of money or bullion was held in the Treasury.

Exclusive of the bonds issued to the Pacific Railways (provision having been made by law to secure the Treasury against both principal and interest) and the Navy pension fund (which was in no sense a debt, the principal being the property of the United States). The Statement of the Public Debt included the railroad bonds from issuance and the Navy fund from Sept. 1, 1896, until the Statement of June 30, 1890.

III.

The following three tables group respectively: population, and immigration figures; the distribution of the population by geographic region; the distribution of the population by size of area density.

TABLE III-1

ESTIMATED POPULATION OF THE UNITED STATES AND TOTAL YEARLY IMMIGRATION, 1850-1880

Population (in thousands)		Immigrants (Actual figures)	
1850	23,261	1850	369,980
1851	24,086	1851	379,466
1852	24,911	1852	371,603
1853	25,736	1853	368,645
1854	26,561	1854	427,833
1855	27,386	1855	200,877
1856	28,212	1856	200,436
1857	29,037	1857	251,306
1858	29,862	1858	123,126
1859	30,687	1859	121,282
1860	31,513	1860	153,640
1861	32,351	1861	91,918
1862	33,188	1862	91,985
1863	34,026	1863	176,282
1864	34,863	1864	193,418
1865	35,701	1865	248,120
1866	36,538	1866	318,568
1867	37,376	1867	315,722
1868	38,213	1868	138,840
1869	39,051	1869	352,768
1870	39,905	1870	387,203
1871	40,938	1871	321,350
1872	41,972	1872	404,806
1873	43,006	1873	459,803
1874	44,040	1874	313,339
1875	45,073	1875	227,498
1876	46,107	1876	169,986
1877	47,141	1877	141,857
1878	48,174	1878	138,469
1879	49,208	1879	177,826
1880	50,262	1880	457,257

SOURCE: Historical Statistics of the U.S. (1960), pp. 7 and 56-59.

TABLE III-2

POPULATION BY STATES AND REGIONS, 1850-1880

[Insofar as possible, population shown is that of present area of State.]

State	1850	1860	1870	1880
New England	2,728,116	3,135,283	3,487,924	4,010,529
Maine	583,169	628,279	626,915	648,936
New Hampshire	317,976	326,073	318,300	346,991
Vermont	314,120	315,098	330,551	332,286
Massachusetts	994,514	1,231,066	1,457,351	1,783,085
Rhode Island	147,545	174,620	217,353	276,531
Connecticut	370,792	460,147	537,454	622,700
Middle Atlantic	5,898,735	7,458,985	8,810,806	10,496,878
New York	3,097,394	3,880,735	4,382,759	5,082,871
New Jersey	489,555	672,035	906,096	1,131,116
Pennsylvania	2,311,786	2,906,215	3,521,951	4,282,891
East North Central	4,523,260	6,926,884	9,124,517	11,206,668
Ohio	1,980,329	2,339,511	2,665,260	3,198,062
Indiana	988,416	1,350,428	1,680,637	1,978,301
Illinois	851,470	1,711,951	2,539,891	3,077,871
Michigan	397,654	749,113	1,184,059	1,636,937
Wisconsin	305,391	775,881	1,054,670	1,315,497
West North Central	880,335	2,169,832	3,856,594	6,157,443
Minnesota	6,077	172,023	439,706	780,773
Iowa	192,214	674,913	1,194,020	1,624,615
Missouri	682,044	1,182,012	1,721,295	2,168,380
North Dakota		4,837[b]	2,405	36,909
South Dakota			11,776	98,268
Nebraska		28,841	122,993	452,402
Kansas		107,206	364,399	996,096
South Atlantic	4,679,090	5,364,703	5,853,610	7,597,197
Delaware	91,532	112,216	125,015	146,608
Maryland	583,034	687,049	780,894	934,943
Dist. of Columbia	51,687	75,080	131,700	177,624
Virginia	1,119,348	1,219,630	1,225,163	1,512,565
West Virginia	302,313	376,688	442,014	618,457
North Carolina	869,039	992,622	1,071,361	1,399,750
South Carolina	668,507	703,708	705,606	995,577
Georgia	906,185	1,057,286	1,184,109	1,542,180
Florida	87,445	140,424	187,748	269,493
East South Central	3,363,271	4,020,991	4,404,445	5,585,151
Kentucky	982,405	1,155,684	1,321,011	1,648,690
Tennessee	1,002,717	1,109,801	1,258,520	1,542,359

State	1850	1860	1870	1880
Alabama	771,623	964,201	996,992	1,262,505
Mississippi	606,526	791,305	827,922	1,131,597
West South Central	940,251	1,747,667	2,029,965	3,334,220
Arkansas	209,897	435,450	484,471	802,525
Louisiana	517,762	708,002	726,915	939,946
Oklahoma				
Texas	212,592	604,216	818,579	1,591,749
Mountain	72,927	174,923	315,385	653,119
Montana			20,595	39,159
Idaho			14,999	32,610
Wyoming			9,118	20,789
Colorado		34,277	39,864	194,327
New Mexico	61,547	93,516[c]	91,874	119,565
Arizona			9,658	40,440
Utah	11,380	40,273[d]	86,786	143,963
Nevada		6,857[e]	42,491	62,266
Pacific	105,891	444,053	675,125	1,114,578
Washington	1,201[a]	11,594[f]	23,955	75,116
Oregon	12,093	52,465	90,923	174,768
California	92,597	379,994	560,247	864,694

SOURCE: Historical Statistics of the U.S. (1960), pp. 12-13.

[a] Parts of Oregon Territory taken to form part of Washington Territory in 1853 and 1859.
[b] Dakota Territory.
[c] Includes area taken to form part of Arizona Territory in 1863.
[d] Utah Territory exclusive of that part of present State of Colorado taken to form Colorado Territory in 1861.
[e] Nevada Territory as organized in 1861.
[f] Includes population of Idaho and parts of Montana and Wyoming.

TABLE III-3

POPULATION IN URBAN AND RURAL TERRITORY, 1850-1880

	1850	1860	1870	1880
Urban [a]	3,543,716	6,216,518	9,902,361	14,129,735
Rural [b]	19,648,160	25,226,803	28,656,010	36,026,048

SOURCE: Adapted from Historical Statistics of the U.S. (1960), p. 14.

[a] Urban territories include population sizes over 1,000,000 but no less than 2,500. In 1880 there was one urban area with one million or more population. Over half of the urban areas so classified had between 2,500 to 25,000 population.
[b] Rural areas include population sizes of less than 2,500.

IV

The four tables in this unit may be used to appraise whether or not workers' wages were outstripping the cost of goods needed for everyday living. One can also trace the trend of wholesale prices in the economy to get a picture of whether or not producers were doing any better than the workers they employed. An impression of the behavior of prices on a regional basis can also be analyzed with the data of Table IV-1. The articles of Mitchell and Lerner in Part One should be re-read after examining the data in these tables.

TABLE IV-1

INDEXES OF WHOLESALE PRICES, THE UNITED STATES
AND THREE IMPORTANT MARKETS, 1850-1880

[1850-59 = 100]

Year	United States	New York	Philadelphia	Cincinnati
1850	90.6	86.2	88.8	80.3
1855	109.6	112.9	110.4	114.9
1856	109.5	107.7	110.2	113.0
1857	118.5	113.9	112.2	119.5
1858	98.2	95.4	99.7	95.3
1859	101.3	97.5	99.4	106.5
1860	99.6	95.4	98.7	102.7
1861	102.9	91.3	98.1	96.2
1862	119.5	106.7	131.9	—
1863	152.3	136.5	190.6	—
1864	220.9	198.0	288.4	—
1865	210.9	189.8	223.0	—
1866	197.4	178.5	193.2	—
1867	182.7	166.2	176.0	186.1
1868	177.3	162.1	170.4	—
1869	168.4	154.9	156.1	—
1870	149.1	138.5	134.7	—
1875	130.6	121.1	119.1	132.8
1880	109.6	102.6	99.1	109.8

SOURCE: Ethel Hoover, in Joint Economic Committee, Historical and Comparative Rates of Production, Productivity, and Prices, p. 395.

TABLE IV-2

INDEXES OF AVERAGE DAILY WAGES IN ALL INDUSTRIES, IN SELECTED INDUSTRIES, AND BY DEGREE OF SKILL: JANUARY AND JULY, 1860 TO 1880

[January 1860 = 100]

Year and Month	All industries	Cotton textiles and ginghams	Woolen textiles	Metals and metallic goods	Building trades	Stone	Railroads	Illuminating gas	City public works	Degree of skill	
										Unskilled men	Skilled men
1860: January	100	100	100	100	100	100	100	100	100	100	100
July	100	100	103	101	102	100	103	99	100	100	100
1861: January	102	100	106	102	101	128	105	100	100	100	100
July	99	102	107	103	102	91	105	99	91	98	100
1862: January	102	101	108	105	103	96	105	100	99	99	100
July	104	103	111	108	107	90	103	103	99	97	102
1863: January	116	108	120	114	118	100	106	125	122	111	105
July	119	108	114	120	118	113	109	142	123	114	112
1864: January	131	116	122	126	128	143	114	157	144	140	120
July	142	124	128	139	143	135	112	162	169	135	137
1865: January	152	135	142	149	145	155	144	176	175	152	150
July	155	146	142	150	158	151	146	175	178	155	150
1866: January	161	159	149	155	162	172	138	183	181	174	153
July	164	166	153	157	171	158	148	181	182	158	164
1867: January	168	168	149	158	174	168	155	183	186	182	166
July	168	169	148	159	186	162	160	185	188	159	166

1868: January	167	166	141	159	180	178	156	185	186	175	165
July	170	167	145	159	195	175	161	186	190	165	173
1869: January	176	168	149	160	195	196	156	195	192	191	170
July	179	173	146	160	199	205	162	189	191	205	171
1870: January	181	169	147	161	192	200	165	192	210	208	170
July	179	172	147	159	188	201	158	189	202	203	172
1871: January	183	182	148	158	178	188	171	199	213	198	175
July	184	184	149	159	187	198	170	195	204	195	179
1872: January	179	190	148	158	185	186	167	196	198	175	172
July	185	189	148	161	190	203	171	205	201	201	175
1873: January	180	185	149	161	180	182	158	221	196	182	171
July	183	189	150	163	186	198	162	204	195	187	175
1874: January	176	175	145	158	178	182	160	212	199	181	169
July	175	177	149	159	182	180	160	200	193	173	169
1875: January	167	162	150	151	168	167	161	200	193	160	160
July	163	163	152	148	170	161	158	182	181	150	160
1876: January	162	160	148	146	160	169	150	193	190	148	150
July	153	154	144	141	160	141	151	173	166	139	150
1877: January	147	149	139	135	143	140	147	184	150	134	144
July	143	150	144	133	140	130	142	165	140	125	140
1878: January	145	153	144	132	141	133	139	169	143	127	141
July	143	153	147	131	137	130	138	156	134	123	137
1879: January	142	149	142	127	139	125	146	162	135	122	138
July	139	149	143	128	139	125	147	157	123	122	135
1880: January	142	152	143	130	138	124	153	158	133	122	136
July	144	154	144	135	146	133	153	159	135	127	140

SOURCE: Adapted from Historical Statistics of the U.S. (1960), p. 90.

TABLE IV-3

Consumer Price Index, 1850-1880
[1851-59 = 100]

Year	Index	Year	Index
1850	94	1864	178
1855	105	1865	177
1856	103	1866	169
1857	106	1867	159
1858	100	1868	156
1859	101	1869	149
1860	101	1870	143
1861	102	1875	125
1862	114	1880	111
1863	141		

SOURCE: Ethel Hoover in Joint Economic Committee, Historical and Comparative Rates of Production, Productivity, and Prices, p. 397.

TABLE IV-4

Gainful Workers, 1850-1880
[in thousands of persons 10 years old and over]

Year	Total Workers	Year	Total Workers
1850	7,697	1870	12,925
1860	10,533	1880	17,392

SOURCE: Adapted from Historical Statistics of the U.S. (1960), p. 72.

V.

The following four tables contain information on agricultural production and bear directly on the earlier articles of Fite, Lerner, and Sellers. These data should be examined closely and compared with population growth and industrial production. It may also be of interest to note the change in population living in rural areas and the output of the farm population. Also, compare data in this section with imports of farm products into the United Kingdom in Tables VIII-4 and 5.

TABLE V-1

MISCELLANEOUS AGRICULTURAL STATISTICS, DECADE YEARS, 1850-1880

Item	1850	1860	1870	1880
1. Farm population (millions)	15.8	20.1	22.4	27.1
2. Persons engaged in agriculture (thousands)	4,902	6,208	6,850	8,585
3. Number of farms (thousands)	1,449	2,044	2,660	4,009
4. Index of farm wage rates (1910-14 = 100)	49	62	63	53
5. Index of farm machinery prices (1910-14 = 100)	187	161	251	124
6. Index of construction cost (1910-14 = 100)	58	64	92	74
7. Gross product per worker (1910-14 dollars)	294	332	362	439

SOURCE: Town & Rasmussen, "Farm Gross Product . . . ," Trends in the American Economy of the 19th Century, p. 269.

TABLE V-2

VALUE OF FARM GROSS OUTPUT AND PRODUCT, IN CURRENT AND CONSTANT DOLLARS, 1850-1880

[In millions of dollars]

Year	Gross output							Inter-mediate products consumed	Farm gross product, including improvements and manufactures			
	Total	Sales and home consumption of farm products			Livestock inventory changes	Gross rent from farm dwellings	Farm gross product		Total	Farm gross product	Improve-ments to farms	Value of home manu-factures
		Total	Livestock	Crops								
CURRENT DOLLARS												
1850	904	837	414	423	10	57	851	53	914	851	34	29
1860	1,579	1,469	700	769	21	89	1,484	95	1,556	1,484	47	25
1870	2,774	2,553	1,393	1,160	52	169	2,542	232	2,631	2,542	67	22
1880	3,263	3,021	1,498	1,523	39	203	2,967	296	3,045	2,967	68	10
1890	3,397	3,106	1,515	1,591	44	247	3,035	362	3,107	3,035	67	5
1900	4,298	3,912	2,047	1,865	79	307	3,799	499	3,857	3,799	55	3
CONSTANT (1910-14) DOLLARS												
1850	1,521	1,379	826	553	42	100	1,442	79	1,536	1,442	69	25
1860	2,186	1,985	1,088	897	60	141	2,059	127	2,156	2,059	76	21
1870	2,694	2,436	1,436	1,000	74	184	2,479	215	2,597	2,479	106	12
1880	4,129	3,784	2,006	1,778	68	277	3,770	359	3,906	3,770	128	8
1890	4,990	4,604	2,612	1,992	70	316	4,527	463	4,638	4,527	106	5
1900	6,409	5,903	3,100	2,803	109	397	5,740	669	5,837	5,740	94	3

SOURCE: Historical Statistics of the U.S. (1960), p. 284.

TABLE V-3

Number of Cattle, Hogs, Stock Sheep, Horses, and Mules, 1850-1890

Year	Cattle [1,000 head]	Hogs [1,000 head]	Stock Sheep [1,000 head]	Horses [1,000 head]	Mules [1,000 head]
1850[a]	16,779	30,354	21,723	4,337	559
1860[a]	25,620	33,513	22,471	6,249	1,151
1867	28,636	34,489	44,997	6,820	1,000
1868	29,238	33,304	43,808	7,051	1,057
1869	30,060	32,570	39,802	7,304	1,130
1870	31,082	33,781	36,449	7,633	1,245
1870[a]	23,821	25,135	28,478	7,145	1,125
1871	32,107	36,688	34,063	8,054	1,305
1872	33,078	39,296	34,312	8,441	1,360
1873	33,830	39,794	35,782	8,767	1,419
1874	34,821	38,377	36,234	9,055	1,485
1875	35,361	35,834	37,237	9,333	1,548
1876	36,140	35,715	37,477	9,606	1,608
1877	37,333	39,333	38,147	9,910	1,674
1878	39,396	43,375	38,942	10,230	1,746
1879	41,420	43,767	41,678	10,574	1,816
1880	43,347	44,327	44,867	10,903	1,878
1880[a]	39,676	49,773	42,192	10,357	1,813
1890	60,014	48,130	42,693	15,732	2,322
1890[a]	57,649	57,417	40,876	15,266	2,352

a Data comes from the census reports.

SOURCE: Compendium of the Ninth Census of the United States, 1870, pp. 709-710. Also Historical Statistics of the U.S. (1960), p. 290.

VI.

The four tables in this section bear directly on the Cochran-Salsbury argument and the article of Victor Clark. Can one determine from the growth rates of industry groups the general movement of the entire economy? Was the economy in a period of expansion when the War started?

TABLE VI-1

GROWTH OF MANUFACTURING PRODUCTION, 1849-1880

Year	Edwin Frickey's Index [1899 = 100]	Value Added by Manufacturing Current Prices	Prices of 1879
		[In millions of dollars]	
1849		447	488
1859		815	859
1860	16		
1861	16		
1862	15		
1863	17		
1864	18		
1865	17		
1866	21		
1867	22		
1868	23		
1869	25	1,631	1,078
1870	25		
1871	26		
1872	31		
1873	30		
1874	29		
1875	28		
1876	28		
1877	30		
1878	32		
1879	36	1,962	1,962
1880	42		

SOURCE for the Frickey Index: Edwin Frickey, Production in the United States, 1860-1914, Harvard Economic Studies (1947), p. 54, reprinted in Historical Statistics of the United States Colonial Times to 1957, p. 409.

SOURCE: for "Value Added by Manufacturing": Robert E. Gallman, "Commodity Output in the United States, 1839-1899," Studies in Income and Wealth, National Bureau of Economic Research (New York), vol. 24, Table A 13 (Princeton, 1960), reprinted in Historical Statistics of the United States Colonial Times to 1957, p. 402.

TABLE VI-2
INDUSTRIAL PRODUCTION, 1850-1880

Year	Pig Iron a [1,000 short tons]	Rails Produced b [1,000 long tons]	Steel Ingots and Castings c [1,000 long tons]	Raw Cotton Consumed d [1,000 bales]	Sugar Refined e [millions of lbs.]	Wheat Flour Milled f [millions of bbls.]
1850	631	—	—	—	—	—
1851	—	—	—	—	—	—
1852	560	—	—	—	—	—
1853	—	—	—	—	—	—
1854	736	—	—	—	—	—
1855	784	—	—	—	—	—
1856	883	—	—	—	—	—
1857	798	—	—	—	—	—
1858	705	—	—	—	—	—
1859	841	—	—	—	—	—
1860	920	183	—	845	788	39.8
1861	732	170	—	842	978	41.6
1862	788	191	—	369	590	42.4
1863	948	246	—	287	607	42.5
1864	1,136	299	—	220	565	42.4
1865	932	318	—	344	733	42.5
1866	1,350	385	—	615	886	42.8
1867	1,462	413	19.6	715	841	44.3
1868	1,603	452	26.8	844	1,149	44.9
1869	1,917	530	31.3	860	1,254	46.8
1870	1,865	554	68.8	797	1,196	47.9
1871	1,912	693	73.2	1,027	1,413	49.0
1872	2,855	893	143.0	1,147	1,454	49.2
1873	2,868	795	198.8	1.116	1,526	51.3
1874	2,689	651	215.7	1,213	1,638	53.6
1875	2,267	708	389.8	1,098	1,642	54.4
1876	2,093	785	533.2	1,256	1,583	56.1
1877	2,315	683	569.6	1,314	1,698	56.5
1878	2,577	788	732.0	1,459	1,778	59.8
1879	3,071	994	935.3	1,457	1,709	61.9
1880	4,295	1,305	1,247.3	1,501	1,988	64.3

a Historical Statistics of the United States Colonial Times to 1957, pp. 365-366.
b Ibid., pp. 416-417.   c Ibid.   d Ibid., p. 415.   e Ibid.   f Ibid.

TABLE VI-3

Mineral Production, 1850-1880

Year	Copper Recoverable from ore mined [short tons]	Iron Ore [long tons]	Lead Production Primary Refined from domestic and foreign ores [short tons]	Zinc Production Primary smelter and slab zinc from domestic and foreign ores [short tons]	Silver thousands of fine troy ounces	Gold thousands of fine troy ounces
1850	728		22,000		39	2,419
1851	1,008		18,500		39	2,661
1852	1,232		15,700		39	2,902
1853	2,240		16,800		39	3,144
1854	2,520		16,500		39	2,902
1855	3,360		15,800		39	2,661
1856	4,480		16,000		39	2,661
1857	5,376		15,800		39	2,661
1858	6,160		15,300	20	39	2,419
1859	7,056		16,400	50	77	2,419
1860	8,064	2,873,000	15,600	800	116	2,225
1861	8,400		14,100	1,500	1,547	2,080
1862	10,580		14,200	1,500	3,480	1,896
1863	9,520		14,800	1,700	6,574	1,935
1864	8,960		15,300	1,800	8,508	2,230
1865	9,520		14,700	2,100	8,701	2,575
1866	9,968		16,100	2,000	7,734	2,588
1867	11,200		15,200	3,200	10,441	2,502
1868	12,992		16,400	3,700	9,281	2,322
1869	14,000		17,500	4,300	9,281	2,395
1870	14,112	3,832,000	17,830	5,400	12,375	2,419
1871	14,560		19,970	6,900	17,789	2,104
1872	14,000		25,750	7,800	22,236	1,742
1873	17,360		41,940	9,600	27,650	1,742
1874	19,600		51,230	13,100	28,868	1,620
1875	20,160	4,018,000	58,590	16,700	24,530	1,619
1876	21,280		62,940	17,000	29,996	1,932
1877	23,520		80,380	15,600	30,778	2,269
1878	24,080		89,130	19,600	35,022	2,477
1879	25,760		90,840	21,300	31,566	1,882
1880	30,240	7,120,000	95,725	25,100	30,319	1,742

SOURCE: Historical Statistics of the United States Colonial Times to 1957, pp. 365-366, 368-371.

TABLE VI-4

PEAKS AND TROUGHS OF LONG SWINGS IN THE RATE OF GROWTH OF OUTPUT AND ECONOMIC ACTIVITY, 1814-1886

		Duration (Years) of	
Peak	Trough	Expansion Phase	Contraction Phase
1814	1819	....	5
1834	1840	15	6
1846	1858	6	12
1864.25	1874.25	6.25	10
1881	1886.5	6.75	5.5

SOURCE: Moses Abramovitz, Joint Economic Committee, Historical and Comparative Rates of Production, Productivity, and Prices, p. 435.

VII.

Transportation statistics are especially important in appraising the long-term impact of the War. Notice the regional data for the War and postwar years in Table VII-3 and 4. Do these data support or refute any generalizations in the articles of Mitchell, Clark, and Cochran?

TABLE VII-1
TRANSPORTATION, 1850-1880

| Year | Railroads | | Merchant Vessels built and documented by type | | | | |
| | Miles of road operated as of Dec. 31 | Miles Built | All Vessels | | Vessels by Type | | |
			Number	Gross tons	Steam (tons)	Sailing[a] (tons)	Canal and Barge (tons)
1850	9,021	1,261	1,360	272,218	56,911	215,307	
1851	10,982	1,274	1,357	298,203	78,197	220,006	
1852	12,908	2,288	1,444	351,493	98,624	252,869	
1853	15,360	2,170	1,710	425,572	109,402	316,170	
1854	16,720	3,442	1,774	535,616	91,037	444,579	
1855	18,374	2,453	2,024	583,450	78,127	505,323	
1856	22,076	1,471	1,703	469,393	74,865	394,528	
1857	24,503	2,077	1,443	378,804	74,459	304,345	
1858	26,968	1,966	1,241	244,712	65,374	179,338	
1859	28,789	1,707	875	156,602	35,305	121,297	
1860	30,626	1,500	1,071	214,798	69,370	145,428	
1861	31,286	1,016	1,146	233,194	60,986	172,208	
1862	32,120	720	864	175,076	55,449	119,627	
1863	33,170	574	1,816	311,045	94,233	216,812	
1864	33,908	947	2,388	415,740	147,499	268,241	
1865	35,085	819	1,789	394,523	146,433	248,090	
1866	36,801	1,404	1,898	336,146	125,183	210,963	
1867	39,050	2,541	1,518	305,594	72,010	233,584	
1868	42,229	2,468	1,802	385,304	63,940	142,742	78,622
1869	46,844	4,103	1,726	275,230	65,066	149,029	61,135
1870	52,922	5,658	1,618	276,953	70,621	146,340	59,992
1871	60,301	6,660	1,755	273,227	87,842	97,179	88,206
1872	66,171	7,439	1,643	209,052	62,210	76,291	70,551
1873	70,268	5,217	2,261	359,246	88,011	144,629	126,606
1874	72,385	2,584	2,147	432,725	101,930	216,316	114,479
1875	74,096	1,606	1,301	297,639	62,460	206,884	28,295
1876	76,808	2,575	1,112	203,586	69,251	118,672	15,663
1877	79,082	2,575	1,029	176,592	47,514	106,331	22,747
1878	81,747	2,428	1,258	235,504	81,860	106,066	47,578
1879	86,556	5,006	1,132	193,031	86,361	66,867	39,803
1880	93,262	n.a.[b]	905	157,410	78,854	59,057	19,499

a Includes canalboats and barges prior to 1868.   b n.a. = not available.

SOURCE: Historical Statistics of the United States Colonial Times to 1957, pp. 427-428, 447-448.

TABLE VII-2

Railroad Mileage Increase by Groups of States

	1850	1860	1870	1880	1890
New England	2,507	3,660	4,494	5,982	6,831
Middle States	3,202	6,705	10,964	15,872	21,536
Southern States	2,036	8,838	11,192	14,778	29,209
Western States and Territories	1,276	11,400	24,587	52,589	62,394
Pacific States and Territories		23	1,677	4,080	9,804

SOURCE: Chauncey M. Depew (ed.), One Hundred Years of American Commerce, 1795-1895, p. 111.

TABLE VII-3

Statement of Tons of Property Arriving at Tide-water, via the Erie Canal[a]

Year	From Western states	From New York State
1850	841,501	530,358
1851	1,045,820	462,857
1852	1,151,978	492,726
1853	1,213,690	637,748
1854	1,094,391	602,167
1855	1,092,876	327,839
1856	1,212,550	374,580
1857	1,019,998	197,201
1858	1,273,099	223,588
1859	1,036,634	414,699
1860	1,896,975	379,086
1861	2,158,425	291,184
1862	2,594,837	322,257
1863	2,279,252	368,437
1864	1,907,136	239,498
1865	1,904,156	174,205
1866	2,235,716	287,948
1867	2,129,405	96,707
1868	2,215,222	163,350
1869	2,028,568	229,121
1870	2,048,947	241,751

a Assembly Document No. 31, Table No. 28, 1877.
SOURCE: Noble Whitford, History of the Canal System of the State of New York, (Albany, 1906), vol. I, p. 910.

TABLE VII-4

Massachusetts Steam Railroad Statistics, 1859-1880

Year	Length of Road in Miles	Length of Double Track in Miles	No. of Passengers Carried	Tons of Freight Transported
1859	1,463	321	12,356,686	3,808,725
1860	1,566	392	12,801,097	4,094,369
1861				
1862	1,608	353	12,020,315	3,877,717
1863	1,414	350	14,043,554	4,595,029
1864	1,406	350	18,206,023	5,177,445
1865	1,405	364	20,278,055	5,277,563
1866	1,254[a]	387	22,126,881	6,046,546
1867	1,232	403	23,660,401	6,113,442
1868	1,264	416	24,916,021	6,537,124
1869	1,241	435	28,126,391	7,378,083
1870	1,257	438	24,721,531[b]	6,859,684[b]
1871	1,361	506	32,816,811	8,934,104
1872	1,804	534	36,059,663	11,472,550
1873	1,734	436	42,398,001	12,431,118
1874				
1875	1,816	440	42,139,697	11,072,312
1876	1,837	439	41,135,229	11,327,502
1877	1,854	440	38,450,823	11,910,663
1878	1,850	452	37,318,427	12,186,545
1879	1,861	450	39,217,634	14,401,877
1880	1,883	454	45,151,152	17,221,567

a Reduction due to exclusion of mileage operated by railroads incorporated in Massachusetts in other states. Such mileage formerly included.

b Figures for a ten-month period only.

SOURCE: Returns of the railroad corporations in Massachusetts 1860-69 and the Massachusetts Railroad Commissioners' Reports 1871-81.

TABLE VII-5

Year	Federal Expenditures for Rivers, etc. Thousands of dollars	Land Grants (in thousands of acres)			
		Total	Railroads	Wagon Roads	Canals
1850	42	....	....	....	......
1851	70	3,752	3,752	....	......
1852	40	1,773	1,773	....	......
1853	489	3,379	2,629	....	750
1854	937	....	....	....	......
1855	791	....	....	....	......
1856	161	14,085	14,085	....	......
1857	268	6,689	6,689	....	......
1858	427	....	....	....	......
1859	290	....	....	....	......
1860	228	....	....	....	......
1861	172	....	....	....	......
1862	37	....	....	....	......
1863	65	31,401	30,877	524	......
1864	102	2,349	2,349	....	......
1865	305	42,794	41,452	941	401
1866	295	200	....	....	200
1867	1,217	25,173	23,535	1,538	100
1868	3,457	....	....	....	......
1869	3,545	105	....	105	......
1870	3,528	129	129	....	......
1871	4,421	3,253	3,253	....	......
1872	4,962	....	....	....	......
1873	6,312				
1874	5,704				
1875	6,434				
1876	5,736				
1877	4,655				
1878	3,791				
1879	8,267				
1880	8,080				

NOTE: Figures include only the area of lands for which title passed to the grantee States and corporations. For the series presented, the areas shown in the instruments of title which were issued for each grant over the years were totaled and shown as of the fiscal year in which the grant was originally enacted, even though in certain instances grants were revived at a later date after the expiration of statutory time limits, while others were enlarged by subsequent legislation.

SOURCE: Historical Statistics of the U. S. Colonial Times to 1957, pp. 233, 239, 455.

VIII.

Compare especially the imports into the United Kingdom originating from the United States. Did the volume of commodity imports warrant concern over tariff levels? Is the wheat vs. cotton thesis supported in the data of Tables VIII-3, 4, and 5?

TABLE VIII-1

VALUE OF EXPORTS AND IMPORTS: 1850-1880 (UNITED STATES)

[In millions of dollars. For years ending September 30, 1790-1842; June 30, 1843-1915; thereafter, calendar years]

Year	Total, gold, silver, and merchandise			Gold			Silver			Merchandise[1]				
	Exports	Imports	Excess of exports (+) or imports (−)	Exports	Imports	Excess of exports (+) or imports (−)	Exports	Imports	Excess of exports (+) or imports (−)	Exports and reexports			General imports	Excess of exports (+) or imports (−)
										Total	Exports of U.S. merchandise	Re-exports		
1850	152	178	−26	5	2	+3	3	3	¹	144	135	9	174	−29
1851	218	216	+2	23	4	+19	7	2	+5	189	179	10	211	−22
1852	210	213	−3	40	4	+36	3	2	+1	167	155	12	207	−40
1853	231	268	−37	25	2	+23	2	2	¹	203	190	14	264	−60
1854	278	305	−26	40	3	+37	1	4	−3	237	215	22	298	−61
1855	275	261	+14	55	1	+54	1	3	−1	219	193	26	258	−39
1856	327	315	+12	45	1	+44	1	3	−2	281	266	15	310	−29
1857	363	361	+2	65	7	+59	4	6	−2	294	279	15	348	−55
1858	325	283	+42	50	12	+38	3	8	−5	272	251	21	263	+9
1859	357	339	+18	61	2	+59	3	5	−3	293	278	15	331	−38
1860	400	362	+38	58	3	+56	8	6	+2	334	316	17	354	−20

TABLE VIII-1 (Continued)

1861	249	336	−86	27	42	−15	2	4	−2	220	205	15	289	−70
1862	228	206	+22	35	14	+22	1	3	−1	191	180	11	189	+1
1863	268	253	+15	62	6	+57	2	4	−2	204	186	18	243	−39
1864	264	330	−65	101	11	+89	5	2	+3	159	144	15	316	−158
1865	234	249	−15	58	6	+52	9	3	+6	166	137	29	239	−73
1866	435	446	−11	71	8	+63	15	3	+12	349	338	11	435	−86
1867	355	418	−62	39	17	+22	22	5	+17	295	280	15	396	−101
1868	376	372	+4	72	9	+64	21	5	+16	282	269	13	357	−75
1869	343	437	−94	36	14	+22	21	6	+15	286	275	11	418	−131
1870	451	462	−11	34	12	+22	25	14	+10	393	377	16	436	−43
1871	541	541	-	67	7	+60	32	14	+17	443	428	14	520	−77
1872	524	640	−116	50	9	+41	30	5	+25	444	428	16	627	−182
1873	607	664	−57	45	9	+36	40	13	+27	522	505	17	642	−120
1874	653	596	+57	34	20	+15	33	9	+24	586	569	17	567	+19
1875	606	554	+52	67	14	+53	25	7	+18	513	499	14	533	−20
1876	597	477	+120	31	8	+23	25	8	+17	540	526	15	461	+80
1877	659	492	+167	27	26	[1]	30	15	+15	602	590	13	451	+151
1878	729	467	+262	9	13	−4	25	16	+8	695	681	14	437	+258
1879	735	466	+269	5	6	−1	20	15	+6	710	698	12	446	+265
1880	853	761	+92	4	81	−77	14	12	+1	836	824	12	668	+168

[1] Less than $500,000.

SOURCE: Historical Statistics of the U.S. (1960), pp. 537-538.

TABLE VIII-2
VALUE OF MERCHANDISE IMPORTS AND DUTIES 1850-1880
(UNITED STATES)

	Value of imports			Duties calculated	Ratio of duties calculated to total imports	
	Total	Free	Dutiable		Free and dutiable	Dutiable
	15	16	17	18	19	20
Year	Mil. dol.	Mil. dol.	Mil. dol.	Mil. dol.	Percent	Percent
1880	628	208	420	183	29.12	43.54
1879	440	143	297	133	30.33	44.90
1878	439	141	297	127	29.00	42.77
1877	440	140	299	128	29.20	42.91
1876	465	140	324	145	31.25	44.76
1875	526	146	380	155	29.36	40.66
1874	568	151	416	161	28.29	38.58
1873	663	178	485	185	27.90	38.12
1872	560	47	513	213	37.99	41.46
1871	500	40	460	202	40.51	44.04
1870	426	20	406	192	44.89	47.13
1869	394	22	373	177	44.76	47.37
1868	345	15	330	161	46.56	48.70
1867	378	17	361	169	44.56	46.66
1866	423	57	366	177	41.81	48.33
1865	210	40	170	81	38.46	47.56
1864	301	38	263	96	32.04	36.69
1863	225	30	195	64	28.28	32.62
1862	178	50	128	47	26.08	36.20
1861	275	67	207	39	14.21	18.84
1860	336	68	268	53	15.67	19.67
1859	317	67	250	49	15.43	19.56
1858	243	55	187	42	17.33	22.44
1857	334	50	284	64	19.09	22.45
1856	296	50	246	64	21.68	26.05
1855	232	30	202	54	23.36	26.83
1854	276	23	254	65	23.52	25.61
1853	250	25	225	58	23.37	25.94
1852	195	22	174	48	24.35	27.38
1851	200	18	183	49	24.26	26.63
1850	164	16	148	40	24.50	27.14

SOURCE: Historical Statistics of the U.S. (1960), p. 539.

TABLE VIII-3

QUANTITIES OF WHEAT AND WHEAT MEAL AND FLOUR, AND OF OTHER KINDS OF GRAIN, IMPORTED INTO THE UNITED KINGDOM — 1858-1872

WHEAT — TOTAL OF GRAIN and FLOUR in equivalent Weight of GRAIN (1 cwt. of wheat flour = 1¼cwt. of wheat in grain).

COUNTRIES	1858	1859	1860	1861	1862	1863	1864	1865	1866	1867	1868	1869	1870	1871	1872
	Cwts.	Cwts.	Cwts.	Cwts.	Cwts.	Cwts.	Cwts.	Cwts.	Cwts.	Cwts.	Cwts.	Cwts.	Cwts.	Cwts.	Cwts.
Russia, North Ports	695,494	885,569	967,801	704,444	674,441	675,312	1,317,454	844,155	1,751,937	1,491,823	1,683,813	1,836,674	1,866,299	3,957,081	2,080,939
South Ports	1,958,389	2,951,885	4,692,170	3,836,039	5,081,348	3,863,622	3,811,956	7,249,834	7,429,495	12,674,971	8,371,525	7,350,562	8,460,545	11,732,862	15,858,038
Sweden	43,879	149,273	142,695	66,352	19,280	26,810	80,479	26,808	30,009	18,244	24,509	62,955	37,322	20,538	44,582
Denmark, Including the Duchies up to 1860.	1,306,406	1,331,891	1,182,280	674,325	419,148	384,894	776,175	687,763	563,007	564,963	817,173	779,884	580,243	293,432	611,283
Germany, exclusive of the Duchies up to 1860	4,210,117	4,561,521	6,904,819	6,658,462	7,930,849	5,728,626	6,842,721	7,224,371	6,801,657	7,873,216	7,224,597	7,546,688	4,487,773	4,258,823	5,183,601
Holland	358,434	218,760	129,808	50,872	12,794	11,708	18,786	51,615	93,096	15,938	60,132	205,760	26,308	12,398	61,912
France	5,581,064	8,124,978	4,583,412	1,359,882	1,961,835	1,857,403	2,854,424	6,058,902	8,023,530	2,140,832	846,863	2,153,350	1,060,120	182,262	4,553,781
Spain	23,250	10,452	548,424	1,297,257	316,882	11,393	1,980	133,855	863,529	452,680	2,982	43,151	8,395	16,990	643,087
Austrian Territories, including Venetia from 1858 to 1860	85,532	61,508	330,132	465,583	831,185	107,379	43,765	612,725	1,390,935	706,819	1,250,515	1,345,786	463,683	836,243	456,966
Turkey	324,688	191,291	288,596	411,277	1,284,590	282,998	355,086	386,142	387,252	1,905,195	1,730,492	1,396,328	361,164	827,265	563,779
—— Wallachia & Moldavia	578,823	131,317	422,068	591,491	474,976	132,526	127,908	188,043	141,181	542,023	1,336,105	990,611	132,382	594,481	266,163
Egypt	2,013,491	1,634,536	858,575	1,474,480	3,304,579	2,322,636	367,462	10,063	33,831	1,471,756	3,237,380	1,020,289	106,701	908,847	2,361,042
British N. America	702,838	170,821	1,310,652	3,387,949	5,118,698	3,198,187	1,831,897	528,456	59,601	835,006	798,505	3,396,511	3,402,690	3,782,776	2,157,170
United States	4,782,785	430,504	9,315,125	15,610,472	21,765,087	11,869,179	10,077,431	1,498,579	986,229	5,091,733	6,753,389	15,320,257	15,057,236	15,625,331	9,634,349
Chile	4	2	33,545	364,246	347,341	282,311	198,231	169,862	341,999	2,097,978	1,477,536	580,349	643,347	589,951	1,677,908
Other Countries	535,747	643,426	131,824	693,574	499,361	132,908	131,448	172,379	474,391	1,253,603	890,529	418,617	211,907	722,947	1,458,296
Total	23,200,941	21,497,734	31,841,926	37,646,705	50,012,394	30,887,892	28,837,203	25,843,552	29,371,679	39,136,780	36,506,045	44,447,772	36,906,115	44,362,227	47,612,896

SOURCE: Statistical Abstract for the United Kingdom in Each of the Last Fifteen Years from 1858-1872 (London, 1873), p. 44.

TABLE VIII-4

Quantities of Maize (Corn) Imported into the United Kingdom — 1858-1872

COUNTRIES	1858	1859	1860	1861	1862	1863	1864	1865	1866	1867	1868	1869	1870	1871	1872
	Cwts.	Cwts.	Cwts.	Cwts.	Cwts.	Cwts.	Cwts.	Cwts.	Cwts.	Cwts.	Cwts.	Cwts.	Cwts.	Cwts.	Cwts.
Russia	1,331,554	1,085,477	1,111,976	528,952	935,070	987,236	1,401,343	1,181,756	461,930	247,460	664,881	604,618	2,511,725	2,086,488	423,851
France	422,087	236,370	643,539	74,966	13,187	42,998	167,129	71,935	464,161	1,000,824	178,461	166,312	371,682	96,623	10,902
Austrian Territories, including Venetia from 1858 to 1860	706,538	552,801	80,289	188,490	—	206,876	79,538	26,617	45,863	526,263	1,079,564	2,927,056	1,225,914	156,049	155,656
Turkey	696,846	798,394	1,116,938	2,404,367	1,704,617	4,314,257	3,682,585	3,159,597	4,768,370	923,652	2,913,608	9,033,781	9,607,806	4,270,220	1,639,615
Wallachia & Moldavia	1,849,701	2,381,876	2,811,660	1,330,384	536,751	1,466,173	629,210	538,251	604,503	107,316	1,113,523	1,974,826	2,213,474	1,278,051	948,413
Egypt	295,637	312,493	137,700	266,049	235,693	431,494	9,238	—	3,903	219,988	537,726	10,866	11,214	75,905	372,001
British North America	5,049	1,470	12,673	506,249	1,425,892	394,440	9,641	302,173	858,578	338,032	339,831	33,847	12,400	1,346,069	3,557,896
United States	1,692,583	14,417	1,844,289	7,385,717	6,511,718	4,548,386	294,263	1,766,305	6,953,811	4,799,385	4,009,770	1,354,844	23,063	7,319,246	16,980,683
Other Countries	503,541	249,429	177,059	559,192	331,890	344,734	12,991	49,399	161,744	387,509	634,862	1,557,963	779,505	196,372	443,653
Total	7,503,536	5,632,727	7,936,123	13,244,366	11,694,818	12,736,594	6,285,938	7,096,033	14,322,863	8,540,429	11,472,226	17,664,113	16,756,783	16,825,023	24,532,670

SOURCE: Statistical Abstract for the United Kingdom in Each of the Last Fifteen Years from 1858-1872, p. 46.

TABLE VIII-5

Quantities of Raw Cotton Imported into the United Kingdom from Various Countries, Total Exported, and Excess of Imports

Years	The United States	Mexico	British West India Islands and British Guiana	New Granada and Venezuela	Brazil	The Mediterranean, exclusive of Egypt	Egypt	British Possessions in the East Indies	China	Japan	Other Countries	Total Imported	Total Exported	Excess of Imports
	Lbs.	Lbs.	Lbs.	Lbs.	Lbs.	Lbs.	Lbs.	Lbs.	Lbs.	Lbs.	Lbs.	Lbs.	Lbs.	Lbs.
1861	819,500,528	—	486,304	154,896	17,290,336	587,104	40,892,096	369,040,448	—	—	9,033,024	1,256,984,736	298,287,920	958,696,816
1862	13,524,224	3,131,520	5,563,376	1,170,736	23,339,008	6,225,856	59,012,464	392,654,528	1,766,016	224	17,585,344	523,973,296	214,714,528	309,258,768
1863	6,394,080	19,278,112	25,181,856	2,623,600	22,603,168	13,806,576	93,552,368	434,420,784	30,856,336	711,424	20,655,824	670,084,128	241,352,496	428,731,632
1864	14,198,688	25,539,024	26,738,992	6,500,368	38,017,504	21,755,216	125,493,648	506,527,392	86,157,008	9,404,304	33,770,240	894,102,384	244,702,304	649,400,080
1865	135,832,480	36,664,880	16,536,912	14,699,328	55,403,152	27,239,072	176,838,144	445,947,600	35,855,792	2,982,896	30,501,744	978,502,000	302,908,928	675,593,072
1866	520,061,136	352,240	3,600,352	11,599,392	68,524,400	11,510,688	118,260,800	615,302,240	5,837,440	46,032	22,419,376	1,377,514,096	388,981,936	988,532,160
1867	528,166,800	2,464	4,810,288	9,713,872	70,430,080	6,780,480	126,285,264	498,317,008	527,184	—	17,852,464	1,262,885,904	350,635,936	912,249,968
1868	574,478,016	—	2,725,856	4,808,160	98,796,768	6,702,304	129,182,928	493,706,640	—	21,504	18,339,440	1,328,761,616	322,713,328	1,006,048,288
1869	457,358,944	40,544	1,695,568	8,085,728	79,417,968	13,506,640	160,450,280	481,440,176	448	—	19,574,936	1,221,571,232	274,289,344	947,281,888
1870	716,248,848	2,016	2,314,256	4,767,056	64,234,688	11,510,912	143,710,448	341,536,608	10,528	—	55,031,760	1,339,367,120	238,175,840	1,101,191,280
1871	1,038,677,920	—	2,671,536	6,582,240	86,158,800	3,777,424	176,166,480	431,209,744	102,144	—	32,793,488	1,778,139,776	362,075,616	1,416,064,160
1872	625,600,080	31,136	1,450,960	7,960,624	112,509,824	8,031,744	177,581,712	443,234,736	252,112	—	32,184,544	1,408,837,472	273,005,040	1,135,832,432
1873	832,573,616	28,448	1,070,160	3,973,088	72,480,800	8,670,816	204,977,136	367,649,744	1,016,848	—	35,155,568	1,527,596,224	220,000,256	1,307,595,968
1874	874,926,864	16,464	502,768	6,391,952	79,501,408	2,195,312	172,317,488	412,025,040	398,832	—	18,588,304	1,566,864,432	258,967,632	1,307,896,800
1875	841,333,472	—	662,928	4,195,632	71,859,536	5,835,760	163,912,336	385,685,552	583,520	—	18,282,432	1,492,351,168	262,853,808	1,229,497,360

SOURCE: Statistical Abstract for the United Kingdom for 1861-1875 (London, 1876), pp. 50-51.

IX

Was the rate of growth in the number and assets of national banks a factor ignored in any of the preceding arguments? Of what significance is the growth of life insurance companies to the post-Civil War development of the economy?

TABLE IX-1

NATIONAL BANKS — NUMBER OF BANKS AND PRINCIPAL ASSETS
AND LIABILITIES: 1863 TO 1880

[Money figures in millions of dollars. As of June 30 or nearest available date]

Year	Number of banks	Total assets or liabilities	Assets		
			Total loans	Total investments [1]	Total cash
1880	2,076	2,036	995	452	518
1879	2,048	2,020	836	715	398
1878	2,056	1,751	835	460	388
1877	2,078	1,774	902	431	371
1876	2,091	1,826	934	427	400
1875	2,076	1,913	973	443	432
1874	1,983	1,852	926	451	430
1873	1,968	1,851	926	445	439
1872	1,853	1,771	872	450	412
1871	1,723	1,703	789	456	422
1870	1,612	1,566	719	453	361
1869	1,619	1,564	686	466	382
1868	1,640	1,572	656	507	384
1867	1,636	1,494	589	522	361
1866	1,634	1,476	550	468	439
1865	1,294	1,127	362	[2]394	344
1864	467	252	71	[2]93	86
1863	66	17	6	[2]6	5

	Liabilities		
Year	Total deposits	National bank-notes	Capital accounts
1880	1,085	318	625
1879	1,090	307	615
1878	814	300	629
1877	818	290	656
1876	842	294	679
1875	897	318	687
1874	828	339	676
1873	836	339	662
1872	805	327	626
1871	791	308	594
1870	706	291	562
1869	716	293	549
1868	745	295	530
1867	685	292	512
1866	695	268	494
1865	614	[3] 132	380
1864	147	[3] 126	79
1863	10	......	7

[1] Before 1896, includes securities borrowed.
[2] U. S. Government securities only.
[3] Includes State banknotes outstanding.

SOURCE: Historical Statistics of U.S. (1960), pp. 626-627.

TABLE IX-2
CURRENCY IN CIRCULATION, BY KIND: 1860 TO 1880
[in thousands of dollars]

Year	Gold coin	Gold certificates	Silver dollars	Silver certificates	State banknotes	Subsidiary silver	Fractional currency	Other U.S. currency	U.S. notes	National bank-notes
1880	225,696	7,964	20,111	5,790	......	48,512	......	......	327,895	337,415
1879	110,505	15,280	8,036	414	......	61,347	......	......	301,644	321,405
1878	84,740	24,898	1,209	7	806	58,918	16,368	428	320,906	311,724
1877	78,111	32,298	......	......	909	42,885	20,242	456	337,899	301,289
1876	74,839	24,175	......	......	1,047	26,055	32,939	500	331,447	316,121
1875	64,446	17,549	......	......	964	22,141	37,905	551	349,686	340,547
1874	78,948	18,015	......	......	1,162	14,940	38,234	620	371,421	340,266
1873	62,718	34,251	......	......	1,399	13,679	38,076	701	348,464	338,962
1872	76,575	26,412	......	......	1,701	12,064	36,403	849	346,169	329,037
1871	72,391	17,790	......	......	1,968	12,022	34,446	1,064	343,069	311,406
1870	81,183	32,085	......	......	2,223	8,978	34,379	2,507	324,963	288,648
1869	62,129	29,956	......	......	2,559	5,695	30,442	3,343	314,767	291,750
1868	63,758	17,643	......	......	3,164	6,520	28,999	28,859	328,572	294,369
1867	72,882	18,678	......	......	4,484	7,082	26,306	123,727	319,438	286,764
1866	109,705	10,505	......	......	19,996	8,241	24,687	162,739	327,792	276,013
1865	148,557	......	......	......	142,920	8,713	21,729	236,567	378,917	146,138
1864	184,346	......	......	......	179,158	9,375	19,133	169,252	415,116	31,235
1863	[1]260,000	......	......	......	238,677	[1]11,000	15,884	93,230	312,481	......
1862	[1]283,000	......	......	......	183,792	[1]13,000	......	53,040	72,866	......
1861	266,400	......	......	......	202,006	[1]16,000	......	......	......	......
1860	207,305	......	......	......	207,102	[1]21,000	......	......	......	......

SOURCE: Historical Statistics of U.S. (1960), pp. 648-649.
[1] Total stock; circulation not available.

TABLE IX-3

PRIVATE INSURANCE

ASSETS, EARNING RATE, LIABILITIES, AND CAPITAL AND SURPLUS OF U.S. LIFE INSURANCE COMPANIES: 1854 TO 1880

[In millions of dollars, except net rate of interest earned on assets. As of December 31]

Year	Assets						Net rate of interest earned on assets	Liabilities		Capital and surplus
	Total	Bonds	Stocks	Mortgages	Real estate	Other [1]		Total	Policy reserves	
1880	418.1	124.8	(²)	164.8	51.6	76.9	5.48	346.5	338.8	71.6
1879	401.7	116.2	(²)	173.8	49.2	62.5	5.83	336.3	328.3	65.4
1878	404.1	112.8	(²)	189.1	42.8	59.4	5.94	339.6	329.5	64.5
1877	396.4	100.8	(²)	201.1	31.6	62.9	6.37	334.8	326.3	61.6
1876	407.4	85.7	(²)	217.9	29.2	74.6	6.55	346.3	337.5	61.1
1875	403.1	73.9	(²)	219.7	22.6	86.9	6.79	342.3	334.1	60.8
1874	387.3	65.3	(²)	210.1	18.3	93.6	6.89	328.4	320.3	58.9
1873	360.1	56.6	(²)	189.8	15.0	98.7	6.93	311.5	300.2	48.6
1872	335.2	54.7	(²)	164.3	12.5	103.7	6.90	288.3	277.4	46.9
1871	302.6	52.4	(²)	134.9	10.8	104.5	.....	254.6	243.3	48.0
1870	269.5	48.1	(²)	108.0	9.0	104.4	.....	221.0	209.3	48.5

Year									
1869	229.1	45.1	(²)	83.6	7.0	93.4	.....	180.3	170.9	48.8
1868	176.8	40.9	(²)	58.0	4.8	73.1	.....	135.8	126.0	41.0
1867	125.6	33.2	(²)	37.0	3.6	51.8	.....	88.6	81.2	37.0
1866	91.6	28.3	(²)	23.7	2.3	37.3	.....	65.6	59.8	26.0
1865	64.2	22.4	(²)	16.5	1.7	23.6	.....	49.3	42.8	14.9
1864	49.0	.....	.....	.....	.....	.....	.....	34.7	31.0	14.3
1863	37.8	.....	.....	.....	.....	.....	.....	28.6	24.0	9.2
1862	30.1	.....	.....	.....	.....	.....	.....	23.8	17.5	6.3
1861	26.7	.....	.....	.....	.....	.....	.....	18.3	15.3	8.4
1860	24.1	.....	.....	.....	.....	.....	.....	17.1	14.4	7.0
1859	20.5	.....	.....	.....	.....	.....	.....	15.4	.....	5.1
1858	15.9	.....	.....	.....	.....	.....	.....	.....	.....	.....
1857	14.0	.....	.....	.....	.....	.....	.....	.....	.....	.....
1856	15.0	.....	.....	.....	.....	.....	.....	.....	.....	.....
1855	12.7	.....	.....	.....	.....	.....	.....	.....	.....	.....
1854	11.4	.....	.....	.....	.....	.....	.....	.....	.....	.....

¹ Includes cash, policy loans, collateral loans, due and deferred premiums, and all other assets.
² Incuded with bonds.
SOURCE: Historical Statistics of U.S. (1960), p. 676.

ACKNOWLEDGMENTS

An editor, for better or worse, imposes his own tastes and interests in selecting the few out of the many studies that attract his attention. I admit to the charge openly. While I take sole responsibility for the final selections, I must thank Paul Goodman and Stephen Salsbury, both of Harvard University, for their generous assistance in all ways. Mr. Salsbury, in addition to preparing the original essay printed for the first time in this volume, also gathered much of the original data reproduced in the statistical supplement. Ruth Cohen of the Harvard Business School was also extremely helpful in solving many of the secretarial problems that confront every editor. Acknowledgment to the authors and publishers for permission to reprint their work is noted below.

Agricultural History Society, for Eugene Lerner, "Southern Output and Agricultural Income, 1860-1880", from *Agricultural History*, vol. XXXIII (July, 1959), pp. 117-125. Also reprinted by permission of the author.

University of Chicago Press and the *Journal of Political Economy*:

Wesley C. Mitchell, *A History of the Greenbacks* (Chicago: University of Chicago Press, 1903), pp. 392-402 and 403-320.

Eugene Lerner, "Money, Wages and Prices in the Confederacy," *Journal of Political Economy*, vol. LXII (Feb., 1955), pp. 20-40. Also reprinted by permission of the author.

Harvard University Press and the Quarterly Journal of Economics, for:
Emerson D. Fite, "Agricultural Development of the West During the Civil War," *Quarterly Journal of Economics*, vol. XX (Feb., 1906), pp. 259-276.

Mississippi Valley Historical Association and the *Mississippi Valley Historical Review* for the following:

Howard K. Beale, "The Tariff and Reconstruction," *Mississippi Valley Historical Review*, vol. XXXV (Jan., 1930), pp. 276-294.

Stanley Coben, "Northeastern Business and Radical Reconstruction: A Re-Examination," *Mississippi Valley Historical Review*, vol. XLVI (June, 1959), pp. 67-90. Also reprinted by permission of the author.

Thomas C. Cochran, "Did the Civil War Retard Industrialization?", *Mississippi Valley Historical Review*, vol. XLVIII (Sept., 1961), pp. 197-210. Also reprinted by permission of the author.

James L. Sellers, "The Economic Incidence of the Civil War in the South," *Mississippi Valley Historical Review*, vol. XIV (Sept., 1927), pp. 179-191. Also reprinted by permission of the author.

Harvard University Press for the following:
Victor S. Clark, "Manufacturing Development During the Civil War," *Military Historian and Economist*, vol. III (1918), pp. 92-100.

The text is set in W. A. Dwiggins's Electra with Trade Gothic for the tables and Ludlow Garamond display. It has been composed by Carr Composition Company in association with the printer. Designed by Charles Wilton (cover) and Walter T. Tower Jr. (text), it is printed by The Nimrod Press, Boston, on Crocker-Burbank's Saturn Book. It is flexiback bound by The Riverside Press, Cambridge.